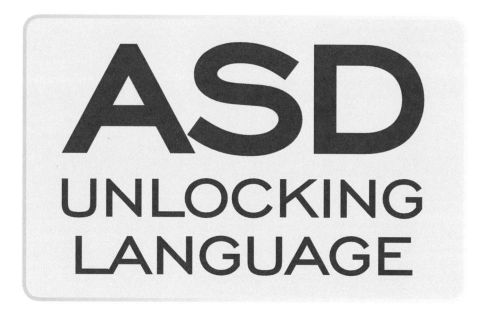

A Program to Teach
Language and Communication

Marion Blank, Ph.D. & Suzanne Goh, M.D.

ASD Unlocking Language: A program to teach language and communication

TABLE OF CONTENTS

Overview 1

PART 1: Pre-Language Skills 11

    Activity A Matching Pictures 13

    Activity B Sequencing Body Movements 41

    Activity C Sequencing Visual Patterns 63

    Activity D Building Receptive Language 85

APPENDIX A: Materials for Pre-Language Activities 135

PART 2: Language Skills 155

    Level 1   Two-Word Phrases 157

    Level 2   Simple Noun-Verb Sentences 173

    Level 3   Expanding Sentence Structure 183

    Level 4   Sentences Introducing a Subject 193

    Level 5   Sentences Describing Actions 203

    Level 6   Sentences Describing Potential Actions 213

    Level 7   Sentences Discussing the Non-Present 223

    Level 8   Sentences in the Past Tense 233

    Level 9   Sentences in the Future Tense 243

    Level 10   Sentence Combinations 6 to 8 words in Length 253

    Level 11   Sentence Combinations up to 10 Words in Length ... 263

    Level 12   Compound Sentences up to 12 Words in Length 273

    Level 13   Starting Questions 283

    Level 14   Questions About Action 293

    Level 15   Questions About Location 303

    Level 16   Questions that use "Which one" for Identification ... 313

    Level 17   Questions about Desire and Ability 323

    Level 18   Questions Using "Not" 333

    Level 19   Questions that Refer to Past Actions 343

    Level 20   Questions that Refer to Future Actions 353

    Level 21   Yes/No Questions 363

    Level 22   Introducing "You" and "I" 373

    Level 23   Questions about "what has been said" 383

    Level 24   Summarizing Events 395

APPENDIX B: Pictures for Language Activities 405

OVERVIEW

Introduction

Life with limited language is difficult to imagine and even more difficult to live. Though in the past this has been the case for many children on the autism spectrum, careful instruction can enable the majority to attain a high level of skill in this vital area.

What is ASD Unlocking Language and what can it accomplish?

ASD Unlocking Language is a program designed to teach effective language and communication to children with autism spectrum disorders and other developmental conditions that affect language. Upon successful completion of the program, children are able to understand and talk about

- past, present, and future events in their home life, such as eating, playing, bathing, and dressing
- past, present, and future events in the outside world, such as visits to the supermarket, a trip to the zoo, and activities at school
- simple stories and other early literacy skills

Mastery of these skills enables children to become more **active** participants in the world around them. As many parents and professionals have told us, the level of language achieved through this program is beyond what most have thought to be possible.

The program may be implemented by a parent, teacher, therapist, or other dedicated adult.

Who is the program for?

The program is for children who meet the following criteria:

- In language—the ability to say at least two words in sequence, either spontaneously or through imitation, such as "go home," "bye bye," "want cookie." While behaviors like these are fragmentary, they are significant indicators that the child has the perceptual and motor base required for spoken language.
- In behavior—the willingness to respond effectively to adult guidance. To benefit from language instruction, a child must be able to cooperate in the teaching process.

If a foundation of cooperation is not yet present, it can be established through the behavioral program outlined in *Spectacular Bond: Reaching the Child with Autism* by Dr. Marion Blank, Dr. Suzanne Goh, and Susan Deland. It is advisable to postpone ASD Unlocking Language until the Spectacular Bond program has been completed.

For children who do not meet the language criteria described above, a different program—ASD Reading—may be more appropriate (see www.ASDreading.com). Although most children learn to speak before they learn to read, this is not a fixed sequence. Children on the autism spectrum have strengths in visual processing that enable many to read before they learn to speak.

How is the program organized?

ASD Unlocking Language is organized into short daily sessions lasting about 20 to 30 minutes each. Sessions take place once per day, four or five days per week. Skills taught in the lessons are also practiced outside the session in real-world settings. Depending on the child's skill and rate of progress, the full program takes from 6 to 18 months to complete. There are two components to the program: Pre-Language Skills and Language Skills.

Components of the program

The two components of the program are outlined below.

PART 1: Pre-Language Skills

Key Pre-Language Skills

- **Attention** — maintaining selective and sustained focus
- **Sequencing** — processing and retaining information that comes in over the course of time
- **Memory** — holding in mind a set of information, such as pictures, words, or sentences

Certain cognitive skills are needed before children can begin to understand and produce spoken language. While these "cognitive precursors" have received little attention, their role in development is critical. The Pre-Language section is designed to teach these skills.

Four activities are used in this section, with each aimed at fostering attention, sequencing, and memory:

- **Activity A: Matching Pictures** — The child sees one or more pictures and selects — either through direct matching or by memory — identical picture(s) from a set of choices.
- **Activity B: Sequencing Body Movements** — The child sees the adult perform a sequence of movements, such as tapping the head and then the knee. The child then imitates the same movements.
- **Activity C: Sequencing Visual Patterns** — The child sees a card with one or more colored squares in a row. Then, either via direct matching or memory, the child reproduces the pattern by tapping in sequence the appropriate colored squares on a separate board.
- **Activity D: Building Receptive Language** — The child carries out requests made by the adult to perform certain actions using a set of small objects (e.g., dolls, animals, etc.). The objects for this activity may be purchased online or in stores (a "shopping list" is provided in this workbook).

Copies of the materials in this workbook may be photocopied for your own personal use to ensure that you have a back up in the event that any part is lost or damaged.

PART 2: Language Skills

With the Pre-Language skills in place, the child moves on to the Language Skills. They are organized into 24 levels. As the program progresses, the child is taught to understand and use language of increasing length and complexity.

Elementary Sentence Structure	*Level 1*	Two-Word Phrases
	Level 2	Simple Noun-Verb Sentences
	Level 3	Expanding Sentence Structure
Advanced Sentence Structure	*Level 4*	Sentences Introducing a Subject
	Level 5	Sentences Describing Actions
	Level 6	Sentences Describing Potential Actions
	Level 7	Sentences Discussing the Non-present
	Level 8	Sentences in the Past Tense
	Level 9	Sentences in the Future Tense
	Level 10	Sentence Combinations 6 to 8 Words in Length
	Level 11	Sentence Combinations up to 10 Words in Length
	Level 12	Compound Sentences up to 12 Words in Length
Questions	*Level 13*	Starting Questions
	Level 14	Questions about Action
	Level 15	Questions about Location
	Level 16	Questions that use "Which one" for Identification
	Level 17	Questions about Desire and Ability
	Level 18	Questions using "Not"
	Level 19	Questions that refer to Past Actions
	Level 20	Questions that refer to Future Actions
Expanding the Language Forms	*Level 21*	Yes/No Questions
	Level 22	Introducing "You" and "I"
	Level 23	Questions About "What Has Been Said"
	Level 24	Summarizing Events

The workbooks have been designed to include four types of language activities:

- **Following Commands** — The child carries out a request that the adult has made.
- **Verbal Imitation** — The child repeats a phrase or sentence that the adult has said.
- **Answering Questions** — The child answers a question that the adult has asked.
- **Sentence Completion** — The child completes a sentence that the adult has started.

These forms appear simple, but they have enormous power. When combined and centered on a specific topic, they begin to approximate the flow of natural conversation. The introduction of new material is done in a slow, carefully paced manner that gives children the sense that verbal communication is within their power.

How do I get started?

This workbook provides all the information you need to carry out the program effectively, including

- the materials to be used,
- the language and actions required of the adult and the child, and
- ways to handle difficulties that may arise.

In preparing for the program, it is helpful to practice with someone other than the child. This allows you to become familiar with the materials and the format of the workbooks, thereby helping the sessions run smoothly when you start working with the child. Remember, there is no need to rush. Spend time reviewing the materials and practicing with them. You may also find it helpful to refer to the resources available online at www.ASDReading.com. The website includes images and videos that demonstrate the techniques used in the program. You may also submit questions through our website.

General Guidelines

Sessions

You should aim to complete one teaching session per day, four or five days per week.

In Part 1 of the program (Pre-Language Skills), a teaching session includes four lessons — one from each activity (A, B, C, & D). From one day to the next, vary the order in which the different activities are presented. For example, on one day you might begin with Activity A, then go to Activity C, then D, then B. On another day, you might begin with Activity B, then go to D, then C, then A. The workbooks can be presented in any order. This variation helps the child develop flexibility.

In Part 2 of the program (Language Skills), a teaching session includes one lesson composed of 25 items.

Set-up

Workspace: The sessions should be carried out in a quiet room with no TV, computer, or other distractions. The work area, if possible, should not be in the child's room. The workspace should be free of clutter with no food, drink, or other items on or near the table. It is preferable to carry out the full session without a break. If necessary, particularly at the outset, you can provide one break during a session. However, do not let the child leave the work area. Just permit him or her to sit quietly and "take a rest."

Position: The adult should sit next to or across from the child at a small table or desk. The child should sit in a firm chair with his or her feet touching the floor. (If necessary, place a stool under the child's feet). Position the material so that the child sees it clearly. Position yourself so that you can see what the child is doing and are close enough to support the child's hand when needed (hand support is explained in more detail below).

Adult's Manner: Your goal is to convey a sense of calm control. Throughout the session, be "business-like." Limit your language to only what is specified in the workbooks. By keeping your language simple, you are helping the child to focus more effectively on the tasks at hand.

The activities are structured so that there are no rewards such as food, toys, or "high-fives." Correct responses are acknowledged solely with comments such as "good" or "very nice" and these are not offered for every correct response. Though often not given the attention it merits, the mastery of skills is empowering and, on its own, serves as the most effective reward a child can receive. As the children learn to recognize the power they have to deal with the world, their confidence soars and they become far more involved in teaching activities — without the need for external rewards.

Child's Behavior: The goal is to have the child sit quietly and attend to the adult throughout the session. If a child is not yet able to do this, the program should be delayed and then restarted in one to two months. In the intervening time, it is recommended that you implement the behavioral program outlined in ***Spectacular Bond: Reaching the Child with Autism*** (available on Amazon.com). This offers a complete step-by-step guide that enables a child to achieve the behavioral foundation needed for learning.

Hand Support

Many of the activities require some level of fine motor skill and this can be challenging for children on the autism spectrum. To handle these difficulties, particularly early in the program, it is extremely valuable to support or stabilize the child's hand. This technique is referred to as "hand support." This type of support is significantly different from the commonly used "hand-over-hand" assistance.

"Hand Support" vs. "Hand-over-hand" assistance	
Hand Support	To support or stabilize the child's hand, hold it at the wrist or palm **but do not move it**. The support reduces the motor demands of the task so that the child can concentrate on the cognitive demands. It also allows you to prevent the child from making incorrect responses or other inappropriate movements. Many children benefit greatly from hand stabilization, but they often are not given this help. Unfortunately, hand support is mistakenly viewed as the adult leading the child to a correct response. This is not the case. Hand support is best viewed as providing the child with "training wheels" that will be removed once the child gains greater motor proficiency. As Ido Kedar, a young man with autism writes, *"It helps many autistic people to have someone touch or even support their arm….This is due to our trouble initiating [movements] and getting our bodies to obey our minds. This slight touch seems to help unlock the sort of paralysis I have described."* (Ido in Autismland)
"Hand-over-Hand" Assistance	"Hand-over-hand" is a commonly used technique where the adult actively moves the child's hand. In this program we use hand-over-hand assistance on occasion to model a response for the child if such modeling is needed. After the response has been modeled, however, the child then has to perform the action independently. Independent action means that the child is completing the action on his or her own. An action that is completed with the use of **hand support** (as described above) is considered independent because the adult has not moved the child's hand. However, an action completed with **hand-over-hand assistance** — in which the adult has actively moved the child's hand — is not considered independent.

Handling Incorrect Responses

In any learning situation, children will for a variety of reasons produce incorrect responses at times. Regardless of the cause, it is important to prevent incorrect responses from occurring too frequently.

Many activities in this program require the child to use a range of hand movements. If the child begins an incorrect movement or goes to an incorrect choice, hold the hand firmly so that the error cannot be made. With the action prevented, the child has the opportunity to consider alternative answers. In other words, hand stabilization allows you to prevent errors and to provide the child with the opportunity to "think before acting."

If the child does produce an incorrect response, *immediately* stop him or her by firmly holding the child's hands in yours and shaking your head "No." In doing so, you prevent the child from continuing on. **In other words, the child should not be allowed to complete an incorrect trial if you can prevent it from happening.**

Once you've taken hold of the child's hands, continue to hold them for one to two minutes while you maintain a calm expression. This may seem like a long period of time to wait, but this distinct pause in activity sends an important message. It tells the child that a particular range of actions is not acceptable. It also leads the child to acknowledge your presence and realize the importance of attending more carefully to what you are requesting. After the delay, say, "Let's do it again." Then start the item again from the beginning using hand support to prevent an incorrect response.

If the child still does not provide a correct response when the trial is repeated, model the correct response. In the case of an action, **use the traditional hand-over-hand movement in which you actively move the child's hand.** Once the correct response has been modeled, start the item again from the beginning so the child can execute (with hand support) the correct response. Later on, in Part 2, some activities require a spoken response. If the child does not offer it, you model it by saying the expected response. Then start the trial again from the beginning.

Many activities in the program require memory. If the child gives an incorrect response for one of these items, repeat the item without requiring memory (that is, allow the child to see the model card while he or she carries out the task). Once the child does this correctly, repeat the item again, but turn the model card over so that the child carries out the task from memory.

These techniques for handling incorrect responses are critical to the success of the program. It may be helpful for you to practice these techniques with a spouse, friend, or older child.

You may also find it helpful to review these instructions during the course of the program. Additional support materials and sample videos can be found at www.ASDReading.com.

ASD Unlocking Language and "Real Life"

The ultimate goal of any language program is to improve the child's understanding and use of language in real life, not just in teaching sessions. This is more likely to happen if parents follow the guidelines below in the language that is used with the child throughout the day:

- **Using commands and questions:** Two of the most common forms of language are

  - *Commands* – where a child is expected to do something (such as "Go get the cup") and
  - *Questions* – where a child is expected to say something in response (such as "What is that boy doing?" "The boy is playing.")

  Each requires a response which a child may or may not get right. The chances of getting them right (and avoiding failure) increase enormously if they are phrased to be similar to the kinds of commands and questions that the child is encountering in the program. Accordingly if a child has not yet reached the point in the program where questions are posed, parents should not be asking the child questions in the exchange of daily life. Then when the child does reach the question answering part of the program, parents should keep note of the forms being learned and then be vigilant so that the questions used in daily exchange are restricted to those forms. Doing this creates a consistent language world for the child that greatly eases his or her mastery of this vital realm.

- **Using comments:** Comments are the other common language form. In commenting, a person simply makes a statement, such as "It is raining." If a listener chooses to respond to a comment, that's perfectly fine. But responses are not required. This makes it an ideal form to use with the children. Even when they have very limited language expression, comments expose them to relatively rich language forms. For example, if the child and adult are outside and cars are going by, the adult might say, "There are so many cars here, and they are going fast. But they have to stop at that light. They have to wait there." Note that the comments are in the form of statements and not questions. Basically, as long as the child is calm and at ease, an adult can comment about anything that is happening and can do so at any level felt to be appropriate. Since they impose no demand for a response, comments leave the child to decide whether or not to attend. With the pressure removed, the children increasingly begin to listen. The end result is an expanded language base that occurs smoothly and easily.

PART
1

PRE-LANGUAGE
SKILLS

What are "Pre-Language" Skills?

Language instruction for children on the spectrum is vital. Equally important, though less well recognized, is the need to teach a range of pre-language skills prior to teaching language itself. The skills we are referring to are ones that serve as the cognitive foundation on which language rests.

For instance, in typical development, children move from single words to two- and three-word phrases within a relatively short period of time. Soon after that, full sentences emerge, so that by two to three years of age amazingly intricate conversations are taking place. These transitions take place so smoothly it can be easy to overlook a simple fact: **the changes are possible because a broad range of underlying pre-language skills are already in place.**

One such skill, for example, is sequencing. Without this skill, production of connected sets of words is not possible. Failure to recognize and teach pre-language skills is largely responsible for the fact that, despite years of instruction, a high percentage of children with ASD speak almost exclusively in single words or two-word phrases.

The Pre-Language activities are designed to overcome this problem. They are organized into four activities. Each begins at the simplest level possible (attending to a single unit) and proceeds to more advanced levels (attending to and holding in mind sequences up to four units).

As you will see, most of the Pre-Language activities rely on visual processing rather than auditory processing. This may seem unusual since the sequences of spoken language rest primarily in the auditory realm. However, this approach allows the children to draw on their relative strength in visual processing. In this way, the child's inherent abilities are being utilized to help foster the development of new skills—namely, those skills that are needed for language. From the perspective of the child on the spectrum, the world of language becomes far less daunting.

ACTIVITY A
MATCHING PICTURES

Overview

These activities are designed to build the child's skill in visual scanning and visual memory. In each item you show the child a set of 3 to 6 pictures like the ones below.

You then show the child a picture that matches one of the choices above.

You set down the picture; the child then selects the matching picture from the set of choices and places it on top of your picture.

Materials

1. *Pictures:* Two sets of thirty pictures (provided in Appendix A). The pictures represent objects from five different categories: people, animals, toys, food, and clothing. Many parents find it helpful to make a color copy of these images as a back-up in case the original is damaged or lost.
   - Cut out each picture.
   - To ensure that the pictures remain durable, either (a) laminate them or (b) mount each on a small piece of cardboard approximately 2 inches by 2 inches in size.

- ☐ If the child finds it difficult to pick up the cards, it is helpful to stick a small piece of foam in the center of the back of each card. This elevates the card off the work surface, enabling the child to pick it up more easily. We suggest the Outer Space self-adhesive shapes (http://amzn.to/17cv3cU) or Creative Hands Foam Sheets (http://amzn.to/18L22Ic) (available at Amazon.com).
- ☐ On the back of the card, near the upper left corner, also write the letter indicating the category (P = people; A = animal; T = toy; F = food; C = clothing) and the number — using the number that appears next to the card at the end of this workbook (i.e., A1, T4, F3, etc.).

2. *Piece of cardboard:* A blank piece of white cardboard approximately 8 inches long and 6 inches wide. This will be used in Levels 3 to 6 to cover the Model in those items where the child is required to select the matching pictures from memory.
3. *Work Surface:* A black foam pad or black cardboard, at least 18 inches by 18 inches in size, set on the desk to serve as a clear work surface on which to place the cards.

Levels

There are six levels in this activity, starting with matching one picture that is in view and progressing to four pictures that are hidden from view. As the levels progress, more difficult items are introduced but simpler items from earlier levels are always maintained.

The Lesson Chart

Each level has 12 lessons and each lesson has 12 items, shown in a chart like the one below.

Sample Chart for Level 1 Lesson 1											
Model Card	P1	A1	T1	F1	C1	P2	T2	C2	A2	F2	P3	C3
# of Choices	3	4	3	3	5	3	3	4	4	3	3	5
✔ or ✘												
Total ✔: _____ (Enter Total in Summary Table)								Date: _____				

In the lesson chart, the row marked **Model Card** identifies the letter and number of the picture card to be used. Cards that begin with the letter **A** represent **Animals**, **C** represent **Clothing**, **F** represent **Food**, **P** represent **People**, and **T** represent **Toys**.

The row marked **# of Choices** indicates how many cards are presented to the child as choices from which to select the matching card. *The Choices should include pictures from two or more* *different categories and must always include the picture that matches the Model.* (For example, if the Model is a picture of an apple, then the choices should include an apple and pictures from two other categories, such as clothes, toys, people, or animals.)

Procedure

1. Prior to the session, it is helpful to organize the cards so that administration of the lesson proceeds more smoothly. This means selecting all the cards that you will need for item 1 and placing them in a pile. Do the same for item 2, item 3, and so on. If you use this technique of administration, it may be helpful to create an additional set of picture cards so that when you reach higher levels (where more cards are needed in each item) you will have enough.

2. Sit at a table either next to, around the corner, or across from the child. The position should allow you both to view the pictures clearly.

3. Place the **Choices** on the top half of the mat.

4. Then place the **Model** on the bottom half of the mat.

5. Point to the Model and say, "Put the same one here." The child should pick up the matching card from the Choices and place it on the Model. (Place your finger directly on top of the Model so the child understands to place the matching card directly on top). Do not accept any other action (e.g., the child cannot hand you the matching picture). If needed, hold the child's hands to help him or her carry out the desired action. Once the child understands how to complete the activities (usually within a few items), you no longer need to say, "Put the same one here." Simply show the Model and wait silently for the child to select the correct picture from the Choices.

    DO NOT NAME THE PICTURES. IF THE CHILD NAMES THEM, DO NOT COMMENT AND DO NOT REPEAT WHAT THE CHILD HAS SAID.

6. Follow the procedures outlined in the General Guidelines for handling incorrect responses and providing hand support.

7. If the child gives a correct response on the 1ˢᵗ try, place a ✔ in the corresponding box. If the child gives an incorrect response, place an X in the box and then repeat the item until the child gives a correct response. (You only score the 1ˢᵗ response, but the item is repeated until it is done correctly.)

8. Only items with a ✔ are considered a correct response. Record the total number of correct responses at the bottom of the lesson chart. Also record the total in the Summary Table provided at the start of each level.

9. When the child has a score of 9 or higher on 3 out of 4 successive lessons in a level, move on to the next level. If you reach Lesson 12, and this has not yet happened, repeat the

material (starting with Lesson 1) and continue until the child has achieved criterion to move on. If this does not happen within 24 lessons, stop the program for a month and then start again.

LEVEL 1
Matching One Picture (with Picture in View)

In Level 1, the model is a single picture, and the set of choices varies in number from two to five. The choices should be arranged in varied positions from one trial to the next (e.g., side by side next to each other, one above the other vertically, diagonally, or laid out in no particular pattern).

Level 1 Summary Table
(to be filled in at the completion of each lesson)

Lesson	1	2	3	4	5	6	7	8	9	10	11	12
Date												
Total # Correct Responses												

When the child attains a score of 9 or more correct responses in 3 of 4 consecutive lessons, move on to the next level.

Level 1 Lesson 1											
Model Card	A1	C1	F1	P1	T1	A2	C2	F2	P2	T2	A3	C3
# of Choices	2	2	2	2	2	2	3	2	3	3	2	3
✔ or ✘												

Total ✔: _____ (Enter Total in Summary Table)   Date: _____

Level 1 Lesson 2											
Model Card	T2	P2	F2	C2	A2	T3	P3	F3	C3	A3	T4	P4
# of Choices	2	3	3	2	3	4	2	3	4	3	4	4
✔ or ✘												

Total ✔: _____ (Enter Total in Summary Table)   Date: _____

Level 1 Lesson 3											
Model Card	A3	C3	F3	P3	T3	A4	C4	F4	P4	T4	A5	C5
# of Choices	3	2	4	3	2	4	2	3	4	5	3	4
✔ or ✘												

Total ✔: _____ (Enter Total in Summary Table)   Date: _____

Level 1 Lesson 4											
Model Card	T4	P4	F4	C4	A4	T5	P5	F5	C5	A5	T6	P6
# of Choices	3	4	3	3	4	3	2	5	3	4	3	4
✔ or ✘												

Total ✔: _____ (Enter Total in Summary Table)   Date: _____

Level 1 Lesson 5

Model Card	A5	C5	F5	P5	T5	A6	C6	F6	P6	T6	A1	C1
# of Choices	4	3	4	2	5	3	2	4	4	4	3	5
✔ or ✘												

Total ✔: _____ (Enter Total in Summary Table)   Date: _____

Level 1 Lesson 6

Model Card	T6	P6	F6	C6	A6	T1	P1	F1	C1	A1	T2	P2
# of Choices	3	5	3	2	4	4	4	3	3	3	5	3
✔ or ✘												

Total ✔: _____ (Enter Total in Summary Table)   Date: _____

Level 1 Lesson 7

Model Card	A1	C1	F1	P1	T1	A2	C2	F2	P2	T2	A3	C3
# of Choices	4	4	3	4	4	2	3	4	3	3	4	2
✔ or ✘												

Total ✔: _____ (Enter Total in Summary Table)   Date: _____

Level 1 Lesson 8

Model Card	T2	P2	F2	C2	A2	T3	P3	F3	C3	A3	T4	P4
# of Choices	3	3	2	3	3	4	3	3	4	3	4	4
✔ or ✘												

Total ✔: _____ (Enter Total in Summary Table)   Date: _____

Level 1 Lesson 9

Model Card	A3	C3	F3	P3	T3	A4	C4	F4	P4	T4	A5	C5
# of Choices	3	2	4	3	3	4	3	3	4	5	2	4
✔ or ✘												

Total ✔: _____ (Enter Total in Summary Table)   Date: _____

Level 1 Lesson 10

Model Card	T4	P4	F4	C4	A4	T5	P5	F5	C5	A5	T6	P6
# of Choices	3	4	2	3	4	3	3	5	3	4	3	4
✔ or ✘												

Total ✔: _____ (Enter Total in Summary Table)   Date: _____

Level 1 Lesson 11

Model Card	A5	C5	F5	P5	T5	A6	C6	F6	P6	T6	A1	C1
# of Choices	4	3	4	2	5	3	3	4	4	4	2	5
✔ or ✘												

Total ✔: _____ (Enter Total in Summary Table)   Date: _____

Level 1 Lesson 12

Model Card	T6	P6	F6	C6	A6	T1	P1	F1	C1	A1	T2	P2
# of Choices	3	5	3	3	4	4	4	2	3	3	5	3
✔ or ✘												

Total ✔: _____ (Enter Total in Summary Table)   Date: _____

LEVEL 2
Matching Two Pictures (with Pictures in View)

In Level 2, the matching of single pictures is maintained while the matching of 2 pictures is introduced. When the model has more than one picture, arrange the pictures in a row, either horizontally or vertically. The child can select the matching pictures in any order he or she chooses. (This activity is focused not on sequencing, but rather on developing visual scanning of an increasingly complex field.)

Level 2 Summary Table
(to be filled in at the completion of each lesson)

Lesson	1	2	3	4	5	6	7	8	9	10	11	12
Date												
Total # Correct Responses												

When the child attains a score of 9 or more correct responses in 3 of 4 consecutive lessons, move on to the next level.

Level 2 Lesson 1											
Model Card	A1 C1	F1	T1 A2	C2 F2	P2	A3 C3	F3 P3	T3	C4	P4 T4	A5 C5	F5
# *of Choices*	4	3	5	4	4	5	3	2	5	4	3	5
✔ or ✘												

Total ✔: _____ (Enter Total in Summary Table)   Date: _____

Level 2 Lesson 2											
Model Card	T5	C6 F6	P6 T6	A1	F1	T1 A2	C1 F2	P1 T2	A2	F2 P3	T2	C2 F3
# *of Choices*	2	4	5	3	5	3	4	4	5	4	5	3
✔ or ✘												

Total ✔: _____ (Enter Total in Summary Table)   Date: _____

Level 2 Lesson 3											
Model Card	P2 T3	A3	F3 P4	T3 A4	C3	P3 T4	A4 C5	F4	T4 A5	C4	P4 T5	A5
# *of Choices*	4	3	5	4	2	4	5	3	5	4	3	5
✔ or ✘												

Total ✔: _____ (Enter Total in Summary Table)   Date: _____

Level 2 Lesson 4											
Model Card	F5	T5 A6	C5 F6	P5	A6 C1	F6 P1	T6	C6 F1	P6	A1 C2	F1 P2	T1
# *of Choices*	5	3	4	5	4	5	3	3	2	5	4	4
✔ or ✘												

Total ✔: _____ (Enter Total in Summary Table)   Date: _____

Level 2 Lesson 5

Model Card	C1	P1 T2	A2 C3	F2	T2 A3	C2	P2 T3	A3 C4	F3	T3	C3 F4	P3 T4
# of Choices	4	4	5	3	4	2	3	5	4	4	3	5
✔ or ✘												

Total ✔: _____ (Enter Total in Summary Table)   Date: _____

Level 2 Lesson 6

Model Card	A4 C5	F4	T4 A5	C4	P4 T5	A4 C5	F5	T5 A6	C5 F6	P5	A5 C6	F6
# of Choices	5	3	5	4	4	4	5	4	5	2	3	3
✔ or ✘												

Total ✔: _____ (Enter Total in Summary Table)   Date: _____

Level 2 Lesson 7

Model Card	A1 C1	F1	T1	C2 F2	P2 T2	A3 C3	F3	T3 A4	C4	P4 T4	A5	F5 P5
# of Choices	4	3	5	4	3	5	2	4	5	4	3	5
✔ or ✘												

Total ✔: _____ (Enter Total in Summary Table)   Date: _____

Level 2 Lesson 8

Model Card	T5	C6 F6	P6 T6	A1	F1 P2	T1 A2	C1	P1 T2	A2	F2 P3	T2	C2 F3
# of Choices	3	4	5	3	5	4	2	4	5	3	5	4
✔ or ✘												

Total ✔: _____ (Enter Total in Summary Table)   Date: _____

Level 2 Lesson 9											
Model Card	P2 T3	A3	F3 P4	T3 A4	C3	P3 T4	A4 C5	F4	T4	C4 F5	P4 T5	A5
# of Choices	4	3	5	4	2	3	5	4	5	3	4	5
✔ or ✘												
Total ✔: _____ (Enter Total in Summary Table)								Date: _____			

Level 2 Lesson 10											
Model Card	F5 P6	T5	C5 F6	P5 T6	A6 C1	F6 P1	T6	C6 F1	P6 T1	A1	F1	T1 A2
# of Choices	5	3	4	5	4	5	3	4	3	5	2	4
✔ or ✘												
Total ✔: _____ (Enter Total in Summary Table)								Date: _____			

Level 2 Lesson 11											
Model Card	C1 F2	P1	A2 C3	F2	T2 A3	C2 F3	P2 T3	A3	F3 P4	T3 A4	C3	P3 T4
# of Choices	4	4	5	3	5	4	3	2	5	3	5	4
✔ or ✘												
Total ✔: _____ (Enter Total in Summary Table)								Date: _____			

Level 2 Lesson 12											
Model Card	A4 C5	F4 P5	T4	C4 F5	P4 T5	A4	F5 P6	T5 A6	C5	P5 T6	A5	F6 P1
# of Choices	5	3	2	4	4	3	5	4	5	4	3	4
✔ or ✘												
Total ✔: _____ (Enter Total in Summary Table)								Date: _____			

LEVEL 3
Matching Two Pictures (with Pictures in View) and Matching One Picture (from Memory)

At this level, some items require memory. These items are indicated in gray. For these items, show the child the Model and then cover it with the piece of white cardboard so the child can no longer see the Model. The child then places the matching picture on top of the cardboard. At the end of the item, expose the model so that the child sees that his or her choice was correct. Easier items from Levels 1 and 2 continue as well. (The intermixing of easier and more difficult items eases the demands of the activity, making the activity more appealing for the children.)

Reminder: if the child gives an incorrect response for an item requiring memory, repeat the item without requiring memory (that is, allow the child to see the picture while he or she selects the matching picture and places it on top of the Model). Once the child does this correctly, repeat the item again, but cover the Model so that the child selects the matching picture from memory.

Level 3 Summary Table
(to be filled in at the completion of each lesson)

Lesson	1	2	3	4	5	6	7	8	9	10	11	12
Date												
Total # Correct Responses												

When the child attains a score of 9 or more correct responses in 3 of 4 consecutive lessons, move on to the next level.

BOXES IN GRAY REPRESENT ITEMS THAT REQUIRE MEMORY

Level 3 Lesson 1											
Model Card	P1 A1	T1	C2 P2	A3	F4 T4	C5	P6 F6	A2	F3 C3	P4	C5 T5	A6
# of Choices	4	3	4	4	5	3	4	4	4	3	4	5
✔ or ✘												
Total ✔: _____ (Enter Total in Summary Table)								Date: _____			

Level 3 Lesson 2											
Model Card	T2	P2 F2	P3	C3 T3	F3 A3	T4	F4 P4	F5	C5 T5	F5 P5	A6 C6	T6
# of Choices	5	4	3	4	4	5	4	5	4	4	4	3
✔ or ✘												
Total ✔: _____ (Enter Total in Summary Table)								Date: _____			

Level 3 Lesson 3											
Model Card	A3 F3	C3	T3	P4 F4	A4	C5 P5	A5 F5	T5	F6	A6	T1 F1	P1 C1
# of Choices	4	3	5	4	4	5	4	3	5	4	4	4
✔ or ✘												
Total ✔: _____ (Enter Total in Summary Table)								Date: _____			

Level 3 Lesson 4											
Model Card	C4 T4	P4	A5 C5	F5 T5	C6	F6	T6	F1 C1	T1 A1	C2	P2 A2	T2 F2
# of Choices	4	5	4	4	5	3	4	5	4	5	4	4
✔ or ✘												
Total ✔: _____ (Enter Total in Summary Table)								Date: _____			

Level 3 Lesson 5

Model Card	P5 A5	T5	C6 P6	A1	F1 T1	C1	P2 F2	A2	F2	P2	C3 T3	A3 F3
# of Choices	4	3	4	5	4	4	4	5	4	3	5	4
✔ or ✘												

Total ✔: _____ (Enter Total in Summary Table)   Date: _____

Level 3 Lesson 6

Model Card	T6 A6	P6 F6	P1	C1	F1 A1	T2 C2	F2 P2	F3	C3 T3	F4	A4 C4	T4
# of Choices	4	5	5	4	4	4	4	3	4	4	4	4
✔ or ✘												

Total ✔: _____ (Enter Total in Summary Table)   Date: _____

Level 3 Lesson 7

Model Card	P1 A1	T1	C2 P2	A3	F4 T4	C5	P6 F6	A2	F3 C3	P4	C5	A6 F6
# of Choices	4	3	4	4	5	3	4	4	4	3	4	5
✔ or ✘												

Total ✔: _____ (Enter Total in Summary Table)   Date: _____

Level 3 Lesson 8

Model Card	T2 A2	P2 F2	P3	C3 T3	A4	T4 C4	F4 P4	F5	C5 T5	F5	A6 C6	T6
# of Choices	5	4	3	4	4	5	4	5	4	4	4	3
✔ or ✘												

Total ✔: _____ (Enter Total in Summary Table)   Date: _____

Level 3 Lesson 9											
Model Card	A3 F3	C3	T3	P4	A4 T4	C5 P5	A5 F5	T5	F6 C6	A6	T1	P1 C1
# of Choices	4	3	5	4	4	5	4	3	5	4	4	4
✔ or ✘												

Total ✔: _____ (Enter Total in Summary Table)   Date: _____

Level 3 Lesson 10											
Model Card	C4 T4	P4	A5 C5	F5 T5	C6 P6	F6	T6	F1 C1	T1	C2	P2 A2	T2 F2
# of Choices	4	5	4	4	5	3	4	5	4	5	4	4
✔ or ✘												

Total ✔: _____ (Enter Total in Summary Table)   Date: _____

Level 3 Lesson 11											
Model Card	P5 A5	T5	C6 P6	A1	F1 T1	C1	P2 F2	A2	F2	P2	C3 T3	A3 F3
# of Choices	4	3	4	5	4	4	4	5	4	3	5	4
✔ or ✘												

Total ✔: _____ (Enter Total in Summary Table)   Date: _____

Level 3 Lesson 12											
Model Card	T6 A6	P6 F6	P1	C1 T1	F1	T2 C2	F2	F3	C3 T3	F4 P4	A4 C4	T4
# of Choices	4	5	5	4	4	4	4	3	4	4	4	4
✔ or ✘												

Total ✔: _____ (Enter Total in Summary Table)   Date: _____

LEVEL 4
Matching Three Pictures (with Pictures in View) and Matching Two Pictures (from Memory)

At this level, the child matches up to three pictures in view and two from memory. Once again, easier items from the earlier levels are maintained.

Level 4 Summary Table
(to be filled in at the completion of each lesson)

Lesson	1	2	3	4	5	6	7	8	9	10	11	12
Date												
Total # Correct Responses												

When the child attains a score of 9 or more correct responses in 3 of 4 consecutive lessons, move on to the next level.

BOXES IN GRAY REPRESENT ITEMS THAT REQUIRE MEMORY

Level 4 Lesson 1											
Model Card	A1 F1 P1	F2 T2	C2	A2 P2	C3 F3 T3	A4 C4	C5 F5 P5	A5 T5	F6	T6	C1 T1	A1 F1
# of Choices	5	4	3	4	5	4	5	4	3	3	4	4
✔ or ✘												
Total ✔: _____ (Enter Total in Summary Table)									Date: _____			

Level 4 Lesson 2											
Model Card	A2 P2 T2	F3 P3	C3	T3 A3	A4 C4 F4	A5	F5 P5	C5 T5	C6 F6 T6	F6 A6	C1 P1	P2 T2
# of Choices	5	4	3	4	6	3	4	4	5	4	4	5
✔ or ✘												
Total ✔: _____ (Enter Total in Summary Table)									Date: _____			

Level 4 Lesson 3											
Model Card	A3 C3 F3	P3 T3	F4	A4 T4	A5 C5 P5	F5 T5	A6 C6 F6	C1 P1	T1	A1	C2 F2	P2 T2
# of Choices	5	4	3	4	5	4	6	4	3	5	4	4
✔ or ✘												
Total ✔: _____ (Enter Total in Summary Table)									Date: _____			

Level 4 Lesson 4											
Model Card	C4 P4 T4	A4 F4	C5	F5 T5	C6 F6 P6	A6	P1 T1	F1 C1	A2 C2 T2	F2 P2	A3 F3 T3	C3 P3
# of Choices	5	4	3	4	6	3	4	4	5	4	5	4
✔ or ✘												
Total ✔: _____ (Enter Total in Summary Table)									Date: _____			

Level 4 Lesson 5

Model Card	A5 F5 P5	F6 T6	C6	A6 P6	C1 F1 T1	A2 C2	C3 F3 P3	A4 T4	F4	T5	C5 T5	A5 F5
# of Choices	5	4	3	4	6	4	5	4	3	4	4	4
✔ or ✘												

Total ✔: _____ (Enter Total in Summary Table)   Date: _____

Level 4 Lesson 6

Model Card	A6 P6 T6	F1 P1	C1	T1 A1	A2 C2 F2	A3	F3 P3	C3 T3	C4 F4 T4	A5 F5	C5 P5	P6 T6
# of Choices	5	4	3	4	5	4	4	4	6	4	4	5
✔ or ✘												

Total ✔: _____ (Enter Total in Summary Table)   Date: _____

Level 4 Lesson 7

Model Card	A1 F1 P1	F2 T2	C2	A2 P2	C3 F3 T3	A4 C4	C5 F5 P5	A5 T5	F6	T6	C1 T1	A1 F1
# of Choices	5	4	3	4	5	4	5	4	3	3	4	4
✔ or ✘												

Total ✔: _____ (Enter Total in Summary Table)   Date: _____

Level 4 Lesson 8

Model Card	A2 P2 T2	F3 P3	C3	T3 A3	A4 C4 F4	A5	F5 P5	C5 T5	C6 F6 T6	F6 A6	C1 P1	P2 T2
# of Choices	5	4	3	4	6	3	4	4	5	4	4	5
✔ or ✘												

Total ✔: _____ (Enter Total in Summary Table)   Date: _____

Level 4 Lesson 9

Model Card	A3 C3 F3	P3 T3	F4	A4 T4	A5 C5 P5	F5 T5	A6 C6 F6	C1 P1	T1	A1	C2 F2	P2 T2
# of Choices	5	4	3	4	5	4	6	4	3	5	4	4
✔ or ✘												

Total ✔: _____ (Enter Total in Summary Table)   Date: _____

Level 4 Lesson 10

Model Card	C4 P4 T4	A4 F4	C5	F5 T5	C6 F6 P6	A6	P1 T1	F1 C1	A2 C2 T2	F2 P2	A3 F3 T3	C3 P3
# of Choices	5	4	3	4	6	3	4	4	5	4	5	4
✔ or ✘												

Total ✔: _____ (Enter Total in Summary Table)   Date: _____

Level 4 Lesson 11

Model Card	A5 F5 P5	F6 T6	C6	A6 P6	C1 F1 T1	A2 C2	C3 F3 P3	A4 T4	F4	T5	C5 T5	A5 F5
# of Choices	5	4	3	4	6	4	5	4	3	4	4	4
✔ or ✘												

Total ✔: _____ (Enter Total in Summary Table)   Date: _____

Level 4 Lesson 12

Model Card	A6 P6 T6	F1 P1	C1	T1 A1	A2 C2 F2	A3	F3 P3	C3 T3	C4 F4 T4	A5 F5	C5 P5	P6 T6
# of Choices	5	4	3	4	5	4	4	4	6	4	4	5
✔ or ✘												

Total ✔: _____ (Enter Total in Summary Table)   Date: _____

LEVEL 5
Matching Four Pictures (with Pictures in View) and
Matching Three Pictures (from Memory)

At this level, the child matches up to four pictures in view and three from memory. Once again, easier items from the earlier levels are maintained.

Level 5 Summary Table
(to be filled in at the completion of each lesson)

Lesson	1	2	3	4	5	6	7	8	9	10	11	12
Date												
Total # Correct Responses												

When the child attains a score of 9 or more correct responses in 3 of 4 consecutive lessons, move on to the next level.

BOXES IN GRAY REPRESENT ITEMS THAT REQUIRE MEMORY

Level 5 Lesson 1

Model Card	C1 F1 P1 T1	A2 C2 F2	T3	C4 P4	A5 F5 P5	C6 F6 T6	A3 C3 P3 T3	F4 P4	A5 F5 T5	C6	C2 F2 P2 T2	A1 P1
# of Choices	5	4	3	4	5	4	6	4	3	5	4	4
✔ or ✗												

Total ✔: _____ (Enter Total in Summary Table)   Date: _____

Level 5 Lesson 2

Model Card	A2 F2 P2 T2	C3 P3 T3	A4	C5 F5	A6 C6 T6	F1 P1 T1	A2 C2 P2	T3	C3 F3 P3	A4 F4	C5 T5	F6 P6
# of Choices	6	5	3	4	5	5	5	3	5	4	4	6
✔ or ✗												

Total ✔: _____ (Enter Total in Summary Table)   Date: _____

Level 5 Lesson 3

Model Card	A1 C2 F3 T4	A2 F3 P4	T5	A5 T6	C1 F2 P3	A4 F5 T6	A3 C4 F5 P6	C4 T5	A2 F3 P4 T5	A6	A3 C4 F5 T6	A1 C2
# of Choices	6	5	3	4	5	5	6	4	6	3	6	4
✔ or ✗												

Total ✔: _____ (Enter Total in Summary Table)   Date: _____

Level 5 Lesson 4

Model Card	A3 F4 P5 T6	A1 C2 F3	P6	C6 F6	A2 C3 T4	C1 F2 P3	A4 T5 F6	C6	F4 P5 T6	A4 F5	C3 P4	A1 C2 P3 T4
# of Choices	6	5	3	4	5	5	4	3	5	4	4	6
✔ or ✗												

Total ✔: _____ (Enter Total in Summary Table)   Date: _____

Level 5 Lesson 5

Model Card	C3 F4 P5 T6	A4 C5 F6	T1	C2 P3	A1 F2 P3	C1 F2 T3	A3 C4 P5 T6	F5 P6	A3 F4 T5	C6	C4 F5 P6 T1	A4 P5
# of Choices	6	5	3	4	5	5	6	4	5	3	6	4
✔ or ✘												

Total ✔: _____ (Enter Total in Summary Table)   Date: _____

Level 5 Lesson 6

Model Card	A1 F2 P3 T4	C5 P6 T1	A6	C5 F6	A6 C1 T2	F6 P1 T2	A5 C6 P1	T2	C3 F4 P5	A2 F3	C1 T2	F1 P2
# of Choices	6	5	3	4	5	5	5	3	5	4	4	6
✔ or ✘												

Total ✔: _____ (Enter Total in Summary Table)   Date: _____

Level 5 Lesson 7

Model Card	C1 F1 P1 T1	A2 C2 F2	T3	C4 P4	A5 F5 P5	C6 F6 T6	A3 C3 P3 T3	F4 P4	A5 F5 T5	C6	C2 F2 P2 T2	A1 P1
# of Choices	6	5	3	4	5	5	6	4	5	3	6	4
✔ or ✘												

Total ✔: _____ (Enter Total in Summary Table)   Date: _____

Level 5 Lesson 8

Model Card	A2 F2 P2 T2	C3 P3 T3	A4	C5 F5	A6 C6 T6	F1 P1 T1	A2 C2 P2	T3	C3 F3 P3	A4 F4	C5 T5	F6 P6
# of Choices	6	5	3	4	5	5	5	3	5	4	4	6
✔ or ✘												

Total ✔: _____ (Enter Total in Summary Table)   Date: _____

Level 5 Lesson 9											
Model Card	A1 C2 F3 T4	A2 F3 P4	T5	A5 T6	C1 F2 P3	A4 F5 T6	A3 C4 F5 P6	C4 T5	A2 F3 P4 T5	A6	A3 C4 F5 T6	A1 C2
# of Choices	6	5	3	4	5	5	6	4	6	3	6	4
✔ or ✘												
Total ✔: _____ (Enter Total in Summary Table)								Date: _____				

Level 5 Lesson 10											
Model Card	A3 F4 P5 T6	A1 C2 F3	P6	C6 F6	A2 C3 T4	C1 F2 P3	A4 F5 T6	C6	F4 P5 T6	A4 F5	C3 P4	A1 C2 P3 T4
# of Choices	6	5	3	4	5	5	4	3	5	4	4	6
✔ or ✘												
Total ✔: _____ (Enter Total in Summary Table)								Date: _____				

Level 5 Lesson 11											
Model Card	C3 F4 P5 T6	A4 C5 F6	T1	C2 P3	A1 F2 P3	C1 F2 T3	A3 C4 P5 T6	F5 P6	A3 F4 T5	C6	C4 F5 P6 T1	A4 P5
# of Choices	6	5	3	4	5	5	6	4	5	3	6	4
✔ or ✘												
Total ✔: _____ (Enter Total in Summary Table)								Date: _____				

Level 5 Lesson 12											
Model Card	A1 F2 P3 T4	C5 P6 T1	A6	C5 F6	A6 C1 T2	F6 P1 T2	A5 C6 P1	T2	C3 F4 P5	A2 F3	C1 T2	F1 P2
# of Choices	6	5	3	4	5	5	5	3	5	4	4	6
✔ or ✘												
Total ✔: _____ (Enter Total in Summary Table)								Date: _____				

LEVEL 6
Matching Four Pictures (from Memory)

At this final level, some of the items require the child to match four pictures from memory.

Level 6 Summary Table
(to be filled in at the completion of each lesson)

Lesson	1	2	3	4	5	6	7	8	9	10	11	12
Date												
Total # Correct Responses												

When the child has achieved a score of 9 or higher in 3 of 4 consecutive lessons, this activity is completed. If the other Pre-Language activities are not yet completed, continue to repeat lessons from Level 6 of this activity at least three times per week while the others are still in progress. Once all the Pre-Language activities have been completed, the child can move on to Part 2: Language Skills.

BOXES IN GRAY REPRESENT ITEMS THAT REQUIRE MEMORY

Level 6 Lesson 1											
Model Card	C5 F6 P1 T2	A4 C5 F6	T1	C3 P4	A1 F2 P3	C2 F3 T4	A3 C4 P5 T6	F1 P2	A2 C3 F4 T5	P3	A1 C2 F3 T4	C5 P6
# of Choices	6	5	3	4	5	5	6	4	6	3	6	4
✔ or ✘												
Total ✔: _____ (Enter Total in Summary Table)									Date: _____			

Level 6 Lesson 2											
Model Card	A4 F5 P6 T1	C1 P2 T3	A6	C2 F3	A3 C4 F5 T6	A1 C2 P3 T4	F2 T3	C4	C5 F6 P1	A2 T3	C4 P5	A6 F1 T2
# of Choices	6	5	3	4	6	6	4	3	5	4	4	6
✔ or ✘												
Total ✔: _____ (Enter Total in Summary Table)									Date: _____			

Level 6 Lesson 3											
Model Card	A5 C6 F1 T2	A2 F3 P4	T4	A5 C6 T1	C2 F3 P4	A4 F5 T6	A1 C2 F3 P4	C2 T3	A3 F4 P5 T6	A6	A2 C3 F4 T5	A4 C5
# of Choices	6	5	3	5	5	5	6	4	6	3	6	4
✔ or ✘												
Total ✔: _____ (Enter Total in Summary Table)									Date: _____			

Level 6 Lesson 4											
Model Card	A6 F1 P2 T3	A5 C6 F1	P2	A4 C5 F6 T1	C1 F2 P3	A3 C4 F5	F3 T4	C5	A4 F5 P6 T1	C2 F3	A5 P6	A1 C2 P3 T4
# of Choices	6	5	3	6	5	5	4	3	6	4	4	6
✔ or ✘												
Total ✔: _____ (Enter Total in Summary Table)									Date: _____			

Level 6 Lesson 5

Model Card	C5 F6 P1 T2	A3 C4 F5	T1	C4 P5	A6 F1 P2	C3 F4 T5	A1 C2 P3 T4	F5 P6	A2 C3 F4 T5	P2	A4 C5 F6 T1	C5 P6
# of Choices	6	5	3	4	5	5	6	4	6	3	6	4
✔ or ✘												

Total ✔: _____ (Enter Total in Summary Table)   Date: _____

Level 6 Lesson 6

Model Card	A4 F5 P6 T1	C2 P3 T4	A3	C4 F5	A2 C3 F4 T5	A1 C2 P3 T4	F5 T6	C1	C2 F3 P4	A5 T6	C5 P6	A6 F1 T2
# of Choices	6	5	3	4	6	6	4	3	5	4	4	6
✔ or ✘												

Total ✔: _____ (Enter Total in Summary Table)   Date: _____

Level 6 Lesson 7

Model Card	A5 C6 F1 T2	A2 F3 P4	T4	A5 C6 T1	C2 F3 P4	A4 F5 T6	A1 C2 F3 P4	C2 T3	A3 F4 P5 T6	A6	A2 C3 F4 T5	A4 C5
# of Choices	6	5	3	5	5	5	6	4	6	3	6	4
✔ or ✘												

Total ✔: _____ (Enter Total in Summary Table)   Date: _____

Level 6 Lesson 8

Model Card	A6 F1 P2 T3	A5 C6 F1	P2	A4 C5 F6 T1	C1 F2 P3	A3 C4 F5	F3 T4	C5	A4 F5 P6 T1	C2 F3	A5 P6	A1 C2 P3 T4
# of Choices	6	5	3	6	5	5	4	3	6	4	4	6
✔ or ✘												

Total ✔: _____ (Enter Total in Summary Table)   Date: _____

Level 6 Lesson 9											
Model Card	A5 C6 F1 T2	A2 F3 P4	T4	A5 C6 T1	C2 F3 P4	A4 F5 T6	A1 C2 F3 P4	C2 T3	A3 F4 P5 T6	A6	A2 C3 F4 T5	A4 C5
# of Choices	6	5	3	5	5	5	6	4	6	3	6	4
✔ or ✘												

Total ✔: _____ (Enter Total in Summary Table)   Date: _____

Level 6 Lesson 10											
Model Card	A6 F1 P2 T3	A5 C6 F1	P2	A4 C5 F6 T1	C1 F2 P3	A3 C4 F5	F3 T4	C5	A4 F5 P6 T1	C2 F3	A5 P6	A1 C2 P3 T4
# of Choices	6	5	3	6	5	5	4	3	6	4	4	6
✔ or ✘												

Total ✔: _____ (Enter Total in Summary Table)   Date: _____

Level 6 Lesson 11											
Model Card	C5 F6 P1 T2	A3 C4 F5	T1	C4 P5	A6 F1 P2	C3 F4 T5	A1 C2 P3 T4	F5 P6	A2 C3 F4 T5	P2	A4 C5 F6 T1	C5 P6
# of Choices	6	5	3	4	5	5	6	4	6	3	6	4
✔ or ✘												

Total ✔: _____ (Enter Total in Summary Table)   Date: _____

Level 6 Lesson 12											
Model Card	A4 F5 P6 T1	C2 P3 T4	A3	C4 F5	A2 C3 F4 T5	A1 C2 P3 T4	F5 T6	C1	C2 F3 P4	A5 T6	C5 P6	A6 F1 T2
# of Choices	6	5	3	4	6	6	4	3	5	4	4	6
✔ or ✘												

Total ✔: _____ (Enter Total in Summary Table)   Date: _____

ACTIVITY B
SEQUENCING BODY MOVEMENTS

Overview

Motor movements, by their very nature, are carried out over time. As such, they represent one of the best domains for developing sequencing skills.

In this activity, you and the child sit facing each other. You perform an action or series of actions on your body, and then the child reproduces, on his or her body, the same action or set of actions.

In executing the activity, the child "mirrors" what you do and uses his or her preferred hand (right hand for a right-hander or left hand for a left-hander). As a result, you will use the opposite side. For example, if the child is to tap his or her right shoulder with the right hand, you use your left hand to tap your left shoulder. That way, from the child's perspective, he or she is tapping the same side as you.

Materials
- Two firm chairs

Levels

There are four levels in this activity. They start with tapping one body part and progress to tapping four body parts in sequence.

The Lesson Chart

Each Level has 12 lessons and each lesson has 12 items, shown in a chart like the one below.

Sample Chart for Level 1 Lesson 1					
Model	Head	Nose	Chest	Shoulder	Belly	Knee
✔ or ✗						
Model	Off Body	Chest	Nose	Shoulder	Belly	Knee
✔ or ✗						
Total ✔: _____ (Enter Total in Summary Table)				Date: _____	

The row marked **Model** indicates where you should tap. *"Off Body"* means that you can tap the table, the floor, or any nearby surface. Items 1 to 6 are in the top row and items 7 to 12 are in the bottom row.

Procedure

1. Both you and the child sit in firm chairs with your feet on the ground or on a stool. Sit near a table or chair that can be used as a surface for tapping *Off Body*. If you prefer, you and the child can be seated on the floor rather than in chairs. If seated on the floor, use the floor for tapping *Off Body*. Face each other directly with about 6 inches separating your knees from the child's.

2. Tap the body part or surface indicated in the chart and say, "Do this." Once the child understands how to complete the activities (usually within a few items), you no longer need to say, "Do this." Simply show the action and then wait silently for the child to imitate it.

3. If the child is right handed, you should tap your left shoulder and left knee, so that the child mirrors you by tapping his or her right shoulder and right knee. If the child is left handed, you should tap your right shoulder and right knee.

4. It is important that the child see the complete sequence before executing any movements. To prevent the child from making incorrect movements or from starting the movements before you have completed the full sequence, use one of your hands to hold both of the child's hands while you demonstrate the movements with your other (free) hand. Once you have demonstrated the movement(s), change your hold so that instead of holding both of the child's hands in one hand, you are holding one of the child's hands in each

of your hands. Hold both hands and wait for the child to move the correct hand in the correct sequence. (See www.ASDReading.com for sample videos).

5. Follow the procedures outlined in the Pre-Language Guidelines for handling incorrect responses. Once the child has learned what is expected and is cooperating easily, you can eliminate the hand support.

    DO NOT NAME THE BODY PARTS. IF THE CHILD NAMES THEM, DO NOT COMMENT AND DO NOT REPEAT WHAT THE CHILD HAS SAID.

6. If the child gives a correct response on the 1st try, place a ✔ in the corresponding box. If the child gives an incorrect response, place an ✘ in the box and then repeat the item until the child gives a correct response.

7. When scoring the lesson, only items with a ✔ are considered to be a correct response. Record the total number of correct responses at the bottom of the lesson chart. Also record the total in the Summary Table provided at the start of each level.

8. When the child has a score of 9 or higher on 3 out of 4 successive lessons in a level, move on to next level. If you reach Lesson 12, and this has not yet happened, repeat the material (starting with Lesson 1) and continue until the child has achieved criterion to move on. If this does not happen within 24 lessons, stop the program for a month and then start again.

LEVEL 1
Imitating One Movement

Level 1 Summary Table
(to be filled in at the completion of each lesson)

Lesson	1	2	3	4	5	6	7	8	9	10	11	12
Date												
Total # Correct Responses												

When the child attains a score of 9 or higher in 3 of 4 consecutive lessons, move on to the next level.

NOTE: Throughout this activity, a right-handed child should tap his or her RIGHT shoulder and knee. A left-handed child should tap his or her LEFT shoulder and knee. This prevents the child from having to reach across the body.

Level 1 Lesson 1

Model	Head	Nose	Chest	Shoulder	Belly	Knee
✔ or ✗						

Model	Off Body	Chest	Nose	Shoulder	Belly	Knee
✔ or ✗						

Total ✔: _____ (Enter Total in Summary Table)   Date: _____

Level 1 Lesson 2

Model	Knee	Belly	Shoulder	Nose	Chest	Off Body
✔ or ✗						

Model	Knee	Belly	Shoulder	Chest	Off Body	Head
✔ or ✗						

Total ✔: _____ (Enter Total in Summary Table)   Date: _____

Level 1 Lesson 3

Model	Shoulder	Head	Chest	Off Body	Nose	Shoulder
✔ or ✗						

Model	Belly	Knee	Off Body	Head	Chest	Nose
✔ or ✗						

Total ✔: _____ (Enter Total in Summary Table)   Date: _____

Level 1 Lesson 4

Model	Chest	Head	Off Body	Knee	Shoulder	Belly
✔ or ✗						

Model	Nose	Head	Chest	Off Body	Knee	Shoulder
✔ or ✗						

Total ✔: _____ (Enter Total in Summary Table)   Date: _____

Level 1 Lesson 5

Model	Head	Nose	Chest	Shoulder	Belly	Knee
✔ or ✘						

Model	Off	Chest	Nose	Shoulder	Belly	Knee
✔ or ✘						

Total ✔: _____ (Enter Total in Summary Table)   Date: _____

Level 1 Lesson 6

Model	Knee	Belly	Shoulder	Nose	Chest	Off Body
✔ or ✘						

Model	Knee	Chest	Shoulder	Belly	Off Body	Head
✔ or ✘						

Total ✔: _____ (Enter Total in Summary Table)   Date: _____

Level 1 Lesson 7

Model	Shoulder	Head	Chest	Off Body	Nose	Shoulder
✔ or ✘						

Model	Belly	Knee	Off Body	Head	Chest	Nose
✔ or ✘						

Total ✔: _____ (Enter Total in Summary Table)   Date: _____

Level 1 Lesson 8

Model	Chest	Head	Off Body	Knee	Shoulder	Belly
✔ or ✘						

Model	Nose	Head	Chest	Off Body	Knee	Shoulder
✔ or ✘						

Total ✔: _____ (Enter Total in Summary Table)   Date: _____

Level 1 Lesson 9

Model	Head	Nose	Chest	Shoulder	Belly	Knee
✔ or ✘						

Model	Off	Chest	Nose	Shoulder	Belly	Knee
✔ or ✘						

Total ✔: _____ (Enter Total in Summary Table)   Date: _____

Level 1 Lesson 10

Model	Knee	Belly	Shoulder	Nose	Chest	Off Body
✔ or ✘						

Model	Knee	Chest	Shoulder	Belly	Off Body	Head
✔ or ✘						

Total ✔: _____ (Enter Total in Summary Table)   Date: _____

Level 1 Lesson 11

Model	Shoulder	Head	Chest	Off Body	Nose	Shoulder
✔ or ✘						

Model	Belly	Knee	Off Body	Head	Chest	Nose
✔ or ✘						

Total ✔: _____ (Enter Total in Summary Table)   Date: _____

Level 1 Lesson 12

Model	Chest	Head	Off Body	Knee	Shoulder	Belly
✔ or ✘						

Model	Nose	Head	Chest	Off Body	Knee	Shoulder
✔ or ✘						

Total ✔: _____ (Enter Total in Summary Table)   Date: _____

LEVEL 2
Imitating Two Movements in Sequence

At this level, the child imitates up to two movements in sequence.

Level 2 Summary Table
(to be filled in at the completion of each lesson)

Lesson	1	2	3	4	5	6	7	8	9	10	11	12
Date												
Total # Correct Responses												

When the child attains a score of 9 or higher in 3 of 4 consecutive lessons, move on to the next level.

Level 2 Lesson 1

Model	Chest	Off Body Knee	Shoulder Belly	Head	Chest Off Body	Knee Shoulder
✔ or ✘						

Model	Head Chest	Off Body	Shoulder Nose	Belly	Knee Chest	Nose Head
✔ or ✘						

Total ✔: _____ (Enter Total in Summary Table)   Date: _____

Level 2 Lesson 2

Model	Head Off Body	Knee Shoulder	Belly	Chest Head	Off Body Knee	Shoulder
✔ or ✘						

Model	Head Off Body	Knee Shoulder	Nose	Belly Knee	Chest	Shoulder Head
✔ or ✘						

Total ✔: _____ (Enter Total in Summary Table)   Date: _____

Level 2 Lesson 3

Model	Knee	Head Chest	Off Body Shoulder	Belly	Head Off Body	Chest Knee
✔ or ✘						

Model	Nose	Belly Head	Off Body Shoulder	Knee Chest	Head	Chest Off Body
✔ or ✘						

Total ✔: _____ (Enter Total in Summary Table)   Date: _____

Level 2 Lesson 4

Model	Head Shoulder	Belly	Shoulder Off Body	Head Chest	Knee Nose	Chest
✔ or ✘						

Model	Head Shoulder	Belly Knee	Off Body	Head Chest	Shoulder Nose	Knee
✔ or ✘						

Total ✔: _____ **(Enter Total in Summary Table)**   **Date:** _____

Level 2 Lesson 5

Model	Chest	Off Body Knee	Shoulder Belly	Head	Chest Off Body	Knee Shoulder
✔ or ✘						

Model	Head Chest	Off Body	Shoulder Nose	Belly	Knee Chest	Nose Head
✔ or ✘						

Total ✔: _____ **(Enter Total in Summary Table)**   **Date:** _____

Level 2 Lesson 6

Model	Head Off Body	Knee Shoulder	Belly	Chest Head	Off Body Knee	Shoulder
✔ or ✘						

Model	Head Off Body	Knee Shoulder	Nose	Belly Knee	Chest	Shoulder Head
✔ or ✘						

Total ✔: _____ **(Enter Total in Summary Table)**   **Date:** _____

Level 2 Lesson 7						
Model	Knee	Head Chest	Off Body Shoulder	Belly	Head Off Body	Chest Knee
✔ or ✘						
Model	Nose	Belly Head	Off Body Shoulder	Knee Chest	Head	Chest Off Body
✔ or ✘						
Total ✔: _____ (Enter Total in Summary Table) Date: _____						

Level 2 Lesson 8						
Model	Head Shoulder	Belly	Shoulder Off Body	Head Chest	Knee Nose	Chest
✔ or ✘						
Model	Head Shoulder	Belly Knee	Off Body	Head Chest	Shoulder Nose	Knee
✔ or ✘						
Total ✔: _____ (Enter Total in Summary Table) Date: _____						

Level 2 Lesson 9						
Model	Chest	Off Body Knee	Shoulder Belly	Head	Chest Off Body	Knee Shoulder
✔ or ✘						
Model	Head Chest	Off Body	Shoulder Nose	Belly	Knee Chest	Nose Head
✔ or ✘						
Total ✔: _____ (Enter Total in Summary Table) Date: _____						

51

Level 2 Lesson 10

Model	Head Off Body	Knee Shoulder	Belly	Chest Head	Off Body Knee	Shoulder
✔ or ✗						

Model	Head Off Body	Knee Shoulder	Nose	Belly Knee	Chest	Shoulder Head
✔ or ✗						

Total ✔: _____ (Enter Total in Summary Table)   Date: _____

Level 2 Lesson 11

Model	Knee	Head Chest	Off Body Shoulder	Belly	Head Off Body	Chest Knee
✔ or ✗						

Model	Nose	Belly Head	Off Body Shoulder	Knee Chest	Head	Chest Off Body
✔ or ✗						

Total ✔: _____ (Enter Total in Summary Table)   Date: _____

Level 2 Lesson 12

Model	Head Shoulder	Belly	Shoulder Off Body	Head Chest	Knee Nose	Chest
✔ or ✗						

Model	Head Shoulder	Belly Knee	Off Body	Head Chest	Shoulder Nose	Knee
✔ or ✗						

Total ✔: _____ (Enter Total in Summary Table)   Date: _____

LEVEL 3
Imitating Three Movements in Sequence

At this level, the child imitates up to three movements in sequence.

Level 3 Summary Table
(to be filled in at the completion of each lesson)

Lesson	1	2	3	4	5	6	7	8	9	10	11	12
Date												
Total # Correct Responses												

When the child attains a score of 9 or higher in 3 of 4 consecutive lessons, move on to the next level.

Level 3 Lesson 1

Model	Head Chest	Shoulder	Belly Nose Knee	Head Belly	Shoulder Chest Off Body	Chest
✔ or ✘						

Model	Nose Head	Knee Belly Chest	Head Shoulder	Belly	Shoulder Nose Knee	Head Belly Chest
✔ or ✘						

Total ✔: _____ (Enter Total in Summary Table)　　　**Date: _____**

Level 3 Lesson 2

Model	Shoulder Head	Chest Belly Head	Off Body	Head Nose	Knee Nose Shoulder	Chest Belly Knee
✔ or ✘						

Model	Shoulder	Belly Head	Chest Knee Off Body	Nose Belly	Off Body Chest Shoulder	Head
✔ or ✘						

Total ✔: _____ (Enter Total in Summary Table)　　　**Date: _____**

Level 3 Lesson 3

Model	Chest Knee Head	Belly	Shoulder Off Body	Chest Shoulder Knee	Head Shoulder	Nose
✔ or ✘						

Model	Knee Head Belly	Chest	Belly Knee	Nose Shoulder	Head Chest Off Body	Shoulder Belly Nose
✔ or ✘						

Total ✔: _____ (Enter Total in Summary Table)　　　**Date: _____**

Level 3 Lesson 4					
Model	Head Knee Nose	Off Body Head	Shoulder	Head Belly Shoulder	Nose Chest Shoulder	Off Body
✔ or ✘					
Model	Belly Chest Head	Shoulder Chest	Belly Nose Knee	Head Belly Chest	Nose Off Body	Head Shoulder
✔ or ✘					
Total ✔: _____ (Enter Total in Summary Table)				Date: _____	

Level 3 Lesson 5					
Model	Head Chest	Shoulder	Belly Nose Knee	Head Belly	Shoulder Chest Off Body	Chest
✔ or ✘					
Model	Nose Head	Knee Belly Chest	Head Shoulder	Belly	Shoulder Nose Knee	Head Belly Chest
✔ or ✘					
Total ✔: _____ (Enter Total in Summary Table)				Date: _____	

Level 3 Lesson 6					
Model	Shoulder Head	Chest Belly Head	Off Body	Head Nose	Knee Nose Shoulder	Chest Belly Knee
✔ or ✘					
Model	Shoulder	Belly Head	Chest Knee Off Body	Nose Belly	Off Body Chest Shoulder	Head
✔ or ✘					
Total ✔: _____ (Enter Total in Summary Table)				Date: _____	

Level 3 Lesson 7						
Model	Chest Knee Head	Belly	Shoulder Off Body	Chest Shoulder Knee	Head Shoulder	Nose
✔ or ✘						
Model	Knee Head Belly	Chest	Belly Knee	Nose Shoulder	Head Chest Off Body	Shoulder Belly Nose
✔ or ✘						

Total ✔: _____ (Enter Total in Summary Table)   **Date:** _____

Level 3 Lesson 8						
Model	Head Knee Nose	Off Body Head	Shoulder	Head Belly Shoulder	Nose Chest Shoulder	Off Body
✔ or ✘						
Model	Belly Chest Head	Shoulder Chest	Belly Nose Knee	Head Belly Chest	Nose Off Body	Head Shoulder
✔ or ✘						

Total ✔: _____ (Enter Total in Summary Table)   **Date:** _____

Level 3 Lesson 9						
Model	Head Chest	Shoulder	Belly Nose Knee	Head Belly	Shoulder Chest Off Body	Chest
✔ or ✘						
Model	Nose Head	Knee Belly Chest	Head Shoulder	Belly	Shoulder Nose Knee	Head Belly Chest
✔ or ✘						

Total ✔: _____ (Enter Total in Summary Table)   **Date:** _____

Level 3 Lesson 10

Model	Shoulder Head	Chest Belly Head	Off Body	Head Nose	Knee Nose Shoulder	Chest Belly Knee
✔ or ✘						

Model	Shoulder	Belly Head	Chest Knee Off Body	Nose Belly	Off Body Chest Shoulder	Head
✔ or ✘						

Total ✔: _____ (Enter Total in Summary Table)   Date: _____

Level 3 Lesson 11

Model	Chest Knee Head	Belly	Shoulder Off Body	Chest Shoulder Knee	Head Shoulder	Nose
✔ or ✘						

Model	Knee Head Belly	Chest	Belly Knee	Nose Shoulder	Head Chest Off Body	Shoulder Belly Nose
✔ or ✘						

Total ✔: _____ (Enter Total in Summary Table)   Date: _____

Level 3 Lesson 12

Model	Head Knee Nose	Off Body Head	Shoulder	Head Belly Shoulder	Nose Chest Shoulder	Off Body
✔ or ✘						

Model	Belly Chest Head	Shoulder Chest	Belly Nose Knee	Head Belly Chest	Nose Off Body	Head Shoulder
✔ or ✘						

Total ✔: _____ (Enter Total in Summary Table)   Date: _____

LEVEL 4
Imitating Four Movements in Sequence

At this level, the child imitates up to four movements in sequence.

Level 4 Summary Table
(to be filled in at the completion of each lesson)

Lesson	1	2	3	4	5	6	7	8	9	10	11	12
Date												
Total # Correct Responses												

When the child has achieved a score of 9 or higher in 3 of 4 consecutive lessons, this activity is completed. If the other Pre-Language activities are not yet completed, continue to repeat a lesson from the highest level of this activity (Level 4) at least three times per week while the others are still in progress. Once all Pre-Language activities have been completed, the child can move on to Part 2: Language Skills.

Level 4 Lesson 1						
Model	Head Belly Chest	Belly Chest Shoulder Off Body	Shoulder	Chest Shoulder Head	Knee Nose	Belly Chest Off Body
✔ or ✘						
Model	Shoulder Head Knee	Chest Shoulder	Head	Shoulder Chest Knee Shoulder	Shoulder Chest	Off Body Head Chest Nose
✔ or ✘						

Total ✔: _____ **(Enter Total in Summary Table)**   **Date:** _____

Level 4 Lesson 2						
Model	Chest Knee Head	Off Body Belly	Nose	Knee Shoulder	Chest Shoulder Nose Knee	Shoulder Chest
✔ or ✘						
Model	Off Body Head	Knee Chest	Belly Shoulder Chest Head	Shoulder Nose	Knee Chest	Head Off Body Shoulder Belly
✔ or ✘						

Total ✔: _____ **(Enter Total in Summary Table)**   **Date:** _____

Level 4 Lesson 3						
Model	Shoulder Chest Body	Head Nose	Chest	Belly Shoulder Chest	Knee Head Shoulder Nose	Chest Shoulder
✔ or ✘						
Model	Off Body Head Chest Knee	Shoulder Off Body	Head	Chest Belly	Belly Knee Nose Off Body	Head Shoulder
✔ or ✘						

Total ✔: _____ **(Enter Total in Summary Table)**   **Date:** _____

Level 4 Lesson 4

Model	Chest Shoulder Head Knee	Shoulder Belly	Off Body	Belly Chest	Knee Chest Shoulder	Head Belly
✔ or ✘						

Model	Off Body Knee	Shoulder Head Chest	Nose Chest Knee Body	Shoulder Knee	Off Body Chest Shoulder Head	Nose Belly Knee
✔ or ✘						

Total ✔: _____ (Enter Total in Summary Table)　　**Date: _____**

Level 4 Lesson 5

Model	Head Belly Chest	Belly Chest Shoulder Off Body	Shoulder	Chest Shoulder Head	Knee Nose	Belly Chest Off Body
✔ or ✘						

Model	Shoulder Head Knee	Chest Shoulder	Head	Shoulder Chest Knee Shoulder	Shoulder Chest	Off Body Head Chest Nose
✔ or ✘						

Total ✔: _____ (Enter Total in Summary Table)　　**Date: _____**

Level 4 Lesson 6

Model	Chest Knee Head	Off Body Belly	Nose	Knee Shoulder	Chest Shoulder Nose Knee	Shoulder Chest
✔ or ✘						

Model	Off Body Head	Knee Chest	Belly Shoulder Chest Head	Shoulder Nose	Knee Chest	Head Off Body Shoulder Belly
✔ or ✘						

Total ✔: _____ (Enter Total in Summary Table)　　**Date: _____**

Level 4 Lesson 7						
Model	Shoulder Chest Body	Head Nose	Chest	Belly Shoulder Chest	Knee Head Shoulder Nose	Chest Shoulder
✔ or ✗						
Model	Off Body Head Chest Knee	Shoulder Off Body	Head	Chest Belly	Belly Knee Nose Off Body	Head Shoulder
✔ or ✗						

Total ✔: _____ (Enter Total in Summary Table)   Date: _____

Level 4 Lesson 8						
Model	Chest Shoulder Head Knee	Shoulder Belly	Off Body	Belly Chest	Knee Chest Shoulder	Head Belly
✔ or ✗						
Model	Off Body Knee	Shoulder Head Chest	Nose Chest Knee Body	Shoulder Knee	Off Body Chest Shoulder Head	Nose Belly Knee
✔ or ✗						

Total ✔: _____ (Enter Total in Summary Table)   Date: _____

Level 4 Lesson 9						
Model	Head Belly Chest	Belly Chest Shoulder Off Body	Shoulder	Chest Shoulder Head	Knee Nose	Belly Chest Off Body
✔ or ✗						
Model	Shoulder Head Knee	Chest Shoulder	Head	Shoulder Chest Knee Shoulder	Shoulder Chest	Off Body Head Chest Nose
✔ or ✗						

Total ✔: _____ (Enter Total in Summary Table)   Date: _____

Level 4 Lesson 10

Model	Chest Knee Head	Off Body Belly	Nose	Knee Shoulder	Chest Shoulder Nose Knee	Shoulder Chest
✔ or ✘						

Model	Off Body Head	Knee Chest	Belly Shoulder Chest Head	Shoulder Nose	Knee Chest	Head Off Body Shoulder Belly
✔ or ✘						

Total ✔: _____ (Enter Total in Summary Table)　　　**Date: _____**

Level 4 Lesson 11

Model	Shoulder Chest Body	Head Nose	Chest	Belly Shoulder Chest	Knee Head Shoulder Nose	Chest Shoulder
✔ or ✘						

Model	Off Body Head Chest Knee	Shoulder Off Body	Head	Chest Belly	Belly Knee Nose Off Body	Head Shoulder
✔ or ✘						

Total ✔: _____ (Enter Total in Summary Table)　　　**Date: _____**

Level 4 Lesson 12

Model	Chest Shoulder Head Knee	Shoulder Belly	Off Body	Belly Chest	Knee Chest Shoulder	Head Belly
✔ or ✘						

Model	Off Body Knee	Shoulder Head Chest	Nose Chest Knee Body	Shoulder Knee	Off Body Chest Shoulder Head	Nose Belly Knee
✔ or ✘						

Total ✔: _____ (Enter Total in Summary Table)　　　**Date: _____**

ACTIVITY C
SEQUENCING VISUAL PATTERNS

Overview

In these activities the child learns to reproduce visual sequences using colored squares. A large piece of cardboard with eight colored squares extending from left to right is placed in front of the child.

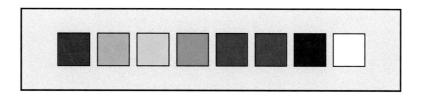

For each item, you then show the child a small card with one or more squares, such as the following.

The child has to tap, on the large cardboard, the colored squares that appear on the small card — tapping them in left to right sequence as shown on the card. (In the example above, the child would tap on the board the blue and then the brown square.)

For all the trials, the tapping sequence goes from left to right (so "yellow blue" is a possible sequence whereas "blue yellow" is not). This procedure has been adopted because it has payoff when the child moves on to the language of reading (i.e., literacy), where left to right sequencing is essential.

Initially the activity involves direct matching where the child sees both the card and the board. But at the higher levels, the small card is shown to the child and then covered so that the child taps the sequence from memory.

(Note: Although the squares are colored, the colors themselves are not the focus of the activity. They serve only as a means to create the sequence. Other materials, such as shapes or shadings would serve as well. The aim of this activity is not to teach colors, but rather to teach the skill of sequencing.)

Materials

1. *Color Board:* Create the color board by laminating and then taping together the two pages provided in Appendix A at the end of this workbook. Alternatively, these can be mounted on a large piece of cardboard, resulting in a board approximately 8 ½ inches wide by 22 inches long.

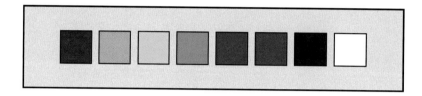

2. *32 Small Cards:* These are also provided in Appendix A. Each card has one or more colored squares. Either laminate the cards or mount each on a small piece of cardboard. Many parents find it helpful to make a color copy as a back up in case the original is damaged or lost.

3. *Work Surface:* In order to create a well-defined workspace, you may find it useful to use the same black foam desk pad or piece of black cardboard that you used for the Picture Matching activities.

4. *OPTIONAL:* A small drinking straw cut to about six inches in length or an unsharpened pencil. Either can be used by the child to tap the squares. (Another option is for the child to use his or her index finger to tap the squares. However, because of difficulties with fine motor coordination, some children find pointing to be difficult. For those children the straw or pencil may be easier).

Levels

There are six levels in this activity. They start with tapping one square with the small card in view and progress to tapping a sequence of four squares without the card in view (so that the child is working from memory). As the levels progress, more difficult items are introduced while the simpler items from earlier levels are maintained.

The Lesson Chart

Each level has 12 lessons and each lesson has 12 items, shown in a chart like the one below.

Sample Chart for Level 1 Lesson 1											
Card #	1-1	1-3	1-6	1-8	1-2	1-4	1-7	1-5	1-2	1-6	1-5	1-4
✔ or ✘												
Total ✔: _____ (Enter Total in Summary Table)							Date: _____				

In the lesson chart see the row marked **Card #.** The two-digit number (e.g., 1-1) identifies the small card to be used. (On each small card, the two digits are located in the upper left corner.)

The first digit represents the number of squares on the card:

- Cards that begin with the number 1 have one square.
- Cards that begin with the number 2 have two squares.
- Cards that begin with the number 3 have three squares.
- Cards that begin with the number 4 have four squares.

The second digit identifies the exact card to use. For example, card 1-1 has a single red square; card 1-2 has a single orange square; etc.

Procedure

1. Place the large color board on the table in front of the child (with the red square to the child's left).

2. Show the child the small card. Be sure to hold the card upright, with the card number in the upper left corner. Then point to the large board in front of the child and say, "Tap the same one here." Once the child understands how to complete the activities, usually within a few items, you no longer need to say, "Tap the same one here." Simply show the Model and wait silently for the child to tap the correct color.

   DO NOT NAME THE COLORS. IF THE CHILD NAMES THEM, DO NOT COMMENT AND DO NOT REPEAT WHAT THE CHILD HAS SAID.

3. Follow the procedures outlined in the General Guidelines for handling incorrect responses and providing hand support.

4. If the child gives a correct response on the first try, place a ✔ in the corresponding box. If the child gives an incorrect response, place an X in the box and then repeat the item until the child gives a correct response.

5. When scoring the lesson, only items with a ✔ are considered a correct response. Record the total number of correct responses at the bottom of the lesson chart. Also record the total in the Summary Table provided at the start of each level.

6. When the child has a score of 9 or higher on 3 out of 4 successive lessons in a level, move on to next level. If you reach Lesson 12, and this has not yet happened, repeat the material (starting with Lesson 1) and continue until the child has a score of 9 or higher on 3 out of 4 successive Lessons.

LEVEL 1
Tapping One Square (with Card in View)

In Level 1, the child sees a card with one square. He or she then has to tap the same colored square on the large color board.

Level 1 Summary Table
(to be filled in at the completion of each lesson)

Lesson	1	2	3	4	5	6	7	8	9	10	11	12
Date												
Total # Correct Responses												

When the child attains a score of 9 or higher in 3 of 4 consecutive lessons, move on to the next level.

Level 1 Lesson 1

Card #	1-1	1-2	1-3	1-4	1-5	1-6	1-7	1-8	1-2	1-6	1-5	1-4
✔ or ✗												

Total ✔: _____ (Enter Total in Summary Table)   Date: _____

Level 1 Lesson 2

Card #	1-6	1-1	1-8	1-4	1-5	1-2	1-7	1-3	1-8	1-1	1-4	1-2
✔ or ✗												

Total ✔: _____ (Enter Total in Summary Table)   Date: _____

Level 1 Lesson 3

Card #	1-4	1-5	1-6	1-7	1-8	1-6	1-2	1-1	1-3	1-7	1-5	1-6
✔ or ✗												

Total ✔: _____ (Enter Total in Summary Table)   Date: _____

Level 1 Lesson 4

Card #	1-5	1-8	1-6	1-1	1-2	1-3	1-7	1-4	1-8	1-1	1-5	1-7
✔ or ✗												

Total ✔: _____ (Enter Total in Summary Table)   Date: _____

Level 1 Lesson 5

Card #	1-1	1-2	1-3	1-4	1-5	1-6	1-7	1-8	1-2	1-6	1-5	1-4
✔ or ✗												

Total ✔: _____ (Enter Total in Summary Table)   Date: _____

Level 1 Lesson 6

Card #	1-6	1-1	1-8	1-4	1-5	1-2	1-7	1-3	1-8	1-1	1-4	1-2
✔ or ✗												

Total ✔: _____ (Enter Total in Summary Table)   Date: _____

Level 1 Lesson 7

Card #	1-4	1-5	1-6	1-7	1-8	1-6	1-2	1-1	1-3	1-7	1-5	1-6
✔ or ✘												

Total ✔: _____ (Enter Total in Summary Table)   Date: _____

Level 1 Lesson 8

Card #	1-5	1-8	1-6	1-1	1-2	1-3	1-7	1-4	1-8	1-1	1-5	1-7
✔ or ✘												

Total ✔: _____ (Enter Total in Summary Table)   Date: _____

Level 1 Lesson 9

Card #	1-1	1-2	1-3	1-4	1-5	1-6	1-7	1-8	1-2	1-6	1-5	1-4
✔ or ✘												

Total ✔: _____ (Enter Total in Summary Table)   Date: _____

Level 1 Lesson 10

Card #	1-6	1-1	1-8	1-4	1-5	1-2	1-7	1-3	1-8	1-1	1-4	1-2
✔ or ✘												

Total ✔: _____ (Enter Total in Summary Table)   Date: _____

Level 1 Lesson 11

Card #	1-4	1-5	1-6	1-7	1-8	1-6	1-2	1-1	1-3	1-7	1-5	1-6
✔ or ✘												

Total ✔: _____ (Enter Total in Summary Table)   Date: _____

Level 1 Lesson 12

Card #	1-5	1-8	1-6	1-1	1-2	1-3	1-7	1-4	1-8	1-1	1-5	1-7
✔ or ✘												

Total ✔: _____ (Enter Total in Summary Table)   Date: _____

LEVEL 2
Tapping Two Squares (with Card in View)

Level 2 uses some cards with one colored square and some cards with two colored squares. If the card shows two colors, the child taps the corresponding colors on the large color board in left-to-right sequence. Hold the small card so that the colors are in the same sequence as they are on the larger board (e.g., a card with yellow and blue should be held so that the yellow is to the left of the blue). In that way, the colors always remain in the same sequence as they appear on the larger board.

Level 2 Summary Table
(to be filled in at the completion of each lesson)

Lesson	1	2	3	4	5	6	7	8	9	10	11	12
Date												
Total # Correct Responses												

When the child attains a score of 9 or higher in 3 of 4 consecutive lessons, move on to the next level.

Level 2 Lesson 1

Card #	1-1	2-6	2-4	1-3	2-3	2-5	2-7	2-2	2-1	1-5	2-6	2-4
✔ or ✗												

Total ✔: _____ (Enter Total in Summary Table)   Date: _____

Level 2 Lesson 2

Card #	2-7	2-6	1-5	2-1	2-5	1-6	2-4	2-7	1-7	2-2	2-3	2-8
✔ or ✗												

Total ✔: _____ (Enter Total in Summary Table)   Date: _____

Level 2 Lesson 3

Card #	1-5	2-1	2-5	1-8	2-6	2-7	1-4	2-2	2-3	2-8	2-5	2-4
✔ or ✗												

Total ✔: _____ (Enter Total in Summary Table)   Date: _____

Level 2 Lesson 4

Card #	2-1	2-5	2-2	2-7	2-4	1-1	2-3	2-6	1-5	2-5	2-1	1-8
✔ or ✗												

Total ✔: _____ (Enter Total in Summary Table)   Date: _____

Level 2 Lesson 5

Card #	1-1	2-6	2-4	1-3	2-3	2-5	2-7	2-2	2-1	1-5	2-6	2-4
✔ or ✗												

Total ✔: _____ (Enter Total in Summary Table)   Date: _____

Level 2 Lesson 6

Card #	2-7	2-6	1-5	2-1	2-5	1-6	2-4	2-7	1-7	2-2	2-3	2-8
✔ or ✗												

Total ✔: _____ (Enter Total in Summary Table)   Date: _____

Level 2 Lesson 7

Card #	1-5	2-1	2-5	1-8	2-6	2-7	1-4	2-2	2-3	2-8	2-5	2-4
✔ or ✗												

Total ✔: _____ (Enter Total in Summary Table)　　　Date: _____

Level 2 Lesson 8

Card #	2-1	2-5	2-2	2-7	2-4	1-1	2-3	2-6	1-5	2-5	2-1	1-8
✔ or ✗												

Total ✔: _____ (Enter Total in Summary Table)　　　Date: _____

Level 2 Lesson 9

Card #	1-1	2-6	2-4	1-3	2-3	2-5	2-7	2-2	2-1	1-5	2-6	2-4
✔ or ✗												

Total ✔: _____ (Enter Total in Summary Table)　　　Date: _____

Level 2 Lesson 10

Card #	2-7	2-6	1-5	2-1	2-5	1-6	2-4	2-7	1-7	2-2	2-3	2-8
✔ or ✗												

Total ✔: _____ (Enter Total in Summary Table)　　　Date: _____

Level 2 Lesson 11

Card #	1-5	2-1	2-5	1-8	2-6	2-7	1-4	2-2	2-3	2-8	2-5	2-4
✔ or ✗												

Total ✔: _____ (Enter Total in Summary Table)　　　Date: _____

Level 2 Lesson 12

Card #	2-1	2-5	2-2	2-7	2-4	1-1	2-3	2-6	1-5	2-5	2-1	1-8
✔ or ✗												

Total ✔: _____ (Enter Total in Summary Table)　　　Date: _____

LEVEL 3
Tapping Two Squares (with Card in View) and Tapping One Square (from Memory)

At this level, some of the items require memory. These items are indicated in gray. For these items, show the child the card, and then turn it face down so that it is no longer in view. The child then has to tap the correct squares from memory.

(**Reminder:** if the child gives an incorrect response for an item requiring memory, repeat the item without requiring memory — that is, allow the child to see the card while he or she taps out the sequence. Once the child does this correctly, repeat the item again, but turn the card over so that the child taps the sequence from memory.)

Level 3 Summary Table
(to be filled in at the completion of each lesson)

Lesson	1	2	3	4	5	6	7	8	9	10	11	12
Date												
Total # Correct Responses												

When the child attains a score of 9 or higher in 3 of 4 consecutive lessons, move on to the next level.

BOXES IN GRAY REPRESENT ITEMS THAT REQUIRE MEMORY

Level 3 Lesson 1												
Card #	2-1	1-4	1-5	2-2	2-5	1-8	2-4	1-5	2-3	1-1	2-6	2-7
✔ or ✘												
Total ✔: _____ (Enter Total in Summary Table) Date: _____												

Level 3 Lesson 2												
Card #	2-2	2-5	1-7	2-4	2-3	2-7	1-5	1-3	2-6	1-8	2-4	1-6
✔ or ✘												
Total ✔: _____ (Enter Total in Summary Table) Date: _____												

Level 3 Lesson 3												
Card #	2-4	1-3	1-8	2-2	2-5	1-5	2-6	1-5	2-7	1-1	2-1	2-3
✔ or ✘												
Total ✔: _____ (Enter Total in Summary Table) Date: _____												

Level 3 Lesson 4												
Card #	2-6	2-3	1-5	2-2	2-1	1-8	1-7	2-5	2-4	1-4	2-7	1-6
✔ or ✘												
Total ✔: _____ (Enter Total in Summary Table) Date: _____												

Level 3 Lesson 5												
Card #	2-1	1-4	1-5	2-2	2-5	1-8	2-4	1-5	2-3	1-1	2-6	2-7
✔ or ✘												
Total ✔: _____ (Enter Total in Summary Table) Date: _____												

Level 3 Lesson 6												
Card #	2-2	2-5	1-7	2-4	2-3	2-7	1-5	1-3	2-6	1-8	2-4	1-6
✔ or ✘												
Total ✔: _____ (Enter Total in Summary Table) Date: _____												

74

Level 3 Lesson 7

Card #	2-4	1-3	1-8	2-2	2-5	1-5	2-6	1-5	2-7	1-1	2-1	2-3
✔ or ✘												

Total ✔: _____ (Enter Total in Summary Table)   Date: _____

Level 3 Lesson 8

Card #	2-6	2-3	1-5	2-2	2-1	1-8	1-7	2-5	2-4	1-4	2-7	1-6
✔ or ✘												

Total ✔: _____ (Enter Total in Summary Table)   Date: _____

Level 32 Lesson 9

Card #	2-1	1-4	1-5	2-2	2-5	1-8	2-4	1-5	2-3	1-1	2-6	2-7
✔ or ✘												

Total ✔: _____ (Enter Total in Summary Table)   Date: _____

Level 3 Lesson 10

Card #	2-2	2-5	1-7	2-4	2-3	2-7	1-5	1-3	2-6	1-8	2-4	1-6
✔ or ✘												

Total ✔: _____ (Enter Total in Summary Table)   Date: _____

Level 3 Lesson 11

Card #	2-4	1-3	1-8	2-2	2-5	1-5	2-6	1-5	2-7	1-1	2-1	2-3
✔ or ✘												

Total ✔: _____ (Enter Total in Summary Table)   Date: _____

Level 3 Lesson 12

Card #	2-6	2-3	1-5	2-2	2-1	1-8	1-7	2-5	2-4	1-4	2-7	1-6
✔ or ✘												

Total ✔: _____ (Enter Total in Summary Table)   Date: _____

LEVEL 4
Tapping Three Squares (with Card in View) and Tapping Two Squares (from Memory)

At this level, the child taps up to three squares in view and two from memory

Level 4 Summary Table
(to be filled in at the completion of each lesson)

Lesson	1	2	3	4	5	6	7	8	9	10	11	12
Date												
Total # Correct Responses												

When the child attains a score of 9 or higher in 3 of 4 consecutive lessons, move on to the next level.

BOXES IN GRAY REPRESENT ITEMS THAT REQUIRE MEMORY

Level 4 Lesson 1

Card #	3-1	2-2	1-1	2-5	3-2	2-4	3-5	2-3	1-7	1-4	2-1	2-5
✔ or ✘												

Total ✔: _____ (Enter Total in Summary Table)   Date: _____

Level 4 Lesson 2

Card #	3-6	2-1	1-3	2-6	3-4	1-8	2-6	2-7	3-7	2-2	2-5	2-4
✔ or ✘												

Total ✔: _____ (Enter Total in Summary Table)   Date: _____

Level 4 Lesson 3

Card #	3-3	2-6	1-6	2-5	3-5	2-7	3-8	2-4	1-4	1-3	2-1	2-2
✔ or ✘												

Total ✔: _____ (Enter Total in Summary Table)   Date: _____

Level 4 Lesson 4

Card #	3-5	2-3	1-7	2-5	3-1	1-5	2-7	2-6	3-2	2-1	3-3	2-2
✔ or ✘												

Total ✔: _____ (Enter Total in Summary Table)   Date: _____

Level 4 Lesson 5

Card #	3-1	2-2	1-1	2-5	3-2	2-4	3-5	2-3	1-7	1-4	2-1	2-5
✔ or ✘												

Total ✔: _____ (Enter Total in Summary Table)   Date: _____

Level 4 Lesson 6

Card #	3-6	2-1	1-3	2-6	3-4	1-8	2-6	2-7	3-7	2-2	2-5	2-4
✔ or ✘												

Total ✔: _____ (Enter Total in Summary Table)   Date: _____

Level 4 Lesson 7

Card #	3-3	2-6	1-6	2-5	3-5	2-7	3-8	2-4	1-4	1-3	2-1	2-2
✔ or ✗												

Total ✔: _____ (Enter Total in Summary Table)   Date: _____

Level 4 Lesson 8

Card #	3-5	2-3	1-7	2-5	3-1	1-5	2-7	2-6	3-2	2-1	3-3	2-2
✔ or ✗												

Total ✔: _____ (Enter Total in Summary Table)   Date: _____

Level 4 Lesson 9

Card #	3-1	2-2	1-1	2-5	3-2	2-4	3-5	2-3	1-7	1-4	2-1	2-5
✔ or ✗												

Total ✔: _____ (Enter Total in Summary Table)   Date: _____

Level 4 Lesson 10

Card #	3-6	2-1	1-3	2-6	3-4	1-8	2-6	2-7	3-7	2-2	2-5	2-4
✔ or ✗												

Total ✔: _____ (Enter Total in Summary Table)   Date: _____

Level 4 Lesson 11

Card #	3-3	2-6	1-6	2-5	3-5	2-7	3-8	2-4	1-4	1-3	2-1	2-2
✔ or ✗												

Total ✔: _____ (Enter Total in Summary Table)   Date: _____

Level 4 Lesson 12

Card #	3-5	2-3	1-7	2-5	3-1	1-5	2-7	2-6	3-2	2-1	3-3	2-2
✔ or ✗												

Total ✔: _____ (Enter Total in Summary Table)   Date: _____

LEVEL 5
Tapping Four Squares (with Card in View) and
Tapping Three Squares (from Memory)

At this level, the child taps up to four squares in view and three from memory.

Level 5 Summary Table
(to be filled in at the completion of each lesson)

Lesson	1	2	3	4	5	6	7	8	9	10	11	12
Date												
Total # Correct Responses												

When the child attains a score of 9 or higher in 3 of 4 consecutive lessons, move on to the next level.

BOXES IN GRAY REPRESENT ITEMS THAT REQUIRE MEMORY

Level 5 Lesson 1

Card #	4-1	3-1	2-2	2-5	3-2	3-7	4-7	2-3	4-5	1-5	4-2	2-2
✔ or ✘												

Total ✔: _____ (Enter Total in Summary Table)   Date: _____

Level 5 Lesson 2

Card #	4-6	3-6	1-1	2-7	3-8	3-3	2-1	1-7	3-5	2-2	2-5	4-7
✔ or ✘												

Total ✔: _____ (Enter Total in Summary Table)   Date: _____

Level 5 Lesson 3

Card #	4-5	3-4	1-8	2-3	2-1	3-6	4-2	2-6	4-7	1-3	4-1	2-4
✔ or ✘												

Total ✔: _____ (Enter Total in Summary Table)   Date: _____

Level 5 Lesson 4

Card #	4-2	3-5	1-6	2-2	3-3	3-8	2-1	1-4	3-7	2-4	2-5	4-6
✔ or ✘												

Total ✔: _____ (Enter Total in Summary Table)   Date: _____

Level 5 Lesson 5

Card #	4-1	3-1	2-2	2-5	3-2	3-7	4-7	2-3	4-5	1-5	4-2	2-2
✔ or ✘												

Total ✔: _____ (Enter Total in Summary Table)   Date: _____

Level 5 Lesson 6

Card #	4-6	3-6	1-1	2-7	3-8	3-3	2-1	1-7	3-5	2-2	2-5	4-7
✔ or ✘												

Total ✔: _____ (Enter Total in Summary Table)   Date: _____

Level 5 Lesson 7

Card #	4-5	3-4	1-8	2-3	2-1	3-6	4-2	2-6	4-7	1-3	4-1	2-4
✔ or ✘												

Total ✔: _____ (Enter Total in Summary Table)   Date: _____

Level 5 Lesson 8

Card #	4-2	3-5	1-6	2-2	3-3	3-8	2-1	1-4	3-7	2-4	2-5	4-6
✔ or ✘												

Total ✔: _____ (Enter Total in Summary Table)   Date: _____

Level 5 Lesson 9

Card #	4-1	3-1	2-2	2-5	3-2	3-7	4-7	2-3	4-5	1-5	4-2	2-2
✔ or ✘												

Total ✔: _____ (Enter Total in Summary Table)   Date: _____

Level 5 Lesson 10

Card #	4-6	3-6	1-1	2-7	3-8	3-3	2-1	1-7	3-5	2-2	2-5	4-7
✔ or ✘												

Total ✔: _____ (Enter Total in Summary Table)   Date: _____

Level 5 Lesson 11

Card #	4-5	3-4	1-8	2-3	2-1	3-6	4-2	2-6	4-7	1-3	4-1	2-4
✔ or ✘												

Total ✔: _____ (Enter Total in Summary Table)   Date: _____

Level 5 Lesson 12

Card #	4-2	3-5	1-6	2-2	3-3	3-8	2-1	1-4	3-7	2-4	2-5	4-6
✔ or ✘												

Total ✔: _____ (Enter Total in Summary Table)   Date: _____

LEVEL 6
Tapping Four Squares (from Memory)

At this level, the child taps up to four squares in view and from memory.

Level 6 Summary Table
(to be filled in at the completion of each lesson)

Lesson	1	2	3	4	5	6	7	8	9	10	11	12
Date												
Total # Correct Responses												

When the child has achieved a score of 9 or higher in 3 of 4 consecutive lessons, this activity is completed. If the other Pre-Language activities are not yet completed, continue to repeat a lesson from the highest level of this activity at least 3 times per week while the others are still in progress. Once all Pre-Language activities have been completed, the child can move on to Part 2: Language Skills.

ACTIVITY C: SEQUENCING VISUAL PATTERNS

BOXES IN GRAY REPRESENT ITEMS THAT REQUIRE MEMORY

Level 6 Lesson 1												
Card #	4-1	3-2	1-4	2-1	3-8	3-3	4-2	2-6	4-7	1-7	4-4	2-2
✔ or ✘												
Total ✔: _____ (Enter Total in Summary Table)								Date: _____				

Level 6 Lesson 2												
Card #	4-2	3-6	1-3	2-5	4-5	4-8	2-4	1-1	3-2	2-3	4-1	4-5
✔ or ✘												
Total ✔: _____ (Enter Total in Summary Table)								Date: _____				

Level 6 Lesson 3												
Card #	4-7	3-3	1-8	4-4	3-5	3-7	4-8	2-7	4-5	1-4	4-1	2-2
✔ or ✘												
Total ✔: _____ (Enter Total in Summary Table)								Date: _____				

Level 6 Lesson 4												
Card #	4-5	3-1	1-5	4-6	3-4	4-7	2-6	1-2	4-8	4-5	2-1	4-2
✔ or ✘												
Total ✔: _____ (Enter Total in Summary Table)								Date: _____				

Level 6 Lesson 5												
Card #	4-1	3-2	1-4	2-1	3-8	3-3	4-2	2-6	4-7	1-7	4-4	2-2
✔ or ✘												
Total ✔: _____ (Enter Total in Summary Table)								Date: _____				

Level 6 Lesson 6												
Card #	4-2	3-6	1-3	2-5	4-5	4-8	2-4	1-1	3-2	2-3	4-1	4-5
✔ or ✘												
Total ✔: _____ (Enter Total in Summary Table)								Date: _____				

Level 6 Lesson 7

Card #	4-7	3-3	1-8	4-4	3-5	3-7	4-8	2-7	4-5	1-4	4-1	2-2
✔ or ✗												

Total ✔: _____ (Enter Total in Summary Table) Date: _____

Level 6 Lesson 8

Card #	4-5	3-1	1-5	4-6	3-4	4-7	2-6	1-2	4-8	4-5	2-1	4-2
✔ or ✗												

Total ✔: _____ (Enter Total in Summary Table) Date: _____

Level 6 Lesson 9

Card #	4-1	3-2	1-4	2-1	3-8	3-3	4-2	2-6	4-7	1-7	4-4	2-2
✔ or ✗												

Total ✔: _____ (Enter Total in Summary Table) Date: _____

Level 6 Lesson 10

Card #	4-2	3-6	1-3	2-5	4-5	4-8	2-4	1-1	3-2	2-3	4-1	4-5
✔ or ✗												

Total ✔: _____ (Enter Total in Summary Table) Date: _____

Level 6 Lesson 11

Card #	4-7	3-3	1-8	4-4	3-5	3-7	4-8	2-7	4-5	1-4	4-1	2-2
✔ or ✗												

Total ✔: _____ (Enter Total in Summary Table) Date: _____

Level 6 Lesson 12

Card #	4-5	3-1	1-5	4-6	3-4	4-7	2-6	1-2	4-8	4-5	2-1	4-2
✔ or ✗												

Total ✔: _____ (Enter Total in Summary Table) Date: _____

ACTIVITY D
BUILDING RECEPTIVE LANGUAGE

Overview

This activity is the only one of the Pre-Language activities that concentrates on language. Aimed at developing receptive language, it enables the child to understand and respond to increasingly complex requests (commands) with no requirement for speaking.

Receptive language activities are common in many intervention programs. However, the focus has typically been on nouns (e.g., *car, house, cup*) and features of those nouns (e.g., *yellow car, big cup,* etc.). By contrast, the activities in this program concentrate on integrating two major language categories—nouns and verbs. Those categories are essential to the development of language. When these categories are initially established via receptive language, the child's mastery of expressive language is eased significantly.

Materials

1. *Small toys (objects):* Small toys representing people, animals, and vehicles, approximately 3 to 5 inches in size.

Objects	Number needed	Recommended toy brands (available at www.amazon.com)
kids (some boys & some girls)	6	*Plan Toy Doll Family* (http://amzn.to/19a4YRo) *KidKraft Doll Family* (http://amzn.to/18D1C7m) *Hape Doll Family* (http://amzn.to/1aD48Kl)
ladies	6	
men	2	
dogs	6	*Toob (Safari LTD)* (http://amzn.to/19P3GGC) (http://amzn.to/14W0HO6) (http://amzn.to/18D2b19) (http://amzn.to/17gjyV2)
frogs	6	
cats	6	
birds	6	
cars	6	*Hot Wheels* (http://amzn.to/19a5WgB) *MatchBox* (http://amzn.to/19hJUmg)
buses	6	*DieCast Bus* (http://amzn.to/19P4dIs)
trucks	6	*MatchBox* (http://amzn.to/19hJUmg)
planes	6	*InAir Planes (WWII 6 piece set)* (http://amzn.to/1bUq3QR)

It's best if the set of objects within a category are not identical. For example, the cars should be different in color and style, the dogs should differ in size and appearance, and so on. The variation encourages flexibility and generalization.

2. *Storage:* One or two utility trays to organize the objects. The trays should have several deep compartments that can store the objects. This will make it easier for you to locate the correct objects during the sessions. We suggest the Stanley Professional Deep Organizer with 10 removable compartments (available on Amazon.com at http://amzn.to/15EliDT).

3. *Work Surface:* In order to create a well-defined work space, you may find it useful to use the same black foam pad or black cardboard that you used for the Picture Matching activities.

Levels

The activity has four levels. Level 1 is aimed at teaching a set of 12 nouns via the use of the single action *"give me."* The child will be responding to requests such as *"give me the car," "give me the frog,"* etc. By Level 4, the requests become longer and more complex. This is achieved by including requests involving two objects and two actions (e.g., *"shake the plane and then hug the lady"*). Levels 1 and 2 have twelve lessons each, and Levels 3 and 4 have six lessons each. The child will complete all lessons in a level before advancing to the next level.

The Lesson Chart

Each lesson has 12 items. Some sample items from an early lesson aimed at teaching the word *"car"* appear below.

	Objects		Adult's Actions & Words	✔ if correct		
	Model	*Choices*		1st	2nd	3rd
1	CAR	car frog dog	holding model *"This is a car. Give me another car."*			
2	CAR	lady car bird	holding model *"This is a car. Give me another car."*			
3		frog car kid dog	*"Give me a car."*			

In the lesson chart, the column labeled **Objects** indicates the objects needed for the lesson. The **Choices** are placed on the table in front of the child. When a new word is first introduced, a **Model** is needed in order to ensure that the child understands the meaning of the word. The model is typically held in the adult's hand, whereas the choices are placed on the table in front of the child.

The column labeled **Adult's Actions & Words** indicates what the adult should do (shown in gray) and say (shown in black). For all items, the child has to use the correct object(s) to perform the correct action(s).

The lessons here are evaluated differently from those in the other Pre-Language activities. In the other activities, a lesson was offered only once. Here, because the language may be new to the child and more challenging, he or she is given up to three opportunities to succeed in any lesson. This is reflected in the lesson chart by the columns labeled **1st, 2nd,** and **3rd.** These columns are for keeping track of correct and incorrect responses. The first column is used when the lesson is carried out for the first time. If the child's performance meets the criteria to move on, the lesson is considered complete and is not repeated. The next day the child moves on to the next lesson. However, if the child does not meet criteria to move on, the lesson is repeated the next day and the scores are recorded in the 2nd column. The same thing can occur a third time, and this is recorded in the 3rd column.

A lesson is not administered more than three times. After the third time, the child proceeds to the next lesson. There are several reasons for allowing the child to move on in this way. First, experience has shown us that children generally have learned the new material after three trials even if their performance does not meet strict criteria for moving on. Second, children may show difficulty early on, but it is important to allow them to move ahead to new material. Most children adapt over time and begin to show success as the program progresses. (Further detail is provided in the following section *Procedures.*)

Procedure

1. Place all objects that are needed for the lesson off to the side of the table so they are accessible to you but out of the child's reach. (NOTE: Do not allow the child to play with these objects either during our outside of the teaching sessions. This rule applies to all materials used in the program.)

2. For each item, set out the **Choices** in front of the child. From one item to the next, vary the arrangement of the **Choices** (e.g., sometimes line the objects in a row, sometimes in a 2x2 arrangement, etc.). The variability encourages flexibility.

3. If the item has a **Model**, hold the model in your hand.

4. Do and say what is shown in the column labeled **Adult's Actions & Words**. For example, in item 1 above, the adult will hold the **Model** and say, "This is a car. Give me another car." By contrast, in item 3 above, the adult offers no model and simply says, "Give me a car."

5. If the child gives a correct response on the first try, place a ✔ in the corresponding box in the 1ˢᵗ column. Only items with a ✔ are considered a correct response. If the child gives an incorrect response, place an ✗ in the box and then repeat the item until the child gives a correct response.

6. Unlike the other Pre-Language activities, this one requires that the child complete every lesson at a level before moving on to the next level. Levels 1 and 2 have 12 lessons. Levels 3 and 4 have 6 lessons.

7. A lesson may occur one, two, or three times, depending on the child's performance. If the child has fewer than 9 correct responses on the first trial, repeat the same lesson the following day and record the child's responses in the 2ⁿᵈ column. If the child again has fewer than 9 correct responses, repeat the same lesson a third time on the following day and record the responses in the 3ʳᵈ column. The maximum number of times a child does the same lesson is three times. After the 3ʳᵈ time, you move on to the next lesson regardless of how many correct responses were given. (If a child is having a great deal of difficulty, it may be useful to postpone the program for 6 to 8 weeks.)

8. Follow the procedures outlined in the General Guidelines for handling incorrect responses and providing hand support.

9. Record the total number of correct responses at the bottom of the lesson chart. Also record the total in the Summary Table provided at the start of each level.

NOTE: If the child has motor difficulties or is making frequent errors, support the child's hand so that he or she can execute the movement more effectively. In providing hand support, hold the child's hand in a way that prevents him or her from reaching for the incorrect object or carrying out incorrect movements. (In other words, do not move the child's hand to the correct object, but do prevent the child from moving to an incorrect object or from performing an incorrect action.)

As described in the General Guidelines, if the child is having clear difficulty in knowing what to do, you can model a correct response by using hand-over-hand movement (in which you actively move the child's hand in order to show the correct response). Following this, you repeat the item until the child can complete the action without prompting or modeling (though you still may be providing hand support—see the General Guidelines for further details).

Outside the Session

As the child learns the language, it is important to begin using the new linguistic forms in real-life settings. For example, once the child has learned to respond to requests that involve handing over objects (e.g., "give me the car"), similar requests should be made during everyday life (e.g., at the dinner table say, "give me the spoon").

At the end of Lesson 1 in each Level, sample items are offered to illustrate the kinds of requests that should be made over the course of the day. These are just examples. Parents should also create their own. **Bringing language from the lesson into real-life settings is an essential part of the program and will become even more important as the child progresses to more complex language.**

LEVEL 1

In Level 1, ten nouns are taught: *car, kid, frog, lady, truck, cat, bird, bus, plane,* and *dog*. They are taught in both the singular and plural form (e.g., kid and kids). While many children are familiar with all the nouns, few are familiar with the plural form. As a result, even if your child knows all the nouns, it is important to have him or her go through this level.

All requests in this level are in the form "give me the ____." It is important that you **do not** gesture with your hand as you make the request (a gesture signals to the child what to do and so enables him or her to carry out the request without listening to the language). Instead, only hold out your hand *after* the child has picked up the object and has reached out to give it to you.

There are 12 Lessons in Level 1, and the child completes all of them before moving on to Level 2. Only one new word is introduced in any lesson. As the lessons advance, any words previously taught re-appear so that the variation in the language steadily increases. Another feature of the lessons is that plurals are taught. An understanding of plurals is essential to mastering language.

Note: For items 7, 8, 9, & 12, the child must give the adult ALL the cars.

Level 1 Lesson 1			Adult's Actions & Words	✔ if correct		
	Objects			Dates: ___ ___ ___ 1st 2nd 3rd		
	Model	Choices		1st	2nd	3rd
1	CAR	car frog dog	holding model *"This is a car. Give me another car."*			
2	CAR	lady car bird	holding model *"This is a car. Give me another car."*			
3	CAR	frog car kid dog	holding model *"This is a car. Give me another car."*			
4		2 kids car	*"Give me a car."*			
5		car truck dog	*"Give me a car."*			
6		bus man car	*"Give me a car."*			
7	2 CARS	2 cars dog kid	holding models *"These are cars. Give me the other cars."*			
8	3 CARS	cat dog 2 cars	holding models *"These are cars. Give me the other cars."*			
9		3 cars bird 2 trucks	*"Give me the cars."*			
10		2 ladies kid car	*"Give me the car."*			
11		man car truck	*"Give me the car."*			
12		2 cars 2 frogs	*"Give me the cars."*			
			Total			

If Total is 9 or higher, move on to the next lesson. If Total is fewer than 9, repeat this lesson the next day. If the child has completed this lesson 3 times, move on to the next lesson regardless of the score.

Level 1 Sample Daily Real-World Exercises

Note: For these activities, you should only use nouns that the child already knows. The items below are only examples.

Setting	Adult's Actions & Words
Home	"Give me the cup."
Home	"Give me the spoons."
Home	"Give me a pen."
Home	"Give me the books."
Home	"Give me a cookie."
Playground	"Give me a rock."
Playground	"Give me a ball."
Restaurant	"Give me the fork."
Restaurant	"Give me the bowl."
Bathroom	"Give me the soap."

NOTE: For items 7, 8, 10, & 12, the child must give the adult ALL the kids.

	Level 1 Lesson 2		Adult's Actions & Words	Dates: _____ _____ _____ 1st 2nd 3rd		
	Objects			**✔ if correct**		
	Model	*Choices*		*1st*	*2nd*	*3rd*
1	KID	kid frog dog	holding model *"This is a kid. Give me another kid."*			
2	KID	kid bird plane	holding model *"This is a kid. Give me another kid."*			
3	KID	frog kid bus	holding model *"This is a kid. Give me another kid."*			
4		2 birds kid	*"Give me a kid."*			
5		kid truck dog	*"Give me a kid."*			
6		bus kid car	*"Give me a kid."*			
7	2 KIDS	2 kids frog dog	holding models *"These are kids. Give me the other kids."*			
8	3 KIDS	cat 3 kids 2 dogs	holding models *"These are kids. Give me the other kids."*			
9		kid bird truck	*"Give me the kid."*			
10		2 kids 2 cars dog	*"Give me the kids."*			
11		car truck kid	*"Give me the kid."*			
12		car 2 frogs 3 kids	*"Give me the kids."*			
			Total			

If Total is 9 or higher, move on to the next lesson. If Total is fewer than 9, repeat this lesson the next day. If the child has completed this lesson 3 times, move on to the next lesson regardless of the score.

Remember to carry out Daily Real-World Exercises each day (see Chart following Level 1 Lesson 1). The items in the chart are only examples. You should create your own and use them regularly throughout the day.

NOTES:

- This lesson is a review of the two words taught so far (car & kid); accordingly, no models are used, and the column for Models does not appear in the chart. Although the child already knows these words, the intermixing can prove challenging, so it is not unexpected to find the child showing some confusion or resistance.

- For items 7 and 9, the child must give ONLY one object. For items 5, 6, 10, & 11, the child must give ALL the objects requested.

Level 1 Lesson 3		Dates: ___ ___ ___ 1st 2nd 3rd			
	Choices	Adult's Actions & Words	**✔ if correct**		
			1st	*2nd*	*3rd*
1	kid frog dog	*"Give me the kid."*			
2	plane kid 2 birds	*"Give me the kid."*			
3	frog car bus	*"Give me the car."*			
4	truck bird car	*"Give me the car."*			
5	2 cars truck 2 dogs	*"Give me the cars."*			
6	bus 2 cars 3 kids	*"Give me the kids."*			
7	3 kids car frog dog	*"Give me a kid."*			
8	cat kid dog	*"Give me a kid."*			
9	2 cars bird truck	*"Give me a car."*			
10	3 cars man plane	*"Give me the cars."*			
11	3 kids car truck	*"Give me the kids."*			
12	car kid 2 frogs	*"Give me a kid."*			
		Total			

If Total is 9 or higher, move on to the next lesson. If Total is fewer than 9, repeat this lesson the next day. If the child has completed this lesson 3 times, move on to the next lesson regardless of the score.

Remember to carry out Daily Real-World Exercises each day (see Chart following Level 1 Lesson 1). The items in the chart are only examples. You should create your own and use them regularly throughout the day.

NOTE: For items with plurals, the child must give all the objects requested.

Level 1 Lesson 4			Adult's Actions & Words	✔ if correct		
	Objects			Dates: ___ ___ ___ 1st 2nd 3rd		
	Model	Choices		1st	2nd	3rd
1	FROG	frog man dog	holding model "This is a frog. Give me another frog."			
2	FROG	lady frog 2 birds	holding model "This is a frog. Give me another frog."			
3	FROG	bird frog bus	holding model "This is a frog. Give me another frog."			
4	2 FROGS	2 birds 2 frogs	holding models "These are frogs. Give me the other frogs."			
5	3 FROGS	3 frogs truck 2 dogs	holding models "These are frogs. Give me the other frogs."			
6		bus frog car	"Give me the frog."			
7		bus frog lady	"Give me the frog."			
8		2 frogs plane 2 dogs	"Give me the frogs."			
9		cat kid dog	"Give me the kid."			
10		car bird truck	"Give me the car."			
11		2 ladies 2 cars dog	"Give me the cars."			
12		frog truck 3 kids	"Give me the kids."			
			Total			

If Total is 9 or higher, move on to the next lesson. If Total is fewer than 9, repeat this lesson the next day. If the child has completed this lesson 3 times, move on to the next lesson regardless of the score.

Remember to carry out Daily Real-World Exercises each day (see Chart following Level 1 Lesson 1). The items in the chart are only examples. You should create your own and use them regularly throughout the day.

NOTES: For items with plurals, the child must give all the objects requested. For items with a singular noun, such as items 11 & 12, the child must give only one object.

Level 1 Lesson 5			Adult's Actions & Words	✔ if correct		
	Objects			Dates: ___ 1st ___ 2nd ___ 3rd		
	Model	Choices		1st	2nd	3rd
1	LADY	lady bird dog	holding model *"This is a lady. Give me another lady."*			
2	LADY	car lady 2 birds	holding model *"This is a lady. Give me another lady."*			
3	LADY	bird lady bus	holding model *"This is a lady. Give me another lady."*			
4	2 LADIES	2 birds 2 ladies	holding models *"These are ladies. Give me the other ladies."*			
5	3 LADIES	2 ladies truck dog	holding models "These are ladies. Give me the other ladies."			
6		bus lady car	*"Give me the lady."*			
7		2 ladies plane 2 dogs	*"Give me the ladies."*			
8		cat 2 kids dog	*"Give me a kid."*			
9		3 cars bird truck	*"Give me the cars."*			
10		frog lady car dog	*"Give me a frog."*			
11		kid truck 3 cars	*"Give me a car."*			
12		car 2 ladies plane	*"Give me a lady."*			
			Total			

If Total is 9 or higher, move on to the next lesson. If Total is fewer than 9, repeat this lesson the next day. If the child has completed this lesson 3 times, move on to the next lesson regardless of the score.

Remember to carry out Daily Real-World Exercises each day (see Chart following Level 1 Lesson 1). The items in the chart are only examples. You should create your own and use them regularly throughout the day.

NOTES: For items with plurals, the child must give all the objects requested. For items with a singular noun, the child must give only one object.

	Objects		Adult's Actions & Words	✔ if correct		
Level 1 Lesson 6	**Model**	**Choices**		**Dates:** ___ 1ˢᵗ ___ 2ⁿᵈ ___ 3ʳᵈ		
	Model	Choices		1ˢᵗ	2ⁿᵈ	3ʳᵈ
1	TRUCK	truck bird dog	holding model "This is a truck. Give me another truck."			
2	TRUCK	car truck 2 birds	holding model "This is a truck. Give me another truck."			
3	TRUCK	man truck bus	holding model "This is a truck. Give me another truck."			
4	3 TRUCKS	2 birds 2 trucks	holding models "These are trucks. Give me the other trucks."			
5	2 TRUCKS	3 trucks car 2 dogs	holding models "These are trucks. Give me the other trucks."			
6		bus truck car	"Give me the truck."			
7		2 trucks plane dog	"Give me a truck."			
8		cat kid dog	"Give me a kid."			
9		3 cars bird truck	"Give me a car."			
10		2 frogs lady 2 dogs	"Give me the frogs."			
11		frog 2 ladies truck	"Give me the ladies."			
12		2 cars kid plane	"Give me a car."			
Total						

If Total is 9 or higher, move on to the next lesson. If Total is fewer than 9, repeat this lesson the next day. If the child has completed this lesson 3 times, move on to the next lesson regardless of the score.

Remember to carry out Daily Real-World Exercises each day (see Chart following Level 1 Lesson 1). The items in the chart are only examples. You should create your own and use them regularly throughout the day.

NOTES: For items with plurals, the child must give all the objects requested. For items with a singular noun, the child must give only one object.

	Objects		Adult's Actions & Words	✔ if correct		
Level 1 Lesson 7	**Model**	**Choices**		Dates: ___ 1st ___ 2nd ___ 3rd		
				1st	*2nd*	*3rd*
1	CAT	cat bird dog	holding model *"This is a cat. Give me another cat."*			
2	CAT	car cat 2 birds	holding model *"This is a cat. Give me another cat."*			
3	CAT	bird cat bus	holding model *"This is a cat. Give me another cat."*			
4	2 CATS	2 birds 2 cats	holding models *"These are cats. Give me the other cats."*			
5	3 CATS	2 cats truck 2 dogs	holding models *"These are cats. Give me the other cats."*			
6		man cat truck	*"Give me the truck."*			
7		cat dog 3 trucks	*"Give me a truck."*			
8		cat 2 dogs 2 kids	*"Give me the kids."*			
9		car bird truck	*"Give me the car."*			
10		3 frogs lady dog	*"Give me a frog."*			
11		frog 3 ladies truck	*"Give me the ladies."*			
12		2 cars kid plane	*"Give me the cars."*			
			Total			

If Total is 9 or higher, move on to the next lesson. If Total is fewer than 9, repeat this lesson the next day. If the child has completed this lesson 3 times, move on to the next lesson regardless of the score.

Remember to carry out Daily Real-World Exercises each day (see Chart following Level 1 Lesson 1). The items in the chart are only examples. You should create your own and use them regularly throughout the day.

NOTES: For items with plurals, the child must give all the objects requested. For items with a singular noun, the child must give only one object.

	Level 1 Lesson 8		Adult's Actions & Words	✔ if correct		
			Dates: _____ _____ _____ 1st 2nd 3rd			
	Objects			1st	2nd	3rd
	Model	*Choices*				
1	BIRD	bird truck dog	holding model *"This is a bird. Give me another bird."*			
2	BIRD	car bird cat dog	holding model *"This is a bird. Give me another bird."*			
3	BIRD	kid bird bus	holding model *"This is a bird. Give me another bird."*			
4	2 BIRDS	plane 3 cats 2 birds	holding models *"These are birds. Give me the other birds."*			
5	3 BIRDS	3 birds truck dog	holding models *"These are birds. Give me the other birds."*			
6		bus bird car	*"Give me the bird."*			
7		3 trucks plane dog	*"Give me a truck."*			
8		2 cats 2 kids dog	*"Give me the kids."*			
9		car bird truck	*"Give me a car."*			
10		frog lady car dog	*"Give me a frog."*			
11		frog 3 ladies 2 trucks	*"Give me the ladies."*			
12		car kid 2 cats	*"Give me a cat."*			
			Total			

If Total is 9 or higher, move on to the next lesson. If Total is fewer than 9, repeat this lesson the next day. If the child has completed this lesson 3 times, move on to the next lesson regardless of the score.

Remember to carry out Daily Real-World Exercises each day (see Chart following Level 1 Lesson 1). The items in the chart are only examples. You should create your own and use them regularly throughout the day.

NOTES: For items with plurals, the child must give all the objects requested. For items with a singular noun, the child must give only one object.

Level 1 Lesson 9			Dates: ____ ____ ____ 1st 2nd 3rd			
	Objects		**Adult's** **Actions &** **Words**	**✔ if correct**		
	Model	*Choices*		*1st*	*2nd*	*3rd*
1	BUS	bus bird dog	holding model *"This is a bus. Give me another bus."*			
2	BUS	car bus bird	holding model *"This is a bus. Give me another bus."*			
3	BUS	bird bus 2 cars	holding model *"This is a bus. Give me another bus."*			
4	3 BUSES	cat 2 kids 3 buses	holding models *"These are buses. Give me the other buses."*			
5	2 BUSES	2 buses truck dog	holding models *"These are buses. Give me the other buses."*			
6		man bus car	*"Give me a car."*			
7		bus plane dog kid	*"Give me the kid."*			
8		cat 2 dogs 2 frogs	*"Give me the frogs."*			
9		car 2 birds 3 ladies	*"Give me the ladies."*			
10		bird dog 3 trucks	*"Give me a truck."*			
11		2 cats lady truck	*"Give me a cat."*			
12		bird plane kid	*"Give me the bird."*			
			Total			

If Total is 9 or higher, move on to the next lesson. If Total is fewer than 9, repeat this lesson the next day. If the child has completed this lesson 3 times, move on to the next lesson regardless of the score.

Remember to carry out Daily Real-World Exercises each day (see Chart following Level 1 Lesson 1). The items in the chart are only examples. You should create your own and use them regularly throughout the day.

NOTES: For items with plurals, the child must give all the objects requested. For items with a singular noun, the child must give only one object.

Level 1 Lesson 10			Dates: ___ ___ ___ 1st 2nd 3rd			
			Adult's Actions & Words	**✔ if correct**		
	Choices			*1st*	*2nd*	*3rd*
1	bus bird dog		*"Give me the bird."*			
2	2 cars bus bird		*"Give me the cars."*			
3	bird bus 2 cars		*"Give me the bus."*			
4	2 cats kid 3 ladies		*"Give me the ladies."*			
5	2 kids truck dog		*"Give me a kid."*			
6	lady bus car frog		*"Give me a frog."*			
7	bus plane 3 cats		*"Give me a cat."*			
8	2 cats dog 2 frogs		*"Give me the frogs."*			
9	2 cars bird 3 ladies		*"Give me the ladies."*			
10	bird dog 3 trucks		*"Give me a truck."*			
11	2 cats lady 2 trucks		*"Give me the cats."*			
12	bird plane kid		*"Give me a kid."*			
			Total			

If Total is 9 or higher, move on to the next lesson. If Total is fewer than 9, repeat this lesson the next day. If the child has completed this lesson 3 times, move on to the next lesson regardless of the score.

Remember to carry out Daily Real-World Exercises each day (see Chart following Level 1 Lesson 1). The items in the chart are only examples. You should create your own and use them regularly throughout the day.

NOTES: For items with plurals, the child must give all the objects requested. For items with a singular noun, the child must give only one object.

Level 1 Lesson 11			Dates: ___ ___ ___			
				1st 2nd 3rd		
	Objects		Adult's Actions & Words	✔ if correct		
	Model	Choices		1st	2nd	3rd
1	PLANE	plane truck dog	holding model *"This is a plane. Give me another plane."*			
2	PLANE	car plane cat dog	holding model *"This is a plane. Give me another plane."*			
3	PLANE	kid plane bus	holding model *"This is a plane. Give me another plane."*			
4	2 PLANES	dog cat 2 planes	holding models *"These are planes. Give me the other planes."*			
5	3 PLANES	3 planes truck dog	holding models *"These are planes. Give me the other planes."*			
6		bus plane man	*"Give me the plane."*			
7		3 trucks 2 dogs	*"Give me a truck."*			
8		cat 2 kids 2 dogs	*"Give me the kids."*			
9		car bird truck	*"Give me a car."*			
10		frog lady car dog	*"Give me a frog."*			
11		2 frogs 3 ladies truck	*"Give me the ladies."*			
12		car plane 2 cats	*"Give me a cat."*			
			Total			

If Total is 9 or higher, move on to the next lesson. If Total is fewer than 9, repeat this lesson the next day. If the child has completed this lesson 3 times, move on to the next lesson regardless of the score.

Remember to carry out Daily Real-World Exercises each day (see Chart following Level 1 Lesson 1). The items in the chart are only examples. You should create your own and use them throughout the day.

NOTES: For items with plurals, the child must give all the objects requested. For items with a singular noun, the child must give only one object.

	Objects		Adult's Actions & Words	✔ if correct		
	Model	*Choices*		*1st*	*2nd*	*3rd*
Level 1 Lesson 12			**Dates:** _____ _____ _____ 1st 2nd 3rd			
1	DOG	bird truck dog	holding model *"This is a dog. Give me another dog."*			
2	DOG	car bird cat dog	holding model *"This is a dog. Give me another dog."*			
3	DOG	kid dog bus	holding model *"This is a dog. Give me another dog."*			
4	2 DOGS	plane cat 3 dogs	holding models *"These are dogs. Give me the other dogs."*			
5	3 DOGS	2 dogs truck 2 birds	holding models *"These are dogs. Give me the other dogs."*			
6		man bird car	*"Give me the bird."*			
7		3 trucks plane dog	*"Give me a truck."*			
8		3 cats 2 kids dog	*"Give me the kids."*			
9		car plane truck	*"Give me a car."*			
10		frog lady car dog	*"Give me a frog."*			
11		frog truck 3 ladies	*"Give me a lady."*			
12		2 cars kid 2 cats	*"Give me the cats."*			
			Total			

If Total is 9 or higher, move on to the next lesson. If Total is fewer than 9, repeat this lesson the next day. If the child has completed this lesson 3 times, move on to the next lesson regardless of the score.

Remember to carry out Daily Real-World Exercises each day (see Chart following Level 1 Lesson 1). The items in the chart are only examples. You should create your own and use them throughout the day.

LEVEL 2

In Level 2, six new verbs (words requiring actions) are taught. This allows you to combine the nouns from Level 1 with different actions. For many children, systematic use of verbs is novel and challenging. It is common for them to have an extensive range of nouns but a paucity of verbs. You may find that the child has greater difficulty at this level compared to Level 1. But with consistent instruction most children master this new language form within several sessions. The actions are performed in the following way:

shake	Lift up the object and move it up and down several times in succession.
turn over	Lift the object slightly and turn it over.
hug	Lift the object and press it with both hands against your chest.
pull	Take a corner or edge of the object & pull it toward you across the table.
make the ____ walk	Move the object across the table, lifting it slightly with each "step."
make the ____ jump	Select the object and move it up and down in a jumping motion at least four times.

If the child has difficulty copying a movement, move his or her hand (in a hand-over-hand manner) so that he or she is able to execute the requested action. Repeat the movement until the child completes the action independently. See www.ASDReading.com for videos of these actions.

> **NOTES:** Directions written in capital letters indicate that the verb is being presented to the child for the first time. In these cases, model the action for the child. For example, if the directions state "SHAKE THE CAR LIKE THIS," take a car in your hand and shake it at the same time that you say the command. Then put aside the car you've been using so it is out of view. Say, "Do that. Shake the car." If the directions are not written in capital letters, do not model the action.

To expand the child's language and increase the child's comfort with singular and plural forms, some items include the words **"this"** and **"these."** For **"this,"** point to any one of the appropriate objects while making the request; for **"these,"** point to multiple objects. For example, when giving the command *"Shake these cars,"* point to the cars that you would like the child to shake. If the item does not include the word *"this"* or *"these,"* then pointing is not needed. There are 12 lessons in Level 2, and the child will complete all of them before moving on to Level 3.

Level 2 Lesson 1			Dates: ___ ___ ___ 1ˢᵗ 2ⁿᵈ 3ʳᵈ				
	Objects		**Adult's Actions & Words**	**✔ if correct**			
	Model	*Choices*			*1ˢᵗ*	*2ⁿᵈ*	*3ʳᵈ*
1	CAR	car frog dog	shaking model *"SHAKE THE CAR LIKE THIS. Do that— shake the car."*				
2	BIRD	lady car bird	shaking model *"SHAKE THE BIRD LIKE THIS. Do that— shake the bird."*				
3	2 KIDS	frog 2 kids dog	shaking models *"SHAKE THE KIDS LIKE THIS. Do that— shake the kids."*				
4	CAT	kid plane cat	shaking model *"SHAKE THE CAT LIKE THIS. Do that— shake the cat."*				
5	TRUCK	car truck dog	shaking model *"SHAKE THE TRUCK LIKE THIS. Do that— shake the truck."*				
6		bus kid car	*"Shake the bus."*				
7		2 cars frog 2 dogs	*"Shake the dogs."*				
8		cat car dog	*"Shake the car."*				
9		car 3 trucks 2 birds	*"Shake the birds."*				
10		frog lady car	*"Shake the lady."*				
11		man dog truck	*"Shake the truck."*				
12		3 cars frog 2 dogs	*"Shake the cars."*				
			Total				

If Total is 9 or higher, move on to the next lesson. If Total is fewer than 9, repeat this lesson the next day. If the child has completed this lesson 3 times, move on to the next lesson regardless of the score.

Remember to carry out Daily Real-World Exercises each day (see Chart following this lesson). The items in the chart are only examples. You should create your own and use them throughout the day.

Level 2 Sample Daily Real-World Exercises

*Only use verbs that the child has already learned in the lessons.

Setting	Adult's Actions & Words
Home	"Give me the apple."
Home (after completing Lesson 1)	"Shake the spoon."
Home (after completing Lesson 1)	"Shake the pens."
Home (after completing Lesson 3)	"Turn over a book."
Home (after completing Lesson 3)	"Turn over the box."
Playground (after completing Lesson 5)	"Hug the rock."
Playground (after completing Lesson 5)	"Hug a ball."
Restaurant (after completing Lesson 7)	"Pull the fork."
Playroom (after completing Lesson 9)	"Make the monkey walk."
Playroom (after completing Lesson 11)	"Make the doll jump."

Level 2 Lesson 2			Dates: _____ _____ _____ 1st 2nd 3rd			
		Choices	Adult's Actions & Words	✔ if correct		
				1st	2nd	3rd
1		cat bird kid	*"Give me the kid."*			
2		2 cars dog bird plane	*"Shake the cars."*			
3		bird kid 3 dogs	*"Shake a dog."*			
4		truck cat dog	*"Give me the truck."*			
5		dog plane 2 trucks	*"Shake the trucks."*			
6		bus dog car	*"Give me the bus."*			
7		plane lady truck	*"Give me the lady."*			
8		car cat dog	*"Shake the cat."*			
9		2 cats bird 2 kids	*"Give me the kids."*			
10		frog kid car plane	*"Shake the plane."*			
11		3 frogs bus truck	*"Give me a frog."*			
12		3 kids car 2 trucks	*"Shake a truck."*			
			Total			

If Total is 9 or higher, move on to the next lesson. If Total is fewer than 9, repeat this lesson the next day. If the child has completed this lesson 3 times, move on to the next lesson regardless of the score.

Remember to carry out Daily Real-World Exercises each day (see Chart following Level 2 Lesson 1). The items in the chart are only examples. You should create your own and use them throughout the day.

Level 2 Lesson 3			Dates: _____ _____ _____ 1st 2nd 3rd			
	Objects		**Adult's Actions & Words**	**✔ if correct**		
	Model	*Choices*		*1st*	*2nd*	*3rd*
1	DOG	dog bird kid	turning over model *"TURN OVER THE DOG LIKE THIS.* *Do that—turn over the dog."*			
2	BIRD	car dog bird	turning over model *"TURN OVER THE BIRD LIKE THIS.* *Do that—turn over the bird."*			
3	3 KIDS	bird 3 kids bus	turning over models *"TURN OVER THE KIDS LIKE THIS.* *Do that—turn over the kids."*			
4	LADY	truck cat lady	turning over model *"TURN OVER THE LADY LIKE THIS.* *Do that—turn over the lady."*			
5	2 TRUCKS	dog 2 trucks man	turning over models *"TURN OVER THE TRUCKS LIKE THIS.* *Do that—turn over the trucks."*			
6		bus dog car	*"Turn over the bus."*			
7		3 kids dog truck	*"Turn over a kid."*			
8		car lady dog	*"Turn over the dog."*			
9		cat truck 2 birds	*"Shake the birds."*			
10		3 planes kid dog	*"Give me the planes."*			
11		frog bus truck	*"Give me the bus."*			
12		2 kids car plane	*"Shake the car."*			
			Total			

If Total is 9 or higher, move on to the next lesson. If Total is fewer than 9, repeat this lesson the next day. If the child has completed this lesson 3 times, move on to the next lesson regardless of the score.

Remember to carry out Daily Real-World Exercises each day (see Chart following Level 2 Lesson 1). The items in the chart are only examples. You should create your own and use them throughout the day.

Level 2 Lesson 4			Dates: ___ ___ ___ 1st 2nd 3rd			
	Choices		Adult's Actions & Words	✔ if correct		
				1st	2nd	3rd
1	bird 2 kids		pointing to one kid *"Turn over this kid."*			
2	car dog bird plane		*"Shake the car."*			
3	bird dog kid		*"Give me the dog."*			
4	3 trucks cat dog		*"Turn over the trucks."*			
5	3 planes truck		pointing to one plane *"Shake this plane."*			
6	bus dog car		*"Turn over the bus."*			
7	bird 2 ladies truck		*"Give me a lady."*			
8	dog 3 cats		pointing to one cat *"Shake this cat."*			
9	cat bird kid		*"Give me the bird."*			
10	3 frogs car 2 planes		*"Shake the frogs."*			
11	frog 2 buses truck		*"Give me the buses."*			
12	3 cars 2 kids		*"Turn over a car."*			
			Total			

If Total is 9 or higher, move on to the next lesson. If Total is fewer than 9, repeat this lesson the next day. If the child has completed this lesson 3 times, move on to the next lesson regardless of the score.

Remember to carry out Daily Real-World Exercises each day (see Chart following Level 2 Lesson 1). The items in the chart are only examples. You should create your own and use them throughout the day.

Level 2 Lesson 5			Adult's Actions & Words	✔ if correct		
			Dates: ___ 1st ___ 2nd ___ 3rd			
	Objects					
	Model	Choices		1st	2nd	3rd
1	BIRD	dog bird man	hugging model "HUG THE BIRD LIKE THIS. Do that — hug the bird."			
2	CAR	car dog bird	hugging model "HUG THE CAR LIKE THIS. Do that — hug the car."			
3	2 KIDS	bird 2 kids bus	hugging models "HUG THE KIDS LIKE THIS. Do that — hug the kids."			
4	TRUCK	truck cat lady	hugging model "HUG THE TRUCK LIKE THIS. Do that — hug the truck."			
5	3 LADIES	dog 3 ladies plane	hugging models "HUG THE LADIES LIKE THIS. Do that — hug the ladies."			
6		bus dog car	"Hug the dog."			
7		2 kids dog 3 trucks	"Turn over the trucks."			
8		car lady dog	"Shake the lady."			
9		cat 3 trucks 2 birds	"Hug the birds."			
10		3 planes kid dog	"Give me a plane."			
11		frog bus truck	"Turn over the bus."			
12		2 kids car plane	"Shake the kids."			
			Total			

If Total is 9 or higher, move on to the next lesson. If Total is fewer than 9, repeat this lesson the next day. If the child has completed this lesson 3 times, move on to the next lesson regardless of the score.

Remember to carry out Daily Real-World Exercises each day (see Chart following Level 2 Lesson 1). The items in the chart are only examples. You should create your own and use them throughout the day.

Level 2 Lesson 6			Dates: _____ _____ _____ 1st 2nd 3rd	✔ if correct		
	Choices		Adult's Actions & Words	1st	2nd	3rd
1	bird 2 dog		pointing to one dog *"Turn over this dog."*			
2	car dog bird plane		*"Shake the plane."*			
3	bird dog 3 kids		*"Give me the kids."*			
4	3 trucks plane		*"Shake a truck."*			
5	2 planes truck		pointing to one plane *"Give me this plane."*			
6	bus dog car		*"Turn over the bus."*			
7	bird 2 ladies 3 trucks		*"Give me the ladies."*			
8	2 dogs 3 cats		pointing to two cats *"Shake these cats."*			
9	cat bird kid		*"Give me the bird."*			
10	3 frogs car plane		*"Shake a frog."*			
11	2 frogs 2 buses truck		*"Give me the buses."*			
12	3 cars 2 kids		pointing to one car *"Turn over this car."*			
			Total			

If Total is 9 or higher, move on to the next lesson. If Total is fewer than 9, repeat this lesson the next day. If the child has completed this lesson 3 times, move on to the next lesson regardless of the score.

Remember to carry out Daily Real-World Exercises each day (see Chart following Level 2 Lesson 1). The items in the chart are only examples. You should create your own and use them throughout the day.

	Level 2 Lesson 7		Adult's Actions & Words	Dates: _____ _____ _____ 1st 2nd 3rd		
	Objects		**Adult's Actions & Words**	**✔ if correct**		
	Model	*Choices*		*1st*	*2nd*	*3rd*
1	BUS	bus dog bird kid	pulling model *"PULL THE BUS LIKE THIS. Do that— pull the bus."*			
2	PLANE	car plane bird	pulling model *"PULL THE PLANE LIKE THIS. Do that— pull the plane."*			
3	2 CARS	bird 2 cars 2 buses	pulling models *"PULL THE CARS LIKE THIS. Do that— pull the cars."*			
4	TRUCK	truck cat lady	pulling model *"PULL THE TRUCK LIKE THIS. Do that— pull the truck."*			
5	3 FROGS	3 dogs 3 frogs plane	pulling models *"PULL THE FROGS LIKE THIS. Do that— pull the frogs."*			
6		bus dog car	*"Pull the dog."*			
7		kid dog 3 cats	pointing to two cats *"Turn over these cats."*			
8		car lady dog	*"Shake the lady."*			
9		cat bird 2 trucks	*"Pull the trucks."*			
10		3 dogs kid	pointing to one dog *"Give me this dog."*			
11		2 birds bus 2 trucks	*"Hug the birds."*			
12		2 kids car man	*"Turn over a kid."*			
			Total			

If Total is 9 or higher, move on to the next lesson. If Total is fewer than 9, repeat this lesson the next day. If the child has completed this lesson 3 times, move on to the next lesson regardless of the score.

Remember to carry out Daily Real-World Exercises each day (see Chart following Level 2 Lesson 1). The items in the chart are only examples. You should create your own and use them throughout the day.

Level 2 Lesson 8			Dates: _____ _____ _____ 1st 2nd 3rd			
		Choices	Adult's Actions & Words	✔ if correct		
				1st	2nd	3rd
1		bird 2 cats	pointing to one cat *"Turn over this cat."*			
2		truck dog bird plane	*"Give me the truck."*			
3		2 birds dog 3 ladies	*"Pull the ladies."*			
4		2 frogs plane	*"Shake a frog."*			
5		2 planes truck	pointing to one plane *"Hug this plane."*			
6		bus dog car	*"Turn over the car."*			
7		3 birds 3 kids truck	*"Give me the kids."*			
8		2 dogs 3 cats	pointing to one dog *"Shake this dog."*			
9		cat bird dog	*"Give me the dog."*			
10		3 frogs car plane	*"Shake a frog."*			
11		frog 2 buses truck	*"Turn over the buses."*			
12		3 cars kid	pointing to one car *"Pull this car."*			
			Total			
If Total is 9 or higher, move on to the next lesson. If Total is fewer than 9, repeat this lesson the next day. If the child has completed this lesson 3 times, move on to the next lesson regardless of the score.						

Remember to carry out Daily Real-World Exercises each day (see Chart following Level 2 Lesson 1). The items in the chart are only examples. You should create your own and use them throughout the day.

Level 2 Lesson 9			Dates: ___ ___ ___ 1st 2nd 3rd			
	Objects		**Adult's** **Actions &** **Words**	**✔ if correct**		
	Model	*Choices*		*1st*	*2nd*	*3rd*
1	KID	bus dog bird kid	making model walk *"MAKE THE KID WALK LIKE THIS.* *Do that—make the kid walk."*			
2	BIRD	car plane bird	making model walk *"MAKE THE BIRD WALK LIKE THIS.* *Do that—make the bird walk."*			
3	2 DOGS	bird 2 dogs 3 buses	making model walk *"MAKE THE DOGS WALK LIKE THIS.* *Do that—make the dogs walk."*			
4	CAT	truck cat lady	making model walk *"MAKE THE CAT WALK LIKE THIS.* *Do that—make the cat walk."*			
5	3 LADIES	dog plane 3 ladies	making models walk *"MAKE THE LADIES WALK LIKE THIS.* *Do that—make the ladies walk."*			
6		bus dog car	*"Make the dog walk."*			
7		kid dog 3 cars	*"Hug a car."*			
8		car lady 2 frogs	*"Shake the frogs."*			
9		cat bird truck	*"Pull the truck."*			
10		3 buses man	pointing to one bus *"Give me this bus."*			
11		2 birds bus 2 trucks	*"Make the birds walk."*			
12		2 cars 2 planes	*"Turn over a plane."*			
			Total			

If Total is 9 or higher, move on to the next lesson. If Total is fewer than 9, repeat this lesson the next day. If the child has completed this lesson 3 times, move on to the next lesson regardless of the score.

Remember to carry out Daily Real-World Exercises each day (see Chart following Level 2 Lesson 1). The items in the chart are only examples. You should create your own and use them throughout the day.

Level 2 Lesson 10			Dates: ___ ___ ___	✔ if correct		
				1st	2nd	3rd
	Choices		**Adult's Actions & Words**	1st	2nd	3rd
1	bird 2 cats		pointing to one cat *"Turn over this cat."*			
2	truck dog bird plane		*"Give me the truck."*			
3	bird 3 dogs 3 ladies		*"Pull the ladies."*			
4	2 frogs plane		*"Shake a frog."*			
5	3 planes truck		pointing to two planes *"Hug these planes."*			
6	bus dog car		*"Make the dog walk."*			
7	bird 3 kids truck		*"Give me the kids."*			
8	2 dogs 3 cats		pointing to one dog *"Shake this dog."*			
9	2 cats 2 birds dog		*"Make the cats walk."*			
10	3 frogs car plane		*"Hug a frog."*			
11	frog 2 buses truck		*"Turn over the buses."*			
12	3 cars kid		pointing to one car *"Pull this car."*			
			Total			

If Total is 9 or higher, move on to the next lesson. If Total is fewer than 9, repeat this lesson the next day. If the child has completed this lesson 3 times, move on to the next lesson regardless of the score.

Remember to carry out Daily Real-World Exercises each day (see Chart following Level 2 Lesson 1). The items in the chart are only examples. You should create your own and use them throughout the day.

115

	Level 2 Lesson 11		Dates: ___ ___ ___ 1st 2nd 3rd			
	Objects		**Adult's Actions & Words**	**✔ if correct**		
	Model	*Choices*		*1st*	*2nd*	*3rd*
1	KID	bus dog kid	making model jump **"MAKE THE KID JUMP LIKE THIS. Do that—make the kid jump."**			
2	LADY	lady plane bird	making model jump **"MAKE THE LADY JUMP LIKE THIS. Do that—make the lady jump."**			
3	2 KIDS	bird 2 kids bus	making models jump **"MAKE THE KIDS JUMP LIKE THIS. Do that—make the kids jump."**			
4	3 LADIES	truck 2 cats 3 ladies	making models jump **"MAKE THE LADIES JUMP LIKE THIS. Do that—make the ladies jump."**			
5		dog kid plane	**"Make the kid jump."**			
6		man dog car	**"Make the dog walk."**			
7		kid dog 3 trucks	**"Hug a truck."**			
8		2 cars lady 2 planes	**"Shake the planes."**			
9		cat bird truck	**"Pull the cat."**			
10		2 birds kid cat	pointing to one bird **"Give me this bird."**			
11		2 ladies kid dog	**"Make a lady jump."**			
12		2 cars 2 planes	**"Turn over a car."**			
			Total			

If Total is 9 or higher, move on to the next lesson. If Total is fewer than 9, repeat this lesson the next day. If the child has completed this lesson 3 times, move on to the next lesson regardless of the score.

Remember to carry out Daily Real-World Exercises each day (see Chart following Level 2 Lesson 1). The items in the chart are only examples. You should create your own and use them throughout the day.

Level 2 Lesson 12		Dates: _____ _____ _____ 1st 2nd 3rd			
	Choices	Adult's Actions & Words	✔ if correct		
			1st	2nd	3rd
1	bird 2 cars	*"Turn over a car."*			
2	truck dog kid plane	*"Make the kid jump."*			
3	bird 2 dogs 3 frogs	*"Pull the frogs."*			
4	2 ladies 3 planes	*"Shake the ladies."*			
5	2 planes 2 trucks	pointing to one truck *"Hug this truck."*			
6	bus dog cat	*"Make the cat walk."*			
7	3 birds truck	*"Give me the birds."*			
8	2 dogs 2 buses	pointing to one bus *"Shake this bus."*			
9	2 cats bird dog	*"Make the dog walk."*			
10	frog car 2 planes	*"Hug a plane."*			
11	3 frogs 2 buses man	*"Turn over the buses."*			
12	3 kids cat	pointing to two kids *"Make these kids jump."*			
		Total			

If Total is 9 or higher, move on to the next lesson. If Total is fewer than 9, repeat this lesson the next day. If the child has completed this lesson 3 times, move on to the next lesson regardless of the score.

Remember to carry out Daily Real-World Exercises each day (see Chart following Level 2 Lesson 1). The items in the chart are only examples. You should create your own and use them throughout the day.

LEVEL 3

In this level no new words are introduced. Using the nouns and verbs already taught, the child carries out the same action on two different objects (e.g. "hug the bird and then the kid").

In all cases, the objects are handled in the order named. For example, if the directions are *"hug the bird and then the kid,"* the child picks up the first object, hugs it, puts it down, then picks up the second object and hugs it. There are six Lessons in Level 3, and the child completes all of them before moving on to Level 4.

NOTE: No Models are used in Levels 3 and 4, so the column for Models no longer appears in the charts.

Level 3 Lesson 1			Dates: _____ _____ _____				
			1st 2nd 3rd				
		Choices	**Adult's Actions & Words**	✔ if correct			
				1st	2nd	3rd
1		bird cat plane	*"Hug the bird and then the cat."*			
2		2 trucks dog bird	pointing to one truck *"Shake this truck."*			
3		bird frog lady	*"Give me the frog and then the lady."*			
4		frog dog plane	*"Make the dog walk."*			
5		2 planes 2 trucks	*"Pull the planes."*			
6		bus dog car	*"Turn over the car and then the bus."*			
7		bird truck 3 kids	pointing to two kids *"Make these kids walk."*			
8		frog car bus	*"Shake the frog and then the car."*			
9		cat bird dog lady	*"Make the lady jump."*			
10		frog car plane	*"Pull the plane and then the car."*			
11		2 frogs 3 buses truck	pointing to two buses *"Give me these buses."*			
12		3 cars kid	*"Hug a car."*			
			Total			

If Total is 9 or higher, move on to the next lesson. If Total is fewer than 9, repeat this lesson the next day. If the child has completed this lesson 3 times, move on to the next lesson regardless of the score.

Remember to carry out Daily Real-World Exercises each day (see Chart following this lesson). The items in the chart are only examples. You should create your own and use them throughout the day.

Level 3 Sample Daily Real-World Exercises

Setting	Adult's Actions & Words
Home	"Give me the apple and then the spoon."
Home	"Shake the pencil and then the box."
Home	"Turn over the book and then the paper."
Home	pointing to two bananas "Give me these bananas."
Home	"Pull the fork and then the spoon."
Playground	"Hug the rock and then the ball."
Playground	pointing to a stick "Shake this stick."
Playroom	pointing to a toy "Pull this toy."
Playroom	"Make the doll walk."
Playroom	"Make the doll jump."

Level 3 Lesson 2		Dates: _____ _____ _____ 1st 2nd 3rd		✔ if correct	
	Choices	**Adult's** Actions & **Words**	*1st*	*2nd*	*3rd*
1	2 cats plane 2 kids	*"Make the kids jump."*			
2	truck dog 2 birds	pointing to one bird *"Make this bird walk."*			
3	bird frog bus	*"Pull the frog and then the bus."*			
4	man dog plane	*"Hug the plane and then the dog."*			
5	2 planes truck	*"Turn over the planes and then the truck."*			
6	2 buses 2 cars	*"Turn over a car and then a bus."*			
7	2 birds 3 kids truck	pointing to two kids *"Shake these kids."*			
8	frog car bus	*"Give me the frog and then the car."*			
9	cat 2 birds 2 ladies	*"Make the ladies jump."*			
10	frog car plane	*"Pull the plane and then the car."*			
11	frog 3 buses truck	pointing to two buses *"Give me these buses."*			
12	3 cats kid	*"Hug a cat."*			
		Total			

If Total is 9 or higher, move on to the next lesson. If Total is fewer than 9, repeat this lesson the next day. If the child has completed this lesson 3 times, move on to the next lesson regardless of the score.

Remember to carry out Daily Real-World Exercises each day (see Chart following Level 3 Lesson 1). The items in the chart are only examples. You should create your own and use them throughout the day.

	Level 3 Lesson 3		Dates: ___ ___ ___ 1st 2nd 3rd			
	Choices		Adult's Actions & Words	✔ if correct		
				1st	2nd	3rd
1	bird cat plane 2 kids		"Give me the cat and then the kids."			
2	truck dog 2 birds		pointing to one bird "Shake this bird."			
3	bird frog bus		"Turn over the bus and then the frog."			
4	2 frogs dog plane		"Hug a frog."			
5	plane dog truck		"Pull the plane and then the truck."			
6	2 buses 2 cars		"Turn over the buses and then the cars."			
7	3 kids		pointing to one kid "Make this kid jump."			
8	frog car bus		"Give me the bus and then the car."			
9	cat 2 birds 2 ladies		"Make the ladies walk."			
10	2 cars 2 planes		"Pull a car and then a plane."			
11	frog 3 trucks		pointing to two trucks "Hug these trucks."			
12	3 cats kid		"Make a cat walk."			
			Total			

If Total is 9 or higher, move on to the next lesson. If Total is fewer than 9, repeat this lesson the next day. If the child has completed this lesson 3 times, move on to the next lesson regardless of the score.

Remember to carry out Daily Real-World Exercises each day (see Chart following Level 3 Lesson 1). The items in the chart are only examples. You should create your own and use them throughout the day.

Level 3 Lesson 4		Dates: ___ ___ ___ 1st 2nd 3rd	✔ if correct		
	Choices	Adult's Actions & **Words**	*1st*	*2nd*	*3rd*
1	bird cat plane	*"Hug the bird and then the cat."*			
2	2 trucks dog bird	pointing to one truck *"Shake this truck."*			
3	bird frog lady	*"Give me the frog and then the lady."*			
4	frog dog plane	*"Make the dog walk."*			
5	2 planes 3 trucks	*"Pull the planes."*			
6	bus dog car	*"Turn over the car and then the bus."*			
7	2 birds 3 kids truck	pointing to two kids *"Make these kids walk."*			
8	frog car bus	*"Shake the frog and then the car."*			
9	cat bird dog lady	*"Make the lady jump."*			
10	frog car plane	*"Pull the plane and then the car."*			
11	frog 3 buses truck	pointing to two buses *"Give me these buses."*			
12	3 cars kid	*"Hug a car."*			
		Total			

If Total is 9 or higher, move on to the next lesson. If Total is fewer than 9, repeat this lesson the next day. If the child has completed this lesson 3 times, move on to the next lesson regardless of the score.

Remember to carry out Daily Real-World Exercises each day (see Chart following Level 3 Lesson 1). The items in the chart are only examples. You should create your own and use them throughout the day.

	Choices	Adult's Actions & Words	✔ if correct		
Level 3 Lesson 5		Dates: _____ _____ _____ 1st 2nd 3rd	1st	2nd	3rd
1	2 birds plane 2 kids	*"Make the kids jump."*			
2	truck dog 2 birds	pointing to one bird *"Make this bird walk."*			
3	man frog bus	*"Pull the frog and then the bus."*			
4	frog dog plane	*"Hug the plane and then the dog."*			
5	2 planes truck	*"Turn over the planes and then the truck."*			
6	2 buses 2 cars	*"Turn over a car and then a bus."*			
7	bird 3 kids 2 trucks	pointing to two kids *"Shake these kids."*			
8	frog car bus	*"Give me the frog and then the car."*			
9	cat bird 2 ladies	*"Make the ladies jump."*			
10	frog car plane	*"Pull the plane and then the car."*			
11	frog 3 buses truck	pointing to two buses *"Give me these buses."*			
12	3 cats kid	*"Hug a cat."*			
		Total			

If Total is 9 or higher, move on to the next lesson. If Total is fewer than 9, repeat this lesson the next day. If the child has completed this lesson 3 times, move on to the next lesson regardless of the score.

Remember to carry out Daily Real-World Exercises each day (see Chart following Level 3 Lesson 1). The items in the chart are only examples. You should create your own and use them throughout the day.

Level 3 Lesson 6		Dates: ___ ___ ___ 1st 2nd 3rd			
	Choices	Adult's Actions & Words	✔ if correct		
			1st	2nd	3rd
1	cat dog 2 planes 2 kids	*"Give me the cat and then the kids."*			
2	truck dog 2 birds	pointing to one bird *"Shake this bird."*			
3	bird frog bus	*"Turn over the bus and then the frog."*			
4	2 frogs dog plane	*"Make the frogs jump."*			
5	plane dog truck	*"Pull the plane and then the truck."*			
6	2 buses 2 cars	*"Turn over the buses and then the cars."*			
7	3 kids	pointing to one kid *"Make this kid jump."*			
8	frog car bus	*"Give me the bus and then the car."*			
9	cat 3 birds 2 ladies	*"Make the ladies walk."*			
10	2 cars 2 planes	*"Pull a car and then a plane."*			
11	frog 3 trucks	pointing to two trucks *"Hug these trucks."*			
12	3 cats kid	*"Make a cat walk."*			
		Total			
If Total is 9 or higher, move on to the next lesson. If Total is fewer than 9, repeat this lesson the next day. If the child has completed this lesson 3 times, move on to the next lesson regardless of the score.					

Remember to carry out Daily Real-World Exercises each day (see Chart following Level 3 Lesson 1). The items in the chart are only examples. You should create your own and use them throughout the day.

LEVEL 4

In Level 4, the child's language expands to handle items containing two different verbs and two different nouns. For example, *"give me the cat and then hug the kid."* The actions are to be carried out in the sequence named. The simpler requests (from Levels 1-3) are maintained and interwoven with the more complex items.

		Adult's Actions & Words	✔ if correct		
Level 4 Lesson 1		Dates: _____ _____ _____ 1st　　2nd　　3rd			
	Choices		*1st*	*2nd*	*3rd*
1	bus bird　car plane	*"Shake the bus and then hug the car."*			
2	3 kids dog bird	pointing to two kids *"Make these kids jump."*			
3	bird dog　cat	*"Give me the dog and then turn over the cat."*			
4	frog　dog plane　bird	*"Make the bird walk and then pull the frog."*			
5	2 planes truck	*"Shake the planes."*			
6	2 ladies 2 kids	pointing to one kid *"Make this kid jump."*			
7	bird 3 cats truck	pointing to two cats *"Make these cats walk."*			
8	2 frogs car　bus	*"Shake a frog."*			
9	2 birds 2 cars	*"Hug the birds and then the cars."*			
10	frog　bus plane	*"Pull the plane and then the bus."*			
11	2 frogs 3 buses truck	*"Give me the buses."*			
12	3 trucks kid	*"Turn over a truck."*			
		Total			

If Total is 9 or higher, move on to the next lesson. If Total is fewer than 9, repeat this lesson the next day. If the child has completed this lesson 3 times, move on to the next lesson regardless of the score.

Remember to carry out Daily Real-World Exercises each day (see Chart following this lesson). The items in the chart are only examples. You should create your own and use them throughout the day.

Level 4 Sample Daily Real-World Exercises

*When using "this" or "these," point to the objects at the same time that the command is given.

Setting	Adult's Actions & Words
Home	"Shake the apple and then give me the fork."
Home	"Hug the pen and then turn over the book."
Home	"Give me the spoon and then the cup."
Home	"Pull this banana."
Home	"Shake these pencils."
Playground	"Hug this stick and then give me the ball."
Playground	"Turn over these rocks."
Playroom	"Pull this toy and then make the doll jump."
Playroom	"Make these dogs walk."
Playroom	"Make the dolls jump."

Level 4 Lesson 2		Adult's Actions & Words	✔ if correct		
	Choices		*1ˢᵗ*	*2ⁿᵈ*	*3ʳᵈ*
1	bird cat bus lady	*"Pull the bus and then make the lady walk."*			
2	truck dog 2 birds	pointing to one bird *"Turn over this bird."*			
3	bird frog bus	*"Turn over the bus and then the frog."*			
4	2 frogs dog plane	*"Give me the dog and then shake the plane."*			
5	2 planes 3 ladies	pointing to two ladies *"Make these ladies jump."*			
6	2 buses 2 cars	*"Shake a bus and then a car."*			
7	2 kids 2 dogs	pointing to one kid *"Make this kid jump and then hug the dogs."*			
8	frog car bus	*"Give me the bus and then the car."*			
9	2 cats bird 2 ladies	*"Make the ladies walk and then shake the bird."*			
10	2 cars 2 trucks	*"Pull a car and then a truck."*			
11	frog 3 cars	pointing to two cars *"Hug these cars."*			
12	3 dogs kid	*"Make a dog walk."*			
		Total			

Dates: _____ _____ _____
1ˢᵗ   *2ⁿᵈ*   *3ʳᵈ*

If Total is 9 or higher, move on to the next lesson. If Total is fewer than 9, repeat this lesson the next day. If the child has completed this lesson 3 times, move on to the next lesson regardless of the score.

Remember to carry out Daily Real-World Exercises each day (see Chart following Level 4 Lesson 1). The items in the chart are only examples. You should create your own and use them throughout the day.

	Level 4 Lesson 3		Dates: ___ ___ ___ 1st 2nd 3rd			
	Choices	Adult's Actions & Words		✔ if correct		
				1st	2nd	3rd
1	bird cat bus lady	*"Give me the bus and then make the lady jump."*				
2	2 trucks 2 birds	pointing to one truck *"Turn over this truck."*				
3	bird frog bus	*"Shake the frog and then the bird."*				
4	2 frogs dog man	*"Make the dog walk and then give me a frog."*				
5	plane 3 ladies	*"Make a lady jump."*				
6	2 buses 2 cars	*"Hug the buses and then the cars."*				
7	2 kids 2 dogs	pointing to one dog *"Make this dog walk and then hug the kids."*				
8	2 frogs car 2 buses	*"Turn over the frogs."*				
9	cat bird 2 ladies	*"Shake the cat and then hug the bird."*				
10	2 cats 2 kids	*"Pull a cat and then a kid."*				
11	frog 3 cars	pointing to two cars *"Hug these cars."*				
12	3 dogs kid	*"Make the kid walk and then make the dogs walk."*				
			Total			
	If Total is 9 or higher, move on to the next lesson. If Total is fewer than 9, repeat this lesson the next day. If the child has completed this lesson 3 times, move on to the next lesson regardless of the score.					

Remember to carry out Daily Real-World Exercises each day (see Chart following Level 4 Lesson 1). The items in the chart are only examples. You should create your own and use them throughout the day.

Level 4 Lesson 4			Dates: ___ ___ ___ 1st 2nd 3rd			
		Choices	Adult's Actions & Words	✔ if correct		
				1st	2nd	3rd
1		bus bird car plane	*"Shake the bird and then hug the plane."*			
2		2 kids dog bird	*"Make the kids jump."*			
3		bird dog cat	*"Give me the dog and then turn over the cat."*			
4		frog dog plane bird	*"Make the bird walk and then pull the frog."*			
5		2 planes 3 trucks	*"Shake the planes."*			
6		2 ladies 2 kids	pointing to one kid *"Make this kid jump."*			
7		bird 3 cats truck	pointing to two cats *"Make these cats walk."*			
8		2 frogs 2 buses	*"Shake a frog and then turn over a bus."*			
9		2 birds 2 cars	*"Hug the birds and then the cars."*			
10		frog bus plane	*"Pull the plane and then the bus."*			
11		2 frogs 3 buses truck	*"Give me the buses."*			
12		3 trucks kid	*"Turn over a truck and then hug the kid."*			
			Total			

If Total is 9 or higher, move on to the next lesson. If Total is fewer than 9, repeat this lesson the next day. If the child has completed this lesson 3 times, move on to the next lesson regardless of the score.

Remember to carry out Daily Real-World Exercises each day (see Chart following Level 4 Lesson 1). The items in the chart are only examples. You should create your own and use them throughout the day.

Level 4 Lesson 5		Adult's Actions & Words	Dates: ___ ___ ___ 1st 2nd 3rd		
	Choices		✔ if correct		
			1st	2nd	3rd
1	bird cat bus lady	"Pull the cat and then make the lady walk."			
2	truck dog 2 birds	pointing to one bird "Turn over this bird."			
3	bird frog bus	"Turn over the bus and then the frog."			
4	2 frogs dog plane	"Give me the dog and then shake the plane."			
5	plane 3 ladies	pointing to one lady "Make this lady jump."			
6	2 buses 2 cars	"Shake a bus and then a car."			
7	2 kids 2 dogs	pointing to one kid "Make this kid jump and then hug the dogs."			
8	man car bus	"Give me the bus and then the car."			
9	cat bird 2 ladies	"Make the ladies walk and then shake the bird."			
10	2 cars 2 trucks	"Pull a car and then a truck."			
11	frog 3 cars	pointing to two cars "Hug these cars."			
12	3 dogs kid	"Make a dog walk."			
		Total			

If Total is 9 or higher, move on to the next lesson. If Total is fewer than 9, repeat this lesson the next day. If the child has completed this lesson 3 times, move on to the next lesson regardless of the score.

Remember to carry out Daily Real-World Exercises each day (see Chart following Level 4 Lesson 1). The items in the chart are only examples. You should create your own and use them throughout the day.

Level 4 Lesson 6			Dates: ___ ___ ___ 1st 2nd 3rd			
	Choices		**Adult's** Actions & **Words**	✔ **if correct**		
				1st	2nd	3rd
1	bird cat bus lady		*"Give me the bus and then make the lady jump."*			
2	2 trucks 2 birds		pointing to one truck *"Turn over this truck."*			
3	bird frog bus		*"Shake the frog and then the bird."*			
4	2 frogs dog plane		*"Make the dog walk and then give me a frog."*			
5	plane 3 ladies		*"Make a lady jump."*			
6	2 buses 2 cars 3 frogs		*"Hug the buses and then the cars."*			
7	2 kids 2 dogs		pointing to one dog *"Make this dog walk and then hug the kids."*			
8	2 frogs car bus		*"Turn over the frogs."*			
9	cat bird 2 ladies		*"Shake the cat and then hug the bird."*			
10	2 cats 2 kids		*"Pull a cat and then a kid."*			
11	2 frogs 3 cars		pointing to two cars *"Hug these cars."*			
12	3 dogs kid		*"Make the kid walk and then make the dogs walk."*			
			Total			
If Total is 9 or higher, move on to the next lesson. If Total is fewer than 9, repeat this lesson the next day. If the child has completed this lesson 3 times, move on to the next lesson regardless of the score.						

Remember to carry out Daily Real-World Exercises each day (see Chart following Level 4 Lesson 1). The items in the chart are only examples. You should create your own and use them throughout the day.

Congratulations! With completion of Level 4, the child has completed the Receptive Language activities. All four Pre-Language activities must be completed before moving on to Part 2: Language Skills. If any Pre-Language activities have not yet been completed, continue to repeat a lesson from the highest level of each completed activity at least 3 times per week while the others are still in progress.

In addition, when you do move on to Part 2, during the early levels, continue some of the Pre-Language activities (see Part 2 for more details). Practice with these familiar skills reinforces the child's comfort and confidence.

Continue to use the language forms from this workbook in daily life outside of the teaching sessions.

See www.ASDReading.com for more ideas on how to expand the child's use of language in real-world settings.

APPENDIX

A

MATERIALS FOR PRE-LANGUAGE ACTIVITIES

PICTURE CARDS for ACTIVITY A (Animals)

Card A1

Card A2

Card A3

Card A4

Card A5

Card A6

PICTURE CARDS for ACTIVITY A (Clothing)

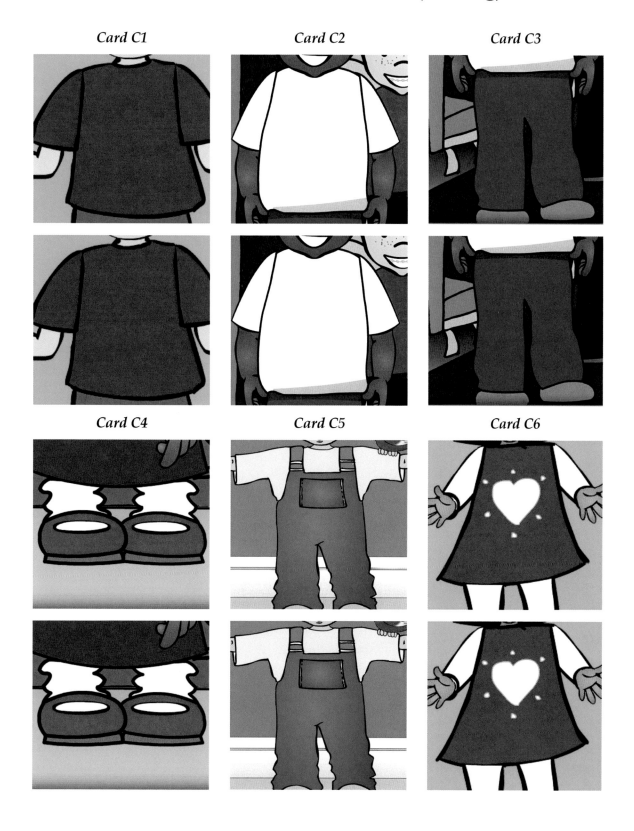

Card C1 Card C2 Card C3

Card C4 Card C5 Card C6

PICTURE CARDS for ACTIVITY A (Food)

Card F1

Card F2

Card F3

Card F4

Card F5

Card F6

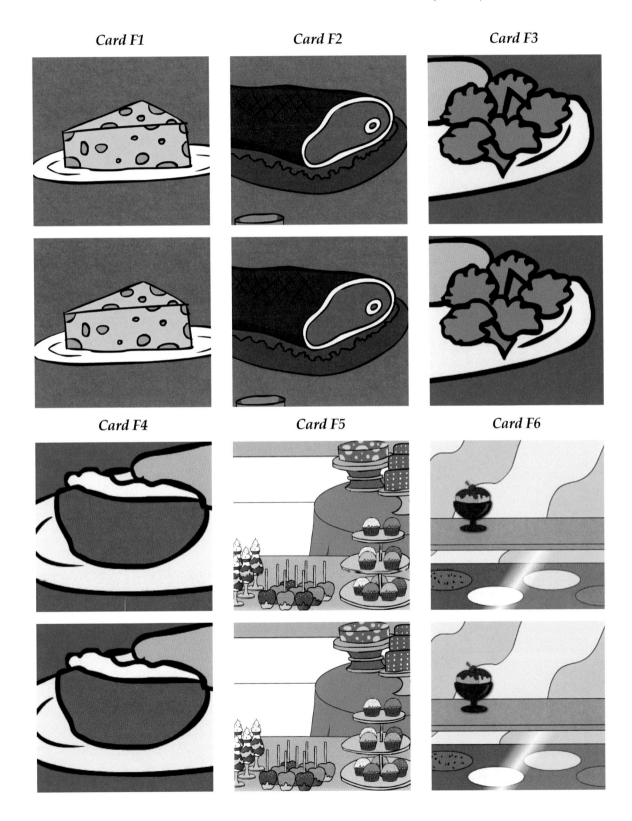

PICTURE CARDS for ACTIVITY A (People)

Card P1

Card P2

Card P3

Card P4

Card P5

Card P6

PICTURE CARDS for ACTIVITY A (Toys)

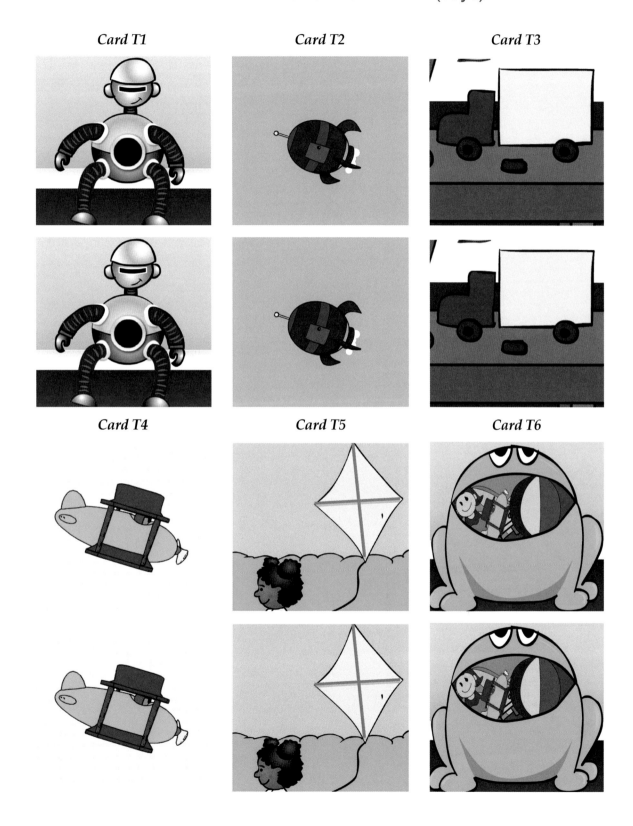

Card T1 Card T2 Card T3

Card T4 Card T5 Card T6

Color Board

Color Board

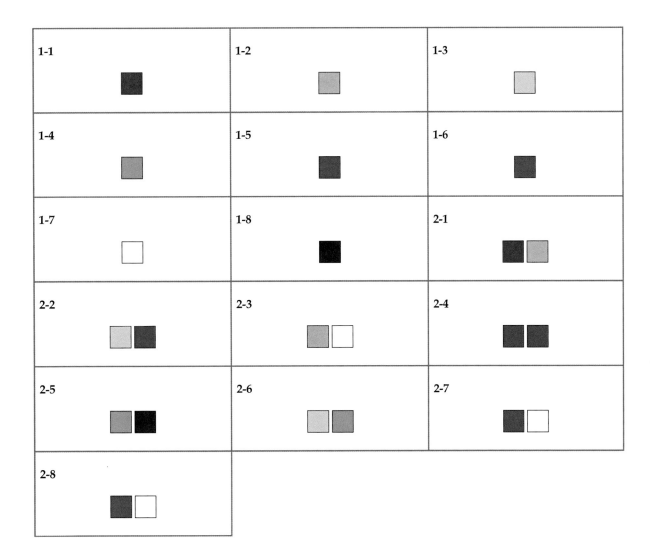

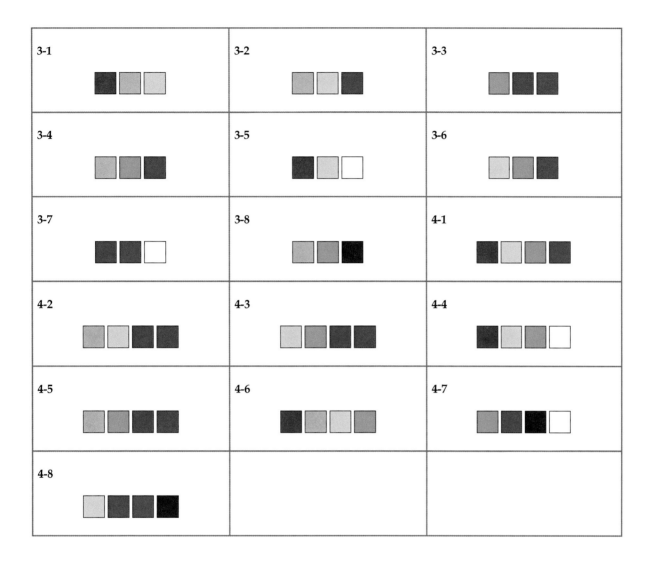

PART
2

LANGUAGE
SKILLS

Elementary Sentence Structure	*Level 1*	Two-Word Phrases
	Level 2	Simple Noun-Verb Sentences
	Level 3	Expanding Sentence Structure
Advanced Sentence Structure	*Level 4*	Sentences Introducing a Subject
	Level 5	Sentences Describing Actions
	Level 6	Sentences Describing Potential Actions
	Level 7	Sentences Discussing the Non-present
	Level 8	Sentences in the Past Tense
	Level 9	Sentences in the Future Tense
	Level 10	Sentence Combinations 6 to 8 Words in Length
	Level 11	Sentence Combinations up to 10 Words in Length
	Level 12	Compound Sentences up to 12 Words in Length
Questions	*Level 13*	Starting Questions
	Level 14	Questions about Action
	Level 15	Questions about Location
	Level 16	Questions that use "Which one" for Identification
	Level 17	Questions about Desire and Ability
	Level 18	Questions using "Not"
	Level 19	Questions that refer to Past Actions
	Level 20	Questions that refer to Future Actions
Expanding the Language Forms	*Level 21*	Yes/No Questions
	Level 22	Introducing "You" and "I"
	Level 23	Questions About "What Has Been Said"
	Level 24	Summarizing Events

LEVEL 1
TWO-WORD PHRASES

Overview

Many children find it relatively easy to say single words. For language to progress, however, it is critical that they learn to combine words. Only with this skill, is it possible to express clear, complete thoughts.

The move from single words to combinations of words must be made carefully. The sequenced production of words is taxing for children with language problems, and it is vital to move slowly and systematically to avoid excessive pressure. The new skills must be built gradually in small increments.

In Level 1 the child masters the important skill of moving from single words to two-word combinations. For children who can already produce some two-word phrases, these exercises will reinforce their basic skills.

In contrast to many programs, the content at this point does not include questions. In getting the child to speak, we do not ask, "What is this?" or "What color is the car?" Questions of this sort tend to elicit, and strengthen, single word responses, rather than advancing the child's production of multi-word sequences. In addition, answering questions can be difficult, leading the children to feel confused and to experience language as something to be avoided.

Imitation, by contrast, is a more effective technique when first teaching a child to speak. It allows the adult to offer a clear model—thereby removing any pressure on the children at this very early stage to formulate the ideas they are going to say. Verbal imitation is the technique used for the activities in Level 1.

Content

The two-word phrases in this level have been carefully selected to be the key building blocks in actual sentences. The phrases contain

- a noun (generally a figure that can perform an action such as *kid, frog, lady*) and
- a "helping word" (or "non-content word") that commonly precedes nouns, such as *the, that, some, etc.*

The nouns taught in this level are

- *boy, girl, kid, lady, man, dog, cat, bird, frog, horse, car, plane, truck, bus*

The non-content words taught in this level are

- *a, the, some, more, this, that, these, those*

In addition to verbal imitation of two-word phrases, the child will also continue to practice following the commands introduced in the Receptive Language activity of the Pre-Language section. Therefore, the child will be using language in two ways:

- producing longer utterances
- following verbal commands.

Materials

The activities require a set of small objects that are used to help link the language to real world experience. (Many of the objects are the same as those used in *Pre-Language Activity D: Building Receptive Language*.)

The objects should be

- approximately 3 to 5 inches in size,
- realistic in appearance (they should not be cartoon characters nor have unrealistic features, such as toy cars with eyes painted on them)

All animals need to be in the standing position. All people should be manipulable so that they can stand or sit. Unless a specific position is indicated (e.g., sitting), any figure of a person should be in standing position.

Objects	Number needed	Recommended toy brands (available at www.amazon.com)
boys	3	*Plan Toy Doll Family* (http://amzn.to/19a4YRo)
girls	3	*KidKraft Doll Family* (http://amzn.to/18D1C7m)
ladies	3	*Hape Doll Family* (http://amzn.to/1aD48Kl)
men	3	
dogs	3	*Toob (Safari LTD)*
frogs	3	(http://amzn.to/19P3GGC)
cats	3	(http://amzn.to/14W0HO6)
birds	3	(http://amzn.to/18D2b19)
horses	3	(http://amzn.to/17gjyV2) (http://amzn.to/15PKJ5A)
cars	3	*Hot Wheels* (http://amzn.to/19a5WgB) *MatchBox* (http://amzn.to/19hJUmg)
buses	3	*DieCast Bus* (http://amzn.to/19P4dIs)
trucks	3	*MatchBox* (http://amzn.to/19hJUmg)
planes	3	*InAir Planes (WWII 6 piece set)* (http://amzn.to/1bUq3QR)
beds	2	*Plan Toys Dollhouse furniture*
chairs	2	(http://amzn.to/16JGT3S) (http://amzn.to/1g9XbEA)

It's best if the objects within a single category are not exactly identical. For example, the 3 cars can differ in color and style; the dogs can differ in size and appearance, etc. This variation fosters flexibility and generalization of the concepts.

Beginning in Level 11, some activities require pictures. The pictures are provided in Appendix B. Cut them out and either laminate them or mount them on pieces of cardboard. You may find it useful to make a back up copy in case the original is damaged or lost.

Procedures

The items in a lesson appear as follows:

	Objects		Adult's Actions & Words	Expected Response*	✔ if correct
	Near Child	*Far from Child*			
1	girl		*"Say — a girl"*	I-Say	
2		dog	*"the dog"*	I	
3		cat	pointing to cat *"A cat is there."*	I/P	
4		frog	*"Give me the frog."*	O/A	

1. At the start of a session, have all objects accessible to you but out of the child's reach. (Do not allow the child to play with these objects either during or outside of the teaching sessions.)

2. As indicated in the column labeled **Objects**, set out the relevant objects. The objects labeled "Near Child" should be placed close to the child on the table. Objects labeled "Far from child" should be placed farther from the child on the table. Figures should be placed in the standing position unless other directions are given in the column labeled Adult's Actions & Words.

3. Follow the actions described in the column labeled **Adult's Actions and Words**. The action is shown in gray. (In Level 1, the adult does not need to carry out any actions, but in Level 2 and above, the adult uses a range of different actions).

4. Then, from the same column, say the relevant words that appear in quotation marks.

5. The response expected from the child is shown in the column labeled **Expected Response**. The abbreviations used are

   - I-Say (which means that the child must imitate what the adult has said without repeating the word *"say"*)
   - I (which means that the child must imitate what the adult has said)
   - P (which means that the child must point to the object that is being referred to)
   - O/A (which means that the child must perform the correct action on the correct object).

6. If the child gives the correct response on the 1ˢᵗ try, mark the item correct by placing a ✔ in the right-hand column.

7. If the child provides an incorrect response or no response to an item, repeat the item until a correct response is given, but leave the right hand column blank. In other words, a ✔ is given only for a response that is correct on the 1ˢᵗ try.

8. Once the child gives the correct response, move on to the next item.

9. After the session is completed, add up the number of ✔s and write down the total.

10. Record the total in the Summary Table located at the beginning of each level.

Ensuring An Effective Response

Obtaining Correct Imitations

In the first several levels, the early items include the instruction **"Say."** This helps the child understand what you are asking him or her to do. Sometimes a child will mistakenly echo the word "say" in his or her response. It is critical not to allow this pattern to take hold. If it does, it tends to reappear throughout the program, interfering with the child's progress. For example, when you reach Level 13 and start asking the child questions, he or she is likely to echo the questions rather than answer them.

To overcome the pattern, the following techniques are helpful.

- Say the directive word (in this case, **"Say"**) in a low voice and the actual words to be imitated in a louder and more animated voice.
- If the child starts to say the directive word, immediately shake your head and say "No" with a firm voice.
- It can be helpful to put your finger over the child's mouth as a cue to not say the word.

Once the feedback has been given, immediately repeat the item, starting from the beginning. After the first few items, once the child is accustomed to the task, the word "say" is no longer needed as part of the instruction.

Providing Hand Support

Hand support, which was introduced in the Pre-Language activities, plays a role in the Language activities as well. Even though many of the Language activities do not require actions, holding the child's hands can serve to increase the child's focus. If the child seems distracted or "tuned out," it is useful to take his or her hands into your hands, and then simply wait. Usually, within a minute, the child will offer an appropriate response. If the child makes an error or displays difficulty, take the child's hands into your own, and then repeat the item as many times as needed for a correct response.

Additional Techniques to Foster Success

Commands — If the child offers an incorrect response or no response, model the correct response by using hand-over-hand assistance. Then have the child complete the action without hand-over-hand assistance (but you may need to still provide hand support). If the command has multiple steps, model each step separately using hand-over-hand assistance. Then have the child complete both parts in sequence without hand-over-hand assistance (but still providing hand support if needed).

Sentence imitation — If the child has difficulty repeating the full sentence, break the sentence into smaller, more manageable, segments. Have the child imitate each segment, and then gradually combine them until the full sentence is repeated.

An important aim of the language program is for the children to distinguish **questions**, **statements**, and **commands**. Each operates differently in conversation and effective mastery of all of them is vital to progress. Therefore, do not allow the child to echo a command or question. The appropriate response to a command is to carry it out. The appropriate response to a question is to answer it.

One final comment before beginning the sessions. As you will see, the language gradually becomes more complex and steadily approaches the natural language of everyday life. At no point, however, are the rules or procedures underlying the language explicitly discussed with the child. For example, we do not say things like, "When I say 'You', you have to answer with 'I'." or "If something is gone, we use words like 'was' or 'did'." There is a strong tendency for skilled language users to resort to this type of explanation when they see someone having difficulty with language. However, it invariably complicates matters and makes the language experience even more complex for someone who is already confused. Instead, our approach is to dissect the underlying skills into the smallest units possible and then systematically provide the many encounters that the child needs until he or she masters each of those units.

Scoring

Each level has 12 lessons and each lesson has 25 items. For each lesson the criterion of success is 20 or more correct of 25 items on the 1st try (80% correct). At the end of each session, record the child's score on the summary table provided at the start of each level.

In the table shown below, the child has achieved success on 3 of the 5 lessons.

Sample Summary Table

(to be filled in at the completion of each lesson)

Lesson	1	2	3	4	5	6	7	8	9	10	11	12
Date	9/4	9/5	9/7	9/8	9/9							
Total # Correct Responses	15	*20*	22	18	24							

When to move on to the next level

Once the child has achieved 20 or more items correct on 3 out of 4 consecutive lessons (as shown in the table above), move on to the next level. The child does not need to complete all 12 lessons in order to move on. However, if the child has not achieved a passing score on 3 of 4 consecutive lessons by the time all 12 lessons have been completed, it may be helpful to take a break for 3-4 weeks, then restart the level from the beginning.

Outside the Session

Maintaining the Pre-Language Tasks: During Levels 1 to 5, it is helpful to maintain some of the activities from the Pre-Language section of the program. After you have completed a Language lesson, select two Pre-Language activities. Carry out one lesson from the highest level of each activity. From one day to the next, vary the Pre-Language activities that you select, so that over the course of a week, all the activities are covered.

Generalizing the Content: A key goal of the program is to have the children use their skills in the real world (outside the sessions). To aid this process, each level includes a set of sample items that you can use in daily life—both inside and outside the home. These are included after Lesson 1 of each level. There is no need to be limited to the examples offered. They are simply illustrations of how the content can be used in a variety of settings. These "real-world" activities are equally as important as the sessions themselves since they show the children how to generalize their newly acquired language.

It may be helpful to review the section in the General Guidelines at the beginning of the workbook (called ASD Unlocking Language and "Real Life"). It is important to follow these guidelines for using commands, questions, and statements in everyday life.

Level 1 Summary Table

(to be filled in at the completion of each lesson)

Lesson	1	2	3	4	5	6	7	8	9	10	11	12
Date												
Total # Correct Responses												

*Criterion for Moving On: Each lesson contains 25 items. Once a child achieves 20 or more items correct on 3 out of 4 consecutive sessions, move on to the next level. (The child does not need to complete all 12 sessions in order to move on). If the child does not achieve criterion within the 12 sessions, take a break for 3-4 weeks, and then restart this level from Lesson 1.

NOTE: At the start of the program, the child may not be able to complete all 25 items in Lesson 1. Do not feel pressured to do so. Attaining a few clear, correct responses is invaluable and is more important than completing the full lesson. Remember that you will repeat an item as many times as needed until the child offers the correct response. If this takes more than 10 minutes for the first item, end the session there. The following day start again at the beginning of Lesson 1. Each day the child should be able to complete more of the items, gradually working up to 25 items.

In Level 1, if the child has difficulty saying "the," substitute "a" as needed.

Level 1 Lesson 1 (repeat, if needed, as Lessons 4, 7, & 10)*								
Objects		Adult's Actions & Words	ER**	✔ if correct				
Near Child	Far from Child			Lesson 1	Lesson 4	Lesson 7	Lesson 10	
1	girl		*"Say — a girl"*	I-Say				
2	cat		*"Say — a cat"*	I-Say				
3	frog		*"Say — the frog"*	I-Say				
4	car		*"Say — the car"*	I-Say				
5	2 cars		"some cars"	I				
6	3 dogs		"some dogs"	I				
7	truck		**"this truck"**	I				
8	*same as above*	2 trucks	"more trucks"	I				
9	bird		**"a bird"**	I				
10	2 birds		"some birds"	I				
11	2 planes		**"these planes"**	I				
12		3 cars	**"those cars"**	I				
13	2 buses		**"these buses"**	I				
14		3 trucks	**"those trucks"**	I				
15	horse		**"a horse"**	I				
16	*same as above*	2 horses	"more horses"	I				
17	lady		**"the lady"**	I				
18	frog		**"this frog"**	I				
19		2 frogs	**"those frogs"**	I				
20	3 kids		"some kids"	I				
21	dog car kid		*"Hug the car and then give me the kid."*	O/A				
22	car dog kid car		pointing to one car **"Shake this car."**	O/A				
23	horse man bus		*"Give me the man and then pull the bus."*	O/A				
24	truck cat cat plane		pointing to one cat **"Hug this cat."**	O/A				

	Level 1 Lesson 1 (continued)							
	Objects		**Adult's Actions & Words**	**ER****	**✔ if correct**			
	Near Child	*Far from Child*			*Lesson 1*	*Lesson 4*	*Lesson 7*	*Lesson 10*
25	horse dog car		*"Turn over the horse and then the dog."*	O/A				
			Total Record the Total in the Level 1 Summary Table.					

*If the child has not attained criteria to move on to the next level after Lesson 3, do the following: after Lesson 3, return to Lesson 1 and repeat the content of Lesson 1. Record the child's responses in the column above labeled Lesson 4. The same content may be repeated again as Lesson 7 and then as Lesson 10, if needed.

**ER=Expected Response: I^{Say} = Imitates (excluding Say); I = Imitates; P = Points; O/A = Correct action on correct object

Level 1 Sample Daily Real-World Exercises		
Setting	**Adult's Actions & Words**	**Expected Response***
Park	standing near a dog *"this dog"*	I
Park	pointing to birds at a distance *"those birds"*	I/P
Park	pointing to a rock *"Give me this rock."*	O/A
Park	pointing to a tree *"a tree"*	I/P
Park	pointing to more trees nearby *"more trees"*	I/P
Home	standing near some toys *"some toys"*	I
Home	pointing to a bed close by *"this bed"*	I/P
Home	pointing to soap at a distance *"that soap"*	I/P
Kitchen	*"Turn over the fork and then shake the cup."*	O/A
Kitchen	pointing to nearby chairs *"these chairs"*	I/P
Kitchen	standing near a table *"a table"*	I
Neighborhood	pointing to some cars *"these cars"*	I/P
Neighborhood	standing near a bike *"the bike"*	I

* I^{-Say} = Imitates (excluding Say); I = Imitates; P = Points; O/A = Correct actions on correct objects

NOTE: In these real-world exercises, pointing is sometimes needed to clarify the meaning of what the adult is saying. It is important to ensure that the child is attending appropriately to what the adult is talking about, but the child does not always need to point when giving a response. Pointing is only required from the child if "I/P" appears in the column Expected Response.

Remember to create additional Daily Real-World Exercises and use them regularly throughout the day. Over time, you will become more and more comfortable integrating these language forms into a variety of settings.

	Objects		Adult's Actions & Words	ER*	✔ if correct			
	Near Child	Far from Child			Lesson 2	Lesson 5	Lesson 8	Lesson 11
			Level 1 Lesson 2 (repeat, if needed, as Lessons 5, 8, & 11)					
1	kid		*"Say — the kid"*	I-Say				
2	cat		*"Say — a cat"*	I-Say				
3	bird		*"Say — the bird"*	I-Say				
4	truck		*"Say — a truck"*	I-Say				
5	2 planes		*"some planes"*	I				
6	3 horses		*"some horses"*	I				
7	bus		*"this bus"*	I				
8	*same as above*	2 buses	*"more buses"*	I				
9		bird	*"that bird"*	I				
10	boy		*"a boy"*	I				
11	2 planes		*"these planes"*	I				
12		3 girls	*"those girls"*	I				
13	2 frogs		*"these frogs"*	I				
14		2 horses	*"those horses"*	I				
15	car		*"a car"*	I				
16	*same as above*	2 cars	*"more cars"*	I				
17	man		*"the man"*	I				
18	dog		*"this dog"*	I				
19		2 dogs	*"some dogs"*	I				
20	3 kids		*"some kids"*	I				
21	plane boy horse		*"Turn over the plane and then give me the horse."*	O/A				
22	car dog kid dog		pointing to one dog *"Shake this dog and then pull the car."*	O/A				
23	bus horse bus bus		pointing to one bus *"Give me that bus."*	O/A				

Level 1 Lesson 2 (continued)								
	Objects		**Adult's Actions & Words**	**ER***	**✔ if correct**			
	Near Child	*Far from Child*			*Lesson 2*	*Lesson 5*	*Lesson 8*	*Lesson 11*
24	truck plane cat plane		pointing to one plane *"Turn over this plane."*	O/A				
25	horse dog car kid		*"Hug the kid and then shake the horse."*	O/A				
				Total Record the Total in the Level 1 Summary Table.				

*ER=Expected Response: I^{-Say} = Imitates (excluding Say); I = Imitates; P = Points; O/A = Correct action on correct object

NOTE: Remember to create Daily Real-World Exercises and use them regularly throughout the day.

Level 1 Lesson 3 (repeat, if needed, as Lessons 6, 9, & 12)								
	Objects		Adult's Actions & Words	ER*	✔ if correct			
	Near Child	Far from Child			Lesson 3	Lesson 6	Lesson 9	Lesson 12
1	truck		"Say—this truck"	I-Say				
2		bus	"Say—that bus"	I-Say				
3	horse		"Say—the horse"	I-Say				
4	boy		"Say—a boy"	I-Say				
5	3 planes		"some planes"	I				
6		2 birds	"some birds"	I				
7	girl		"this kid"	I				
8	same as above	3 boys	"more kids"	I				
9		frog	"that frog"	I				
10	car		"a car"	I				
11	2 dogs		"these dogs"	I				
12		3 kids	"those kids"	I				
13	2 cats		"these cats"	I				
14	same as above		"some cats"	I				
15	lady		"a lady"	I				
16	same as above	2 ladies	"more ladies"	I				
17	bird		"the bird"	I				
18	car		"this car"	I				
19		2 dogs	"those dogs"	I				
20		3 girls	"some girls"	I				
21	girl plane frog		"Hug the girl and then turn over the plane."	O/A				
22	car car dog man		pointing to one car "Give me that car."	O/A				
23	bird lady cat		"Hug the lady and then pull the cat."	O/A				

171

Level 1 Lesson 3 (continued)								
	Objects		Adult's Actions & Words	ER*	✔ if correct			
	Near Child	*Far from Child*			*Lesson 3*	*Lesson 6*	*Lesson 9*	*Lesson 12*
24	boy girl horse girl		*"Give me the kids."*	O/A				
25	boy horse truck		*"Turn over the truck and then shake the horse."*	O/A				
			Total Record the Total in the Level 1 Summary Table.					

*ER=Expected Response: I^{-Say} = Imitates (excluding Say); I = Imitates; P = Points; O/A = Correct action on correct object

NOTE: Remember to create Daily Real-World Exercises and use them regularly throughout the day.

LEVEL 2
SIMPLE NOUN-VERB SENTENCES

Overview

At each level, the introduction of new information needs to be carefully controlled. In Level 1, the length was limited to two words and the structures were limited to noun phrases (resulting in combinations such as *"those kids"* and *"that truck"*). In Level 2, the language remains at the two-word level, but the structures expand to include noun-verb combinations such as *"boy sits,"* *"cats run,"* and *"cars go."* Rather than simply identifying figures, the child is now describing the actions that the figures are performing.

The actions introduced in this level are ones that can easily be demonstrated, such as *sit, walk, run*, and *jump*. (Actions that cannot easily be demonstrated, such as *see* and *feel*, are not taught at this time.) While the verbs are simple, they can still foster important language advances. For example, a single figure may be performing an action (e.g., a dog sitting), while the sentence is in the plural form making a general statement about the capacities of figures like these (e.g.,*"Dogs sit"*). Items like these lead the child to the realization that language can and regularly does go beyond what is immediately in view.

These new combinations also lend themselves to the use of pronouns. For example, a figure referred to initially as *"the boy"* can now be referred to as *"he."* The children may or may not understand the meaning of the pronouns at this stage; the goal is to practice hearing and saying them.

Meaningful language in everyday life rarely consists of single sentences. Instead, sentences link together to create a coherent message. So even at this early stage, consecutive items are linked to maintain focus on a "topic." For example, the child sees several cats and says, *"some cats."* In the next item, the child says, *"They sit."*

In summary, this level has several goals:
- to introduce children to more varied language structures
- to expose them to connected language
- to familiarize them with hearing and saying pronouns
- to show them that figures do not always have to be named (but can be referred to by using pronouns)

The new words introduced in this level are *he, she, it, they, sit, walk, stand, run, go, rest, jump, & fly.* The actions are performed in the following way:

- Sit — place the figure(s) in a seated position either on the table or in a chair (if present).
- Walk — move the figure(s) across the table, lifting it slightly with each "step."
- Stand — place the figure(s) in a standing position.
- Run — this motion is the same as walking but the steps are faster.
- Go — move the vehicle(s) across the table.
- Rest — lay the figure(s) flat on the table or on a bed (if available).
- Jump — move the figure(s) up and down in a jumping motion at least four times.
- Fly — move the figure(s) through the air in a flying motion.

Level 2 Summary Table
(to be filled in at the completion of each lesson)

Lesson	1	2	3	4	5	6	7	8	9	10	11	12
Date												
Total # Correct Responses												

*Criterion for Moving On: Each lesson contains 25 items. Once a child achieves 20 or more items correct on 3 out of 4 consecutive sessions, move on to the next level. (The child does not need to complete all 12 sessions in order to move on). If the child does not achieve criterion within the 12 sessions, take a break for 3-4 weeks, and then restart this level from Lesson 1.

NOTE: Continue to carry out the Pre-Language activities and the Daily Real-World activities. You may find it helpful to refer back to the instructions provided in Level 1 *Outside the Session.*

NOTE: Throughout the program, all figures should be in the standing position unless otherwise noted.

Level 2 Lesson 1 (repeat, if needed, as Lessons 4, 7, & 10)								
	Objects		Adult's Actions & Words	ER*	✔ if correct			
	Near Child	Far from Child			Lesson 1	Lesson 4	Lesson 7	Lesson 10
1	boy		*"Say – a boy"*	I-Say				
2	2 boys		*"Say – some boys"*	I-Say				
3	*same as above*		boys walking *"Boys walk."*	I				
4	*same as above*		boys sitting *"They sit."*	I				
5	lady		*"the lady"*	I				
6	*same as above*	2 ladies	*"more ladies"*	I				
7	*same as above*	*same as above*	far ladies walking *"Ladies walk."*	I				
8	*same as above*	*same as above*	near lady jumping *"Lady jumps."*	I				
9	dog		*"this dog"*	I				
10	*same as above*	dog	pointing to far dog *"that dog"*	I/P				
11	*same as above*	*same as above*	both dogs running *"Dogs run."*	I				
12	plane		*"a plane"*	I				
13	*same as above*		plane flying *"Plane flies."*	I				
14		man bed	*"that man"*	I				
15		*same as above*	man standing *"He stands."*	I				
16		*same as above*	man lying on bed *"He rests."*	I				
17	truck		*"a truck"*	I				
18	*same as above*		truck going *"It goes."*	I				
19	girl		*"this girl"*	I				
20	*same as above*		girl walking *"Girl walks."*	I				

	Objects		Adult's Actions & Words	ER*	✔ if correct			
	Near Child	*Far from Child*			*Lesson 1*	*Lesson 4*	*Lesson 7*	*Lesson 10*
Level 2 Lesson 1 (continued)								
21	car dog kid kid		pointing to one kid *"Shake this kid."*	O/A				
22	truck plane cat cat		pointing to one cat *"Make this cat walk."*	O/A				
23	horse man bus		*"Give me the man and then pull the bus."*	O/A				
24	bus dog car		*"Turn over the bus and then the dog."*	O/A				
25	dog car kid		*"Hug the kid and then give me the car."*	O/A				
				Total Record the Total in the Level 1 Summary Table.				

*ER=Expected Response: I^{Say} = Imitates (excluding Say); I = Imitates; P = Points; O/A = Correct action on correct object

NOTE: Remember to create Daily Real-World Exercises and use them regularly throughout the day.

	Level 2 Sample Daily Real-World Exercises	
Setting	**Adult's Actions & Words**	**Expected Response***
Home	pointing to a pen *"a pen"*	I
Home	pointing to some more pens nearby *"more pens"*	I
Home	*"Give me a pen."*	O/A
Neighborhood	pointing to some cars driving nearby *"these cars"*	I/P
Neighborhood	*"They go."*	I
Playground	standing near a boy playing *"a boy"*	I
Playground	*"He plays."*	I
Park	pointing to some dogs running *"some dogs"*	I
Park	*"They run."*	I
Restaurant	pointing to some kids eating *"some kids"*	I
Restaurant	*"They eat."*	I

* I-Say = Imitates (excluding Say); I = Imitates; P = Points; O/A = Correct actions on correct objects

177

Level 2 Lesson 2 (repeat, if needed, as Lessons 5, 8, & 11)								
	Objects		Adult's Actions & Words	ER*	✔ if correct			
	Near Child	Far from Child			Lesson 2	Lesson 5	Lesson 8	Lesson 11
1	truck		*"Say—this truck"*	I⁻ˢᵃʸ				
2	*same as above*	2 trucks	*"Say—those trucks"*	I⁻ˢᵃʸ				
3	*same as above*	*same as above*	far trucks going *"Trucks go."*	I				
4	3 cats		*"some cats"*	I				
5	*same as above*		two cats running *"Cats run."*	I				
6	*same as above*		two cats walking *"They walk."*	I				
7	*same as above*		all cats lying down *"They rest."*	I				
8	lady		*"a lady"*	I				
9	*same as above*		lady walking *"Ladies walk."*	I				
10	*same as above*		lady jumping *"Ladies jump."*	I				
11	*same as above*		lady sitting *"Ladies sit."*	I				
12	plane		plane flying *"Planes fly."*	I				
13	bird		*"this bird"*	I				
14	*same as above*		bird flying *"Bird flies."*	I				
15	2 frogs		*"some frogs"*	I				
16	*same as above*	2 dogs	*"some dogs"*	I				
17	*same as above*	*same as above*	one frog jumping *"Frog jumps."*	I				
18	*same as above*	*same as above*	both frogs jumping *"Frogs jump."*	I				
19	girl		*"the girl"*	I				
20	*same as above*		girl walking *"Girls walk."*	I				
21	frog bus bus plane		pointing to one bus *"Pull this bus."*	O/A				

Level 2 Lesson 2 (continued)								
	Objects		Adult's Actions & Words	ER*	✔ if correct			
	Near Child	Far from Child			Lesson 2	Lesson 5	Lesson 8	Lesson 11
22	*same as above*		*"Give me the plane and then hug the frog."*	O/A				
23	cat dog cat dog		pointing to one cat *"Make this cat jump."*	O/A				
24	*same as above*		*"Pull the dogs."*	O/A				
25	kid horse	kid car	pointing to far kid *"Turn over that kid and then make the horse run."*	O/A				
				Total Record the Total in the Level 1 Summary Table.				

*ER=Expected Response: I^{Say} = Imitates (excluding Say); I = Imitates; P = Points; O/A = Correct action on correct object

NOTE: Remember to create Daily Real-World Exercises and use them regularly throughout the day.

Level 2 Lesson 3 (repeat, if needed, as Lessons 6, 9, & 12)								
Objects		**Adult's Actions & Words**	**ER***	**✔ if correct**				
Near Child	*Far from Child*			Lesson 3	Lesson 6	Lesson 9	Lesson 12	
1	horse		*"Say—this horse"*	I⁻ˢᵃʸ				
2	*same as above*	2 horses	*"Say—those horses"*	I⁻ˢᵃʸ				
3	*same as above*	*same as above*	near horse walking *"Horse walks."*	I				
4		bus	*"that bus"*	I				
5		*same as above*	bus going *"It goes."*	I				
6	2 birds		*"these birds"*	I				
7	*same as above*		birds flying *"Birds fly."*	I				
8	*same as above*		birds not flying *"They rest."*	I				
9	kid		*"the kid"*	I				
10	*same as above*	2 kids	*"more kids"*	I				
11	*same as above*	*same as above*	all kids jumping *"Kids jump."*	I				
12	*same as above*	*same as above*	all kids sitting *"Kids sit."*	I				
13	2 cats		*"some cats"*	I				
14	*same as above*		both cats running *"Cats run."*	I				
15	*same as above*		both cats walking *"They walk."*	I				
16	*same as above*		one cat walking *"It walks."*	I				
17	frog		*"a frog"*	I				
18	*same as above*		frog jumping *"Frogs jump."*	I				
19	girl		*"the girl"*	I				
20	*same as above*		girl walking *"Girls walk."*	I				
21	horse dog kid cat		*"Turn over the horse."*	O/A				

	Objects		Adult's Actions & Words	ER*	✔ if correct			
	Near Child	Far from Child			Lesson 3	Lesson 6	Lesson 9	Lesson 12
22	*same as above*		*"Make the dog walk and then hug the kid."*	O/A				
23	horse car kid car		*"Make the cars go."*	O/A				
24	car dog horse cat		*"Shake the dog and then hug the cat."*	O/A				
25	*same as above*		*"Give me the car and then pull the horse."*	O/A				

Level 2 Lesson 3 (continued)

Total
Record the Total in the Level 1 Summary Table.

*ER=Expected Response: I⁻Say = Imitates (excluding Say); I = Imitates; P = Points; O/A = Correct action on correct object

NOTE: Remember to create Daily Real-World Exercises and use them regularly throughout the day.

LEVEL 3
EXPANDING SENTENCE STRUCTURE

Overview

Having become familiar with two-word noun phrases (e.g., *these cars*) and noun-verb combinations (e.g., *cars go*), the next step for the child is to expand the length of sentences to three words and to integrate the structures, so that noun-phrases and noun-verb combinations appear in a single sentence such as *"The boy sits."* and *"These birds fly."*

The new forms maintain a focus on "actors" and their actions. "Actor-action" concepts are critical to understanding the world in which we live. Often, these ideas are not emphasized in language programs for ASD, where the focus is on inanimate nouns or features of nouns, such as size, shape and color. So it may take a bit of time for a child to become comfortable with this aspect of language.

The children often have a preference for nouns, but nouns alone are inadequate for meaningful communication. Even a large vocabulary of single word nouns (e.g., *car, boy, house, spoon, cup,* etc.), does not enable a child to formulate and communicate ideas. Only when children become skilled in linking nouns with verbs can they

- begin to understand the complex language that they hear around them and
- produce the more complex language that others need to understand what the children are thinking.

To skilled language users, the advances from Level 2 to Level 3 are barely noticeable. However, children on the spectrum are far more sensitive to change. This is one reason why they often have difficulty with transitions. By making the transitions tiny, they are able to steadily advance.

Level 3 Summary Table
(to be filled in at the completion of each lesson)

Lesson	1	2	3	4	5	6	7	8	9	10	11	12
Date												
Total # Correct Responses												

*Criterion for Moving On: Each lesson contains 25 items. Once a child achieves 20 or more items correct on 3 out of 4 consecutive sessions, move on to the next level. (The child does not need to complete all 12 sessions in order to move on). If the child does not achieve criterion within the 12 sessions, take a break for 3-4 weeks, and then restart this level from Lesson 1.

NOTE: Continue to carry out the Pre-Language activities and the Daily Real-World activities. You may find it helpful to refer back to the instructions provided in Level 1 *Outside the Session.*

NOTE: Throughout the program, all figures should be in the standing position unless otherwise noted.

	Level 3 Lesson 1 (repeat, if needed, as Lessons 4, 7, & 10)							
	Objects		**Adult's Actions & Words**	**ER***	**✔ if correct**			
	Near Child	*Far from Child*			*Lesson 1*	*Lesson 4*	*Lesson 7*	*Lesson 10*
1	bird		*"Say—the bird"*	I⁻ˢᵃʸ				
2	*same as above*		bird flying *"Say—The bird flies."*	I⁻ˢᵃʸ				
3	car		*"a car"*	I				
4	*same as above*		car going *"It goes."*	I				
5	kid		*"this kid"*	I				
6	*same as above*	2 kids	*"those kids"*	I				
7	*same as above*	*same as above*	near kid sitting *"This kid sits."*	I				
8	*same as above*	*same as above*	far kids running *"Those kids run."*	I				
9	*same as above*	*same as above*	pointing to near kid *"Now make this kid run."*	O/A				
10	frog		frog jumping *"Frogs jump."*	I				
11	*same as above*	2 frogs	*"more frogs"*	I				
12	*same as above*	*same as above*	pointing to far frogs *"Make those frogs jump."*	O/A				
13	*same as above*	*same as above*	frogs resting *"The frogs rest."*	I				
14		cat	*"that cat"*	I				
15		*same as above*	cat walking *"That cat walks."*	I				
16		*same as above*	cat running *"It runs."*	I				
17	2 buses		*"these buses"*	I				
18	*same as above*		buses going *"These buses go."*	I				
19		horse	*"that horse"*	I				

Level 3 Lesson 1 (continued)								
Objects		**Adult's Actions & Words**	**ER***	**✔ if correct**				
Near Child	*Far from Child*			*Lesson 1*	*Lesson 4*	*Lesson 7*	*Lesson 10*	
20		*same as above*	horse walking **"That horse walks."**	I				
21		*same as above*	**"Now make the horse jump."**	O/A				
22		2 girls** bed	**"some girls"**	I				
23		*same as above*	**"Make the girls rest."**	O/A				
24		*same as above*	**"Hug the girls and then give me the bed."**	O/A				
25		*same as above*	both girls sitting **"The girls sit."**	I				
			Total Record the Total in the Level 1 Summary Table.					

*ER=Expected Response: I⁻ˢᵃʸ = Imitates (excluding Say); I = Imitates; P = Points; O/A = Correct action on correct object

**As noted earlier, unless a specific position is indicated, all figures should be in standing position (even if a chair or bed is present).

NOTE: Remember to create Daily Real-World Exercises and use them regularly throughout the day.

Level 3 Sample Daily Real-World Exercises		
Setting	**Adult's Actions & Words**	**Expected Response***
Playground	standing near some ladies sitting *"some ladies"*	I
Playground	*"Some ladies sit."*	I
Park	pointing to bird flying *"The bird flies."*	I
Park	standing near a dog resting *"This dog rests."*	I
Restaurant	pointing to some kids at a distance eating *"those kids"*	I/P
Restaurant	*"Those kids eat."*	I
Restaurant	standing near some ladies talking. *"The ladies talk."*	I
Store	point to a man walking *"a man"*	I
Store	*"He walks."*	I
Store	point to a man sitting *"That man sits."*	I/P

* I^{-Say} = Imitates (excluding Say); I = Imitates; P = Points; O/A = Correct actions on correct objects

	Objects		Adult's Actions & Words	ER*	✔ if correct			
	Near Child	Far from Child			Lesson 2	Lesson 5	Lesson 8	Lesson 11
Level 3 Lesson 2 (repeat, if needed, as Lessons 5, 8, & 11)								
1	dog		"Say—a dog"	I⁻ˢᵃʸ				
2	same as above		dog running "Say—A dog runs."	I⁻ˢᵃʸ				
3		truck	"the truck"	I				
4		same as above	truck going "The truck goes."	I				
5	2 boys	boy	pointing to near boys "these boys"	I/P				
6	same as above	same as above	pointing to far boy "that boy"	I/P				
7	same as above	same as above	near boys jumping "These boys jump."	I				
8	same as above	same as above	all boys standing "The boys stand."	I				
9	same as above	same as above	"Give me the boys."	O/A				
10	2 ladies		"some ladies"	I				
11	same as above		ladies sitting "They sit."	I				
12		3 planes	"those planes"	I				
13		same as above	planes flying "Those planes fly."	I				
14		man bed	"that man"	I				
15		same as above	man laying down on bed "That man rests."	I				
16		same as above	man walking "He walks."	I				
17	boy chair		boy sitting in chair "A boy sits."	I				
18		2 boys	boys standing "Some boys stand."	I				
19		same as above	"Make the boys jump."	O/A				
20	2 buses		buses going "These buses go."	I				
21	same as above	bus	far bus going "That bus goes."	I				

188

Level 3 Lesson 2 (continued)								
	Objects		Adult's Actions & Words	ER*	✔ if correct			
	Near Child	Far from Child			Lesson 2	Lesson 5	Lesson 8	Lesson 11
22	same as above	same as above	pointing to near buses *"Turn over these buses."*	O/A				
23		2 horses	*"Make the horses run."*	O/A				
24		same as above	*"Hug the horses."*	O/A				
25		same as above	horses walking *"Horses walk."*	I				
			Total Record the Total in the Level 1 Summary Table.					

*ER=Expected Response: I^{Say} = Imitates (excluding Say); I = Imitates; P = Points; O/A = Correct action on correct object

NOTE: Remember to create Daily Real-World Exercises and use them regularly throughout the day.

Level 3 Lesson 3 (repeat, if needed, as Lessons 6, 9, & 12)								
	Objects		Adult's Actions & Words	ER*	✔ if correct			
	Near Child	Far from Child			Lesson 3	Lesson 6	Lesson 9	Lesson 12
1	lady		*"Say — the lady"*	I⁻ˢᵃʸ				
2	same as above		lady standing *"Say — The lady stands."*	I⁻ˢᵃʸ				
3	truck		*"a truck"*	I				
4	same as above		truck going *"A truck goes."*	I				
5	boy		*"this boy"*	I				
6	same as above	2 boys	*"more boys"*	I				
7	same as above	same as above	near boy walking *"This boy walks."*	I				
8	same as above	same as above	far boys jumping *"Those boys jump."*	I				
9	same as above	same as above	*"Shake the boys and then hug the boys."*	O/A				
10	plane	2 cats	plane flying *"Planes fly."*	I				
11	same as above	same as above	cats standing *"Those cats stand."*	I				
12	same as above	same as above	pointing to both cats *"Make those cats walk."*	O/A				
13	same as above	same as above	cats laying down *"Those cats rest."*	I				
14	girl chair		*"this girl"*	I				
15	same as above		girl sitting in chair *"This girl sits."*	I				
16	same as above		girl running *"She runs."*	I				
17		bus	*"that bus"*	I				
18		same as above	bus going *"That bus goes."*	I				
19	2 birds	same as above	*"these birds"*	I				
20	same as above	same as above	birds flying *"These birds fly."*	I				

	Objects		Adult's Actions & Words	ER*	✔ if correct			
	Near Child	Far from Child			Lesson 3	Lesson 6	Lesson 9	Lesson 12
21	*same as above*	*same as above*	*"Turn over the birds and then give me the bus."*	O/A				
22		man bed	*"that man"*	I				
23		*same as above*	*"Make the man rest."*	O/A				
24		*same as above*	*"Hug the man and then give me the bed."*	O/A				
25		horse	horse standing *"The horse stands."*	I				
			Total Record the Total in the Level 1 Summary Table.					

Level 3 Lesson 3 (continued)

*ER=Expected Response: I^Say = Imitates (excluding Say); I = Imitates; P = Points; O/A = Correct action on correct object

NOTE: Remember to create Daily Real-World Exercises and use them regularly throughout the day.

LEVEL 4

SENTENCES INTRODUCING A SUBJECT

Overview

To keep things simple, the language forms taught in Levels 1 and 2 were limited to two-word phrases and sentences. Now that the children are building up their sentence length, we are going to revisit those forms and present them in the fuller versions in which they typically appear (e.g., *"this kid"* will be replaced with *"This is a kid,"* etc.) The following sentence forms are taught in Level 4:

> *This is a _____. (e.g., This is a frog.)*
> *These are _____. (e.g., These are birds.)*
> *That is a _____. (e.g., That is a horse.)*
> *Those are _____. (e.g., Those are planes.)*
> *A _____ is here. (e.g., A boy is here.)*
> *Some _____ are here. (e.g., Some kids are here.)*
> *A _____ is there. (e.g., A boy is there.)*
> *Some _____ are there. (e.g., Some boys are there.)*

When using these forms, you will often be pointing as you say the words, and you will also be requiring the child to point as he or she says the words. This action is important to clarify the language. For example, three figures may be in view, such as a dog, a bird and a girl. If you say, "This is a girl," the comment is relevant only if you point to the appropriate figure.

You will see the items that require the child to point by the letters "I/P" in the Expected Response column. The "I" represents the fact the imitation is required and the "P" represents the fact that pointing is also required for that particular item. To facilitate the pointing response, it is best to avoid verbal instructions (e.g., do not say, "You have to point.") Instead, just take the child's hand and model the pointing. Repeat the item until the child points independently. You should continue to provide hand support as needed, but be sure that the child is clearly moving his or her arm and that you are not guiding it in any way.

Level 4 Summary Table
(to be filled in at the completion of each lesson)

Lesson	1	2	3	4	5	6	7	8	9	10	11	12
Date												
Total # Correct Responses												

*Criterion for Moving On: Each lesson contains 25 items. Once a child achieves 20 or more items correct on 3 out of 4 consecutive sessions, move on to the next level. (The child does not need to complete all 12 sessions in order to move on). If the child does not achieve criterion within the 12 sessions, take a break for 3-4 weeks, and then restart this level from Lesson 1.

NOTE: Continue to carry out the Pre-Language activities and the Daily Real-World activities. You may find it helpful to refer back to the instructions provided in Level 1 *Outside the Session.*

NOTE: Throughout the program, all figures should be in the standing position unless otherwise noted.

NOTE: For items in which the Expected Response is I/P, be sure that the child points to the relevant object.

Level 4 Lesson 1 (repeat, if needed, as Lessons 4, 7, & 10)								
Objects		**Adult's Actions & Words**	**ER***	**✔ if correct**				
Near Child	*Far from Child*			*Lesson 1*	*Lesson 4*	*Lesson 7*	*Lesson 10*	
1	bird		pointing to bird *"A bird is here."*	I/P				
2	*same as above*		bird flying *"The bird flies."*	I				
3		car	pointing to car *"A car is there."*	I/P				
4		*same as above*	car going *"The car goes."*	I				
5	2 kids		*"These are kids."*	I				
6	*same as above*		one kid running *"This kid runs."*	I				
7		3 dogs	*"Those are dogs."*	I				
8		*same as above*	dogs walking *"The dogs walk."*	I				
9		*same as above*	*"Make the dogs jump and then give me the dogs."*	O/A				
10	frog		pointing to frog *"A frog is here."*	I/P				
11	*same as above*	2 frogs	pointing to far frogs *"More frogs are there."*	I/P				
12	*same as above*	*same as above*	pointing to one far frog *"Make that frog jump."*	O/A				
13	*same as above*	*same as above*	*"Now give me the frogs."*	O/A				
14		lady	*"That is a lady."*	I				
15		*same as above*	lady jumping *"That lady jumps."*	I				
16		*same as above*	lady sitting *"She sits."*	I				
17	2 buses		*"Some buses are here."*	I				

195

Level 4 Lesson 1 (continued)								
	Objects		Adult's Actions & Words	ER*	✔ if correct			
	Near Child	*Far from Child*			Lesson 1	Lesson 4	Lesson 7	Lesson 10
18	*same as above*		buses going "These buses go."	I				
19		cat	"That is a cat."	I				
20		*same as above*	cat walking "The cat walks."	I				
21		*same as above*	"Hug the cat and then give me the cat."	O/A				
22	2 girls bed		pointing to girls "Some girls are here."	I/P				
23	*same as above*		"Make the girls rest."	O/A**				
24		3 planes bus	pointing to planes "Some planes are there."	I/P				
25		*same as above*	"Make the planes fly and then give me the bus."	O/A				
			Total Record the Total in the Level 1 Summary Table.					

*ER=Expected Response: I^Say = Imitates (excluding Say); I = Imitates; P = Points; O/A = Correct action on correct object

**The girls may either be lying down on the table or on the bed.

NOTE: Remember to create Daily Real-World Exercises and use them regularly throughout the day.

Level 4 Sample Daily Real-World Exercises		
Setting	**Adult's Actions & Words**	**Expected Response**
Playground	pointing to a baby *"That is a baby."*	I
Playground	*"Babies cry."*	I
Home	standing near Dad sitting *"Dad is here."*	I
Home	*"He sits."*	I
Park	standing near some boys playing *"The boys play."*	I
Store	pointing to a cart *"A cart is there."*	I/P
Store	pointing to a box *"A box is here."*	I/P
Store	*"Put the box in the cart."*	O/A
Restaurant	pointing to some kids at a distant table *"Some kids are there."*	I/P
Restaurant	*"They eat."*	I

Level 4 Lesson 2 (repeat, if needed, as Lessons 5, 8, & 11)								
Objects		Adult's Actions & Words	ER*	✔ if correct				
Near Child	Far from Child			Lesson 2	Lesson 5	Lesson 8	Lesson 11
1		truck	*"That is a truck."*	I				
2		same as above	truck going *"The truck goes."*	I				
3	lady		*"This is a lady."*	I				
4	same as above		lady standing *"The lady stands."*	I				
5	2 planes	3 boys	pointing to planes *"Some planes are here."*	I/P				
6	same as above	same as above	planes flying *"The planes fly."*	I				
7	same as above	same as above	pointing to boys *"Some boys are there."*	I/P				
8	same as above	same as above	boys walking *"They walk."*	I				
9	same as above	same as above	*"Hug the boys and then turn over the planes."*	O/A				
10		dog	pointing to dog *"A dog is there."*	I/P				
11	2 dogs	same as above	pointing to near dogs *"Some more dogs are here."*	I/P				
12	same as above	same as above	pointing to far dog *"Make that dog run."*	O/A				
13	same as above	same as above	near dogs jumping *"These dogs jump."*	I				
14		2 girls bed	*"Those are girls."*	I				
15		same as above	girls lying on bed *"The girls rest."*	I				
16		same as above	girls standing *"The girls stand."*	I				
17	2 cats		*"These are cats."*	I				
18	same as above		cats jumping *"These cats jump."*	I				
19	horse		*"That is a horse."*	I				
20		same as above	horse walking *"It walks."*	I				

Level 4 Lesson 2 (continued)								
	Objects		Adult's Actions & Words	ER*	✔ if correct			
	Near Child	Far from Child			Lesson 2	Lesson 5	Lesson 8	Lesson 11
21		*same as above*	*"Pull the horse."*	O/A				
22	man		pointing to man *"A man is here."*	I/P				
23	*same as above*		*"Make the man sit."*	O/A				
24		2 cars	pointing to cars *"Some cars are there."*	I/P				
25		*same as above*	*"Shake those cars."*	O/A				
			Total Record the Total in the Level 1 Summary Table.					

*ER=Expected Response: I^-Say^ = Imitates (excluding Say); I = Imitates; P = Points; O/A = Correct action on correct object

NOTE: Remember to create Daily Real-World Exercises and use them regularly throughout the day.

Level 4 Lesson 3 (repeat, if needed, as Lessons 6, 9, & 12)								
	Objects		Adult's Actions & Words	ER*	✔ if correct			
	Near Child	Far from Child			Lesson 3	Lesson 6	Lesson 9	Lesson 12
1		2 frogs	*"Those are some frogs."*	I				
2		same as above	frogs jumping *"The frogs jump."*	I				
3	car		pointing to car *"A car is here."*	I/P				
4	same as above		car going *"It goes."*	I				
5	2 birds		pointing to birds *"Some birds are here."*	I/P				
6	same as above		birds flying *"They fly."*	I				
7	same as above	2 kids	pointing to kids *"Some kids are there."*	I/P				
8	same as above	same as above	kids sitting *"The kids sit."*	I				
9	same as above	same as above	*"Hug the kids and then give me the birds."*	O/A				
10		bus	*"That is a bus."*	I				
11	2 buses	same as above	pointing to near buses *"More buses are here."*	I/P				
12	same as above	same as above	pointing to far bus *"Make that bus go."*	O/A				
13	same as above	same as above	pointing to near buses *"Pull these buses."*	O/A				
14	lady bed		*"This is a lady."*	I				
15	same as above		lady standing *"She stands."*	I				
16	same as above		lady lying on bed *"She rests."*	I				
17	2 dogs		*"These are dogs."*	I				
18	same as above		dogs walking *"These dogs walk."*	I				
19	same as above	frog	pointing to frog *"A frog is there."*	I/P				
20	same as above	same as above	frog jumping *"It jumps."*	I				

	Objects		Adult's Actions & Words	ER*	✔ if correct			
	Near Child	Far from Child			Lesson 3	Lesson 6	Lesson 9	Lesson 12
21	*same as above*	*same as above*	*"Shake the frog and then make the dogs jump."*	O/A				
22	boy		*"This is a boy."*	I				
23	*same as above*		*"Make the boy run."*	O/A				
24		plane	pointing to plane *"A plane is there."*	I/P				
25		*same as above*	*"Make the plane fly."*	O/A				

*(Table title: **Level 4 Lesson 3 (continued)**)*

Total
Record the Total in the Level 1 Summary Table.

*ER=Expected Response: I⁻ˢᵃʸ = Imitates (excluding Say); I = Imitates; P = Points; O/A = Correct action on correct object

NOTE: Remember to create Daily Real-World Exercises and use them regularly throughout the day.

LEVEL 5

SENTENCES DESCRIBING ACTIONS

Overview

The real world is filled with both animate figures such as *kids, dogs,* and *ladies,* and inanimate objects such as *chairs, beds,* and *plates.* For effective social development, the children need to become aware of the abilities and behaviors of animate figures. A key feature distinguishing the two is that animate figures perform actions, whereas inanimate objects generally do not. To assist children in gaining this awareness, at this level, the children are taught to say complete sentences describing actions that various animate figures are performing. (In addition, some inanimate figures are associated with movement such as *planes flying.* These are also discussed at this level.) The following sentence forms are taught:

> *The _____ is _____ing. (e.g., The lady is sitting.)*
> *The _____s are _____ing. (e.g., The dogs are walking.)*

As always, the language forms taught up to this point are also maintained.

Level 5 Summary Table
(to be filled in at the completion of each lesson)

Lesson	1	2	3	4	5	6	7	8	9	10	11	12
Date												
Total # Correct Responses												

*Criterion for Moving On: Each lesson contains 25 items. Once a child achieves 20 or more items correct on 3 out of 4 consecutive sessions, move on to the next level. (The child does not need to complete all 12 sessions in order to move on). If the child does not achieve criterion within the 12 sessions, take a break for 3-4 weeks, and then restart this level from Lesson 1.

NOTE: Continue to carry out the Pre-Language activities and the Daily Real-World activities. You may find it helpful to refer back to the instructions provided in Level 1 *Outside the Session.*

NOTE: Throughout the program, all figures should be in the standing position unless otherwise noted.

Level 5 Lesson 1 (repeat, if needed, as Lessons 4, 7, & 10)								
	Objects		Adult's Actions & Words	ER*	✔ if correct			
	Near Child	Far from Child			Lesson 1	Lesson 4	Lesson 7	Lesson 10
1	boy		pointing to boy "A boy is here."	I/P				
2	same as above		boy sitting "The boy is sitting."	I				
3		dog	"That is a dog."	I				
4		same as above	dog running "That dog is running."	I				
5	2 ladies	3 planes	pointing to ladies "Some ladies are here."	I/P				
6	same as above	same as above	pointing to planes "Some planes are there."	I/P				
7	same as above	same as above	ladies walking "These ladies are walking."	I				
8	same as above	same as above	planes flying "Those planes are flying."	I				
9	same as above	same as above	"Hug the ladies and then give me the planes."	O/A				
10	man		"This is a man."	I				
11	same as above		man walking "He is walking."	I				
12	same as above	2 trucks	"Those are some trucks."	I				
13	same as above	same as above	trucks going "They are going."	I				
14	girl		girl sitting "A girl is sitting."	I				
15	same as above	2 girls	all girls sitting "More girls are sitting."	I				
16	same as above	same as above	near girl jumping "She is jumping."	I				
17	same as above	same as above	"Hug the girls and then give me the girls."	O/A				
18	frog		"This is a frog."	I				

Level 5 Lesson 1 (continued)								
	Objects		Adult's Actions & Words	ER*	✔ if correct			
	Near Child	*Far from Child*			*Lesson* 1	*Lesson* 4	*Lesson* 7	*Lesson* 10
19	*same as above*		frog jumping ***"The frog is jumping."***	I				
20	boy		pointing to boy ***"A boy is here."***	I/P				
21	*same as above*	2 boys	pointing to far boys ***"Some more boys are there."***	I/P				
22	*same as above*	*same as above*	pointing to near boy ***"Make this boy walk."***	O/A				
23		2 buses 2 cars	buses going ***"Those buses are going."***	I				
24		*same as above*	***"Hug the buses and then shake the cars."***	O/A				
25		*same as above*	***"Give me a car and turn over a bus."***	O/A				
				Total Record the Total in the Level 1 Summary Table.				

*ER=Expected Response: I^{-Say} = Imitates (excluding Say); I = Imitates; P = Points; O/A = Correct action on correct object

NOTE: Remember to create Daily Real-World Exercises and use them regularly throughout the day.

Setting	Adult's Actions & Words	Expected Response
Outdoors	pointing to a street light *"A light is there."*	I/P
Outdoors	*"The light is bright."*	I
Outdoors	pointing to some bugs crawling *"Some bugs are here."*	I/P
Outdoors	*"The bugs are crawling."*	I
Playground	pointing to some kids on swings *"Some kids are there."*	I/P
Playground	*"They are swinging."*	I
Kitchen	pointing to Dad cleaning kitchen table *"Dad is here."*	I/P
Kitchen	*"He is cleaning."*	I
Park	pointing to some birds flying *"Some birds are there."*	I/P
Park	*"Those birds are flying."*	I

Level 5 Sample Daily Real-World Exercises
These examples show you how the new language forms taught in this level should be used in daily life.
You should also continue to use the forms taught in prior levels.

Level 5 Lesson 2 (repeat, if needed, as Lessons 5, 8, & 11)								
	Objects		**Adult's Actions & Words**	**ER***	**✔ if correct**			
	Near Child	*Far from Child*			*Lesson 2*	*Lesson 5*	*Lesson 8*	*Lesson 11*
1		cat	*"That is a cat."*	I				
2		same as above	cat walking *"The cat is walking."*	I				
3	bus		*"This is a bus."*	I				
4	same as above		bus going *"The bus is going."*	I				
5	bird	boy	pointing to bird *"A bird is here."*	I/P				
6	same as above	same as above	pointing to boy *"A boy is there."*	I/P				
7	same as above	same as above	bird flying *"The bird is flying."*	I				
8	same as above	same as above	boy running *"The boy is running."*	I				
9	same as above	same as above	*"Turn over the bird and then shake the boy."*	O/A				
10		3 dogs	pointing to dogs *"Some dogs are there."*	I/P				
11		same as above	dogs jumping *"They are jumping."*	I				
12	2 girls		pointing to girls *"Some girls are here."*	I/P				
13	same as above		girls standing *"The girls are standing."*	I				
14	horse		*"This is a horse."*	I				
15	same as above	2 horses	pointing to far horses *"More horses are there."*	I/P				
16	same as above	same as above	near horse running *"This horse is running."*	I				
17	same as above	same as above	*"Hug a horse."*	O/A				
18		2 kids 2 beds	*"Those are kids."*	I				
19		same as above	kids lying on beds *"The kids are resting."*	I				
20	boy chair		boy sitting in chair *"This boy is sitting."*	I				

Level 5 Lesson 2 (continued)								
	Objects		Adult's Actions & Words	ER*	✔ if correct			
	Near Child	Far from Child			Lesson 2	Lesson 5	Lesson 8	Lesson 11
21	*same as above*	2 boys	far boys standing *"Those boys are standing."*	I				
22	*same as above*	*same as above*	pointing to near boy *"Make this boy stand."*	O/A				
23	man 2 planes		man walking *"He is walking."*	I				
24	*same as above*		*"Make the planes fly and then hug the man."*	O/A				
25	*same as above*		*"Give me the planes and then give me the man."*	O/A				
			Total Record the Total in the Level 1 Summary Table.					

*ER=Expected Response: I^{-Say} = Imitates (excluding Say); I = Imitates; P = Points; O/A = Correct action on correct object

NOTE: Remember to create Daily Real-World Exercises and use them regularly throughout the day.

	Objects		Adult's Actions & Words	ER*	✔ if correct			
	Near Child	*Far from Child*			Lesson 3	Lesson 6	Lesson 9	Lesson 12
1	frog		*"This is a frog."*	I				
2	*same as above*		frog jumping *"It is jumping."*	I				
3		2 trucks	*"Those are trucks."*	I				
4		*same as above*	trucks going *"They are going."*	I				
5	dog	plane	dog walking *"The dog is walking."*	I				
6	*same as above*	*same as above*	plane flying *"The plane is flying."*	I				
7	*same as above*	*same as above*	*"Pull the dog and then turn over the plane."*	O/A				
8	2 kids		pointing to kids *"Some kids are here."*	I/P				
9	*same as above*	2 kids	pointing to far kids *"Some more kids are there."*	I/P				
10	*same as above*	*same as above*	kids standing *"The kids are standing."*	I				
11	*same as above*	*same as above*	far kids running *"Some kids are running."*	I				
12	lady bed	car	pointing to lady *"A lady is here."*	I/P				
13	*same as above*	*same as above*	lady lying on bed *"She is resting."*	I				
14	*same as above*	*same as above*	pointing to car *"A car is there."*	I/P				
15	*same as above*	*same as above*	car going *"It is going."*	I				
16	*same as above*	*same as above*	*"Make the lady walk and then pull the car."*	O/A				
17	kid		*"This is a kid."*	I				
18	*same as above*		kid jumping *"The kid is jumping."*	I				
19	dog		pointing to dog *"A dog is here."*	I/P				
20	*same as above*		dog walking *"The dog is walking."*	I				

Level 5 Lesson 3 (repeat, if needed, as Lessons 6, 9, & 12)

	Objects		Adult's Actions & Words	ER*	✔ if correct			
	Near Child	Far from Child			Lesson 3	Lesson 6	Lesson 9	Lesson 12
	Level 5 Lesson 3 (continued)							
21	*same as above*		*"Make the dog jump."*	O/A				
22	girl chair		pointing to girl *"A girl is here."*	I/P				
23	*same as above*		girl sitting in chair *"She is sitting."*	I				
24	*same as above*	2 horses	*"Make the horses run and then hug the girl."*	O/A				
25	*same as above*	*same as above*	*"Make the girl jump and then give me the horses."*	O/A				
				Total				

Record the Total in the Level 1 Summary Table.

*ER=Expected Response: I^Say = Imitates (excluding Say); I = Imitates; P = Points; O/A = Correct action on correct object

NOTE: Remember to create Daily Real-World Exercises and use them regularly throughout the day.

LEVEL 6

SENTENCES DESCRIBING POTENTIAL ACTIONS

Overview

In language programs, there is a tendency to focus on labeling what is in view (e.g., *"a big dog," "a red car,"* etc.) However, effective language does far more than label what one is seeing. We use language to talk about the past, the future, and what is possible. This aspect of language begins very early in typical development. For example, the speech of toddlers regularly extends beyond what is immediately in view (e.g., *"all gone" "where Daddy?"*)

This aspect of language is often assumed to be beyond the capabilities of children with ASD. Fortunately, this is not the case. Through carefully structured language, they can achieve significant progress. ***From this point on, our goal is to teach children to hear and produce language that refers not only to the immediate present but to figures, objects, actions, and ideas that are not immediately within view.***

As a starting point, the children are taught to use words that focus on the ability or desire to perform particular actions (e,g., *can, likes to,* and *wants to*). In other words, what is being described are not particular actions, but rather the potential for those actions.

The following sentence forms are taught in this level:

> _____ can _____. *(e.g., "The dog can walk.")*
> _____want(s) to_____. *(e.g., "The kid wants to sit.")*
> _____like(s) to _____. *(e.g., "The lady likes to rest.")*

One final comment before beginning the sessions: As we pointed out earlier, at no point, are the rules or procedures underlying the language explicitly discussed with the child. For example, we do not say things like "If something is gone, we use words like 'was' or 'did'." There is a strong tendency for skilled language users to resort to this type of explanation when they see someone having difficulty with language. However, it invariably complicates matters and makes the language experience even more complex for the children. Instead, our approach is to dissect the underlying skills into the smallest units possible and then systematically provide the many encounters that the child needs until he or she masters each of those units.

Level 6 Summary Table
(to be filled in at the completion of each lesson)

Lesson	1	2	3	4	5	6	7	8	9	10	11	12
Date												
Total # Correct Responses												

*Criterion for Moving On: Each lesson contains 25 items. Once a child achieves 20 or more items correct on 3 out of 4 consecutive sessions, move on to the next level. (The child does not need to complete all 12 sessions in order to move on). If the child does not achieve criterion within the 12 sessions, take a break for 3-4 weeks, and then restart this level from Lesson 1.

NOTE: Continue to carry out the Daily Real-World activities. You may find it helpful to refer back to the instructions provided in Level 1 *Outside the Session.*

NOTE: Throughout the program, all figures should be in the standing position unless otherwise noted.

	Level 6 Lesson 1 (repeat, if needed, as Lessons 4, 7, & 10)							
	Objects		**Adult's Actions & Words**	**ER***	**✔ if correct**			
	Near Child	*Far from Child*			*Lesson 1*	*Lesson 4*	*Lesson 7*	*Lesson 10*
1	car		pointing to car "*A car is here.*"	I/P				
2	*same as above*		"*It can go.*"	I				
3	*same as above*		car going "*It is going.*"	I				
4		2 boys chair	"*Those are some boys.*"	I				
5		*same as above*	"*They want to sit.*"	I				
6		*same as above*	one boy sitting in chair pointing to boy sitting "*That boy is sitting.*"	I				
7	cat		"*This is a cat.*"	I				
8	*same as above*	2 cats	pointing to far cats "*Some more cats are there.*"	I/P				
9	*same as above*	*same as above*	"*Cats like to run.*"	I				
10	*same as above*	*same as above*	far cats running "*Those cats are running.*"	I				
11	*same as above*	*same as above*	"*Give me the cats.*"	O/A				
12	2 ladies	bus	pointing to the ladies "*Some ladies are here.*"	I/P				
13	*same as above*	*same as above*	"*The ladies want to walk.*"	I				
14	*same as above*	*same as above*	ladies walking "*They are walking.*"	I				
15	*same as above*	*same as above*	pointing to bus "*A bus is there.*"	I/P				
16	*same as above*	*same as above*	"*The bus can go.*"	I				
17	*same as above*	*same as above*	bus going "*It is going.*"	I				

	Objects		Adult's Actions & Words	ER*	✔ if correct			
	Near Child	Far from Child			Lesson 1	Lesson 4	Lesson 7	Lesson 10
18	same as above	same as above	"Make the ladies jump and then turn over the bus."	O/A				
19		bird	"That is a bird."	I				
20		same as above	"The bird likes to fly."	I				
21		same as above	"Make the bird fly."	O/A				
22	2 planes		"These are planes."	I				
23	same as above		"Planes can fly."	I				
24	same as above		"Make the planes fly."	O/A				
25	same as above		"Give me the planes."	O/A				
			Total Record the Total in the Level 1 Summary Table.					

Table heading: Level 6 Lesson 1 (continued)

*ER=Expected Response: I^{Say} = Imitates (excluding Say); I = Imitates; P = Points; O/A = Correct action on correct object

NOTE: Remember to create Daily Real-World Exercises and use them regularly throughout the day.

Setting	Adult's Actions & Words	Expected Response
Level 6 Sample Daily Real-World Exercises These examples show you how the new language forms taught in this level should be used in daily life. You should also continue to use the forms taught in prior levels.		
Neighborhood	standing near a kid riding a bike *"Kids can ride."*	I
Neighborhood	pointing to kid riding a bike *"That kid is riding."*	I
Playground	standing near some kids on swings *"Kids like to swing."*	I
Playground	*"Some kids are swinging."*	I
Playground	pointing to ladies talking *"Some ladies are there."*	I/P
Playground	*"Ladies like to talk."*	I
Playground	*"Those ladies are talking."*	I
Park	pointing to dog running *"That is a dog."*	I
Park	*"Dogs can run."*	I
Park	*"That dog is running."*	I

Level 6 Lesson 2 (repeat, if needed, as Lessons 5, 8, & 11)								
	Objects		Adult's Actions & Words	ER*	✔ if correct			
	Near Child	Far from Child			Lesson 2	Lesson 5	Lesson 8	Lesson 11
1		cat	*"That is a cat."*	I				
2		same as above	*"The cat can walk."*	I				
3		same as above	cat walking *"The cat is walking."*	I				
4	bus		*"This is a bus."*	I				
5	same as above		*"The bus can go."*	I				
6	same as above		bus going *"The bus is going."*	I				
7	bird	boy	pointing to bird *"A bird is here."*	I/P				
8	same as above	same as above	pointing to boy *"A boy is there."*	I/P				
9	same as above	same as above	*"The bird wants to fly."*	I				
10	same as above	same as above	bird flying *"The bird is flying."*	I				
11	same as above	same as above	*"The boy likes to run."*	I				
12	same as above	same as above	boy running *"He is running."*	I				
13	same as above	same as above	*"Shake the bird and then give me the boy."*	O/A				
14	2 girls	3 dogs	pointing to dogs *"Some dogs are there."*	I/P				
15	same as above	same as above	*"They want to jump."*	I				
16	same as above	same as above	dogs jumping *"They are jumping."*	I				
17	same as above	same as above	pointing to girls *"Some girls are here."*	I/P				
18	same as above	same as above	girls standing *"These girls are standing."*	I				
19	same as above	same as above	*"They like to stand."*	I				
20	same as above	same as above	*"Make a girl sit and then pull a dog."*	O/A				

Level 6 Lesson 2 (continued)								
	Objects		Adult's Actions & Words	ER*	✔ if correct			
	Near Child	Far from Child			Lesson 2	Lesson 5	Lesson 8	Lesson 11
21	horse		*"Horses can walk."*	I				
22	*same as above*		*"This horse wants to walk."*	I				
23	*same as above*		*"Make this horse walk."*	O/A				
24		2 kids	*"Kids like to rest."*	I				
25		*same as above*	*"Make those kids rest."*	O/A				
			Total Record the Total in the Level 1 Summary Table.					

*ER=Expected Response: I^{Say} = Imitates (excluding Say); I = Imitates; P = Points; O/A = Correct action on correct object

NOTE: Remember to create Daily Real-World Exercises and use them regularly throughout the day.

Level 6 Lesson 3 (repeat, if needed, as Lessons 6, 9, & 12)								
	Objects		Adult's Actions & Words	ER*	✔ if correct			
	Near Child	Far from Child			Lesson 3	Lesson 6	Lesson 9	Lesson 12
1	frog	2 trucks	*"The frog can jump."*	I				
2	same as above	same as above	frog jumping *"It is jumping."*	I				
3	same as above	same as above	*"Those trucks can go."*	I				
4	same as above	same as above	trucks going *"They are going."*	I				
5	dog	plane	*"Dogs like to walk."*	I				
6	same as above	same as above	*"Planes can fly."*	I				
7	same as above	same as above	*"Make the dog walk and then make the plane fly."*	O/A				
8	2 kids		*"These kids like to jump."*	I				
9	same as above	2 kids	*"Those kids like to sit."*	I				
10	same as above	same as above	pointing to near kids *"Make these kids jump* pointing to far kids *and then make those kids sit."*	O/A				
11	lady bed	car	pointing to lady *"A lady is here."*	I/P				
12	same as above	same as above	*"She wants to rest."*	I				
13	same as above	same as above	lady lying on bed *"She is resting."*	I				
14	same as above	same as above	pointing to car *"A car is there."*	I/P				
15	same as above	same as above	*"Cars can go."*	I				
16	same as above	same as above	car going *"That car is going."*	I				
17	kid dog		*"This kid wants to jump."*	I				
18	same as above		kid jumping *"The kid is jumping."*	I				
19	same as above		*"This dog likes to walk."*	I				

Level 6 Lesson 3 (continued)								
	Objects		Adult's Actions & Words	ER*	✔ if correct			
	Near Child	Far from Child			Lesson 3	Lesson 6	Lesson 9	Lesson 12
20	same as above		dog walking "The dog is walking."	I				
21	same as above		"Shake the dog and then hug the kid."	O/A				
22	girl	bird	"Girls can sit."	I				
23	same as above	same as above	"Make the girl sit."	O/A				
24	same as above	same as above	"Birds can fly."	I				
25	same as above	same as above	"Make the bird fly and then give me the girl."	O/A				
				Total				
			Record the Total in the Level 1 Summary Table.					

*ER=Expected Response: I-Say = Imitates (excluding Say); I = Imitates; P = Points; O/A = Correct action on correct object

NOTE: Remember to create Daily Real-World Exercises and use them regularly throughout the day.

LEVEL 7
SENTENCES DISCUSSING
THE NON-PRESENT

Overview

As noted earlier, a chief goal of the program is to enable children to understand the power of language to communicate about objects, events and ideas that go beyond what is immediately in view. The word "not" serves as an excellent tool to achieve this objective and so this level introduces children to the idea of events that are *not* occurring.

Examples:

(Boy standing) *"This boy is not sitting."*
(Boy is moved to a seated position) *"Now he is sitting."*
(Cat standing) *"The cat is not walking."*
(Cat walking) *"Now the cat is walking."*

Level 7 Summary Table
(to be filled in at the completion of each lesson)

Lesson	1	2	3	4	5	6	7	8	9	10	11	12
Date												
Total # Correct Responses												

*Criterion for Moving On: Each lesson contains 25 items. Once a child achieves 20 or more items correct on 3 out of 4 consecutive sessions, move on to the next level. (The child does not need to complete all 12 sessions in order to move on). If the child does not achieve criterion within the 12 sessions, take a break for 3-4 weeks, and then restart this level from Lesson 1.

NOTE: Continue to carry out the Daily Real-World activities. You may find it helpful to refer back to the instructions provided in Level 1 *Outside the Session.*

NOTE: Throughout the program, all figures should be in the standing position unless otherwise noted.

Level 7 Lesson 1 (repeat, if needed, as Lessons 4, 7, & 10)								
	Objects		Adult's Actions & Words	ER*	✔ if correct			
	Near Child	Far from Child			Lesson 1	Lesson 4	Lesson 7	Lesson 10
1		man	pointing to man "*A man is there.*"	I/P				
2		*same as above*	"*The man is not walking.*"	I				
3		*same as above*	man sitting "*He is sitting.*"	I				
4	girl	2 dogs	pointing to girl "*A girl is here.*"	I/P				
5	*same as above*	*same as above*	"*She wants to jump.*"	I				
6	*same as above*	*same as above*	girl jumping "*Now she is jumping.*"	I				
7	*same as above*	*same as above*	pointing to dogs "*Some dogs are there.*"	I/P				
8	*same as above*	*same as above*	dogs standing "*They are not running.*"	I				
9	*same as above*	*same as above*	dogs standing "*They are standing.*"	I				
10	*same as above*	*same as above*	dogs running "*Now they are running.*"	I				
11	2 birds	kid	pointing to birds "*Some birds are here.*"	I/P				
12	*same as above*	*same as above*	"*They can fly.*"	I				
13	*same as above*	*same as above*	birds flying "*Now they are flying.*"	I				
14	*same as above*	*same as above*	pointing to kid "*A kid is there.*"	I/P				
15	*same as above*	*same as above*	"*The kid is not sitting.*"	I				
16	*same as above*	*same as above*	"*Make the kid sit and then turn over the birds.*"	O/A				
17	truck	3 frogs	pointing to frogs "*Some frogs are there.*"	I/P				

	Objects		Adult's Actions & Words	ER*	✔ if correct			
	Near Child	Far from Child			Lesson 1	Lesson 4	Lesson 7	Lesson 10
			Level 7 Lesson 1 (continued)					
18	*same as above*	*same as above*	*"They are not jumping."*	I				
19	*same as above*	*same as above*	frogs jumping *"Now they are jumping."*	I				
20	*same as above*	*same as above*	pointing to truck *"A truck is here."*	I/P				
21	*same as above*	*same as above*	*"It can go."*	I				
22	*same as above*	*same as above*	truck going *"Now it is going."*	I				
23	*same as above*	*same as above*	*"Pull the truck and then hug the frogs."*	O/A				
24	boy bed		*"This boy likes to rest."*	I				
25	*same as above*		boy lying on bed *"Now he is resting."*	I				
			Total Record the Total in the Level 1 Summary Table.					

*ER=Expected Response: I⁻ˢᵃʸ = Imitates (excluding Say); I = Imitates; P = Points; O/A = Correct action on correct object

NOTE: Remember to create Daily Real-World Exercises and use them regularly throughout the day.

226

Level 7 Sample Daily Real-World Exercises

These examples show you how the new language forms taught in this level should be used in daily life. You should also continue to use the forms taught in prior levels.

Setting	Adult's Actions & Words	Expected Response
Neighborhood	pointing to a kid riding a bike *"That kid is riding."*	I
Neighborhood	pointing to a kid nearby not riding a bike *"This kid is not riding."*	I
Playground	standing near some kids that are not swinging *"Kids like to swing."*	I
Playground	*"These kids are not swinging."*	I
Playground	pointing to a girl sitting at a distance *"That girl is not running."*	I
Playground	*"She is sitting."*	I
Store	Standing near lady working at cash register *"This lady likes to work."*	I
Store	*"This lady is working."*	I
Home	*"Dad wants to eat."*	I
Home	*"Dad is not eating."*	I
Home	Dad eating *"Now dad is eating."*	I

Level 7 Lesson 2 (repeat, if needed, as Lessons 5, 8, & 11)								
	Objects		**Adult's Actions & Words**	**ER***	**✔ if correct**			
	Near Child	*Far from Child*			*Lesson 2*	*Lesson 5*	*Lesson 8*	*Lesson 11*
1		cat	*"That is a cat."*	I				
2		same as above	*"The cat is not walking."*	I				
3		same as above	cat jumping *"The cat is jumping."*	I				
4	bus		*"This is a bus."*	I				
5	same as above		*"The bus is not going."*	I				
6	same as above		bus going *"Now the bus is going."*	I				
7	bird	boy	pointing to bird *"A bird is here."*	I/P				
8	same as above	same as above	*"Birds can fly."*	I				
9	same as above	same as above	*"This bird is not flying."*	I				
10	same as above	same as above	bird flying *"Now the bird is flying."*	I				
11	same as above	same as above	pointing to boy *"A boy is there."*	I/P				
12	same as above	same as above	boy standing *"He is not running."*	I				
13	same as above	same as above	boy standing *"He is standing."*	I				
14	same as above	same as above	*"Give me the bird and then make the boy run."*	O/A				
15	2 dogs	2 girls cat	pointing to dogs *"Some dogs are here."*	I/P				
16	same as above	same as above	*"They are not jumping."*	I				
17	same as above	same as above	dogs jumping *"Now they are jumping."*	I				
18	same as above	same as above	pointing to girls *"Some girls are there."*	I/P				
19	same as above	same as above	*"Those girls can sit."*	I				
20	same as above	same as above	*"They are not sitting."*	I				

	Objects		Adult's Actions & Words	ER*	✔ if correct			
	Near Child	*Far from Child*			*Lesson 2*	*Lesson 5*	*Lesson 8*	*Lesson 11*
21	*same as above*	*same as above*	*"Make the girls sit and then shake the cat."*	O/A				
22	man	bird	*"That bird wants to fly."*	I				
23	*same as above*	*same as above*	*"It is not flying."*	I				
24	*same as above*	*same as above*	*"This man wants to walk."*	I				
25	*same as above*	*same as above*	*"Make the bird fly and then make the man walk."*	O/A				
			Total Record the Total in the Level 1 Summary Table.					

*ER=Expected Response: I-Say = Imitates (excluding Say); I = Imitates; P = Points; O/A = Correct action on correct object

NOTE: Remember to create Daily Real-World Exercises and use them regularly throughout the day.

	Objects		Adult's Actions & Words	ER*	✔ if correct			
	Near Child	**Far from Child**			Lesson 3	Lesson 6	Lesson 9	Lesson 12
Level 7 Lesson 3 (repeat, if needed, as Lessons 6, 9, & 12)								
1	frog	2 trucks	*"This frog is not jumping."*	I				
2	*same as above*	*same as above*	frog jumping *"Now it is jumping."*	I				
3	*same as above*	*same as above*	*"Those trucks can go."*	I				
4	*same as above*	*same as above*	trucks going *"Now they are going."*	I				
5	dog	plane	*"Dogs like to walk."*	I				
6	*same as above*	*same as above*	*"Planes can fly."*	I				
7	*same as above*	*same as above*	*"This dog is not walking."*	I				
8	*same as above*	*same as above*	*"That plane is not flying."*	I				
9	*same as above*	*same as above*	*"Make the dog walk and then make the plane fly."*	O/A				
10	2 boys		*"These boys like to jump."*	I				
11	*same as above*		*"They are not jumping."*	I				
12	*same as above*		*"Make the boys jump and then hug the boys."*	O/A				
13	man chair	car	pointing to man *"A man is here."*	I/P				
14	*same as above*	*same as above*	man standing *"He is not sitting."*	I				
15	*same as above*	*same as above*	man standing *"He is standing."*	I				
16	*same as above*	*same as above*	pointing to car *"A car is there."*	I/P				
17	*same as above*	*same as above*	*"Cars can go."*	I				
18	*same as above*	*same as above*	*"That car is not going."*	I				
19	kid dog		*"This kid wants to jump."*	I				
20	*same as above*		kid jumping *"Now the kid is jumping."*	I				

Level 7 Lesson 3 (continued)								
	Objects		Adult's Actions & Words	ER*	✔ if correct			
	Near Child	Far from Child			Lesson 3	Lesson 6	Lesson 9	Lesson 12
21	same as above		*"This dog likes to walk."*	I				
22	same as above		*"It is not walking."*	I				
23	same as above		*"Make the dog walk."*	O/A				
24	girl	horse	*"Girls can sit."*	I				
25	same as above	same as above	*"Make the girl sit and then make the horse run."*	O/A				
			Total Record the Total in the Level 1 Summary Table.					

*ER=Expected Response: I⁻ˢᵃʸ = Imitates (excluding Say); I = Imitates; P = Points; O/A = Correct action on correct object

NOTE: Remember to create Daily Real-World Exercises and use them regularly throughout the day.

LEVEL 8

SENTENCES IN THE PAST TENSE

Overview

Many aspects of language go beyond what is immediately in view. One key set involves references to the past. References to the past are abundant in the language that children hear others use (e.g., "We went to the park yesterday." "Remember when we saw the little kitten?" etc.) Once children gain an understanding of the past tense, their understanding of the language that they hear from others increases dramatically. In this level, the language introduces children to describing actions in the past tense (that is, actions that did occur but are no longer occurring).

Examples:

The man was walking.
Those frogs were jumping.

Level 8 Summary Table
(to be filled in at the completion of each lesson)

Lesson	1	2	3	4	5	6	7	8	9	10	11	12
Date												
Total # Correct Responses												

*Criterion for Moving On: Each lesson contains 25 items. Once a child achieves 20 or more items correct on 3 out of 4 consecutive sessions, move on to the next level. (The child does not need to complete all 12 sessions in order to move on). If the child does not achieve criterion within the 12 sessions, take a break for 3-4 weeks, and then restart this level from Lesson 1.

NOTE: Continue to carry out the Daily Real-World activities. You may find it helpful to refer back to the instructions provided in Level 1 *Outside the Session.*

NOTE: Throughout the program, all figures should be in the standing position unless otherwise noted in the column labeled Adult's Actions & Words.

	Level 8 Lesson 1 (repeat, if needed, as Lessons 4, 7, & 10)						
	Objects		Adult's Actions & Words	ER*	✔ if correct		
	Near Child	Far from Child			Lesson 1	Lesson 4	Lesson 7	Lesson 10
1		lady	lady standing "That is a lady."	I				
2		same as above	lady standing "The lady can run."	I				
3		same as above	lady running "Now she is running."	I				
4		same as above	lady standing "She was running."	I				
5	2 birds		"These are some birds."	I				
6	same as above		"They want to fly."	I				
7	same as above		birds flying "Now they are flying."	I				
8	same as above		birds not flying "They were flying."	I				
9		3 cars	"Those are some cars."	I				
10		same as above	"Make the cars go."	O/A				
11		same as above	"The cars were going."	I				
12		same as above	"Now they are not going."	I				
13	boy		"This is a boy."	I				
14	same as above		"He likes to walk."	I				
15	same as above		boy walking "He is walking."	I				
16	same as above		boy standing "Now he is not walking."	I				
17		2 cats	"Those are cats."	I				
18		same as above	"The cats are not jumping."	I				
19		same as above	one cat jumping "Now that cat is jumping."	I				

	Objects		Adult's Actions & Words	ER*	✔ if correct			
	Near Child	Far from Child			Lesson 1	Lesson 4	Lesson 7	Lesson 10
Level 8 Lesson 1 (continued)								
20		same as above	*"The cat was jumping."*	I				
21	plane	2 buses	*"Make the buses go."*	O/A				
22	same as above	same as above	*"The buses were going."*	I				
23	same as above	same as above	*"Now the buses are not going."*	I				
24	same as above	same as above	*"Make the plane fly."*	O/A				
25	same as above	same as above	*"The plane was flying."*	I				
				Total Record the Total in the Level 1 Summary Table.				

*ER=Expected Response: I-Say = Imitates (excluding Say); I = Imitates; P = Points; O/A = Correct action on correct object

NOTE: Remember to create Daily Real-World Exercises and use them regularly throughout the day.

Level 8 Sample Daily Real-World Exercises

These examples show you how the new language forms taught in this level should be used in daily life.
You should also continue to use the forms taught in prior levels.

Setting	Adult's Actions & Words	Expected Response
Playground	pointing to a kid running *"That kid is running."*	I
Playground	wait until kid stops running *"That kid was running."*	I
Playground	*"Now the kid is standing."*	I
Playground	standing near a girl who is talking *"The girl is talking."*	I
Playground	waiting until girl stops talking *"Now the girl is not talking."*	I
Store	standing near a lady walking *"Ladies can walk."*	I
Store	*"The lady is walking."*	I
Store	waiting until lady stops walking *"The lady was walking."*	I
Home	*"Dad likes to sleep."*	I
Home	*"Dad was sleeping."*	I
Home	*"Now dad is not sleeping."*	I

Level 8 Lesson 2 (repeat, if needed, as Lessons 5, 8, & 11)								
	Objects		Adult's Actions & Words	ER*	✔ if correct			
	Near Child	Far from Child			Lesson 2	Lesson 5	Lesson 8	Lesson 11
1		dog	*"That is a dog."*	I				
2		*same as above*	*"The dog is not running."*	I				
3		*same as above*	dog running *"Now the dog is running."*	I				
4		*same as above*	dog standing *"The dog was running."*	I				
5	2 trucks		pointing to trucks *"Some trucks are here."*	I/P				
6	*same as above*		*"These trucks are not going."*	I				
7	*same as above*		trucks going *"Now the trucks are going."*	I				
8	*same as above*		*"The trucks were going."*	I				
9	man chair		*"This is a man."*	I				
10	*same as above*		*"He can sit."*	I				
11	*same as above*		*"He is not sitting."*	I				
12		bird	bird flying *"The bird is flying."*	I				
13		*same as above*	bird not flying *"The bird was flying."*	I				
14		3 girls	girls standing *"Those girls are standing."*	I				
15		*same as above*	girls sitting *"They were standing."*	I				
16		*same as above*	girls sitting *"Now they are sitting."*	I				
17	2 frogs		pointing to frogs *"Some frogs are here."*	I/P				
18	*same as above*		*"They are not jumping."*	I				
19	*same as above*		frogs jumping *"Now they are jumping."*	I				

	Objects		Adult's Actions & Words	ER*	✔ if correct			
	Near Child	Far from Child			Lesson 2	Lesson 5	Lesson 8	Lesson 11
Level 8 Lesson 2 (continued)								
20	*same as above*		frogs not jumping *"The frogs were jumping."*	I				
21	lady bed	kid	*"This lady wants to rest."*	I				
22	*same as above*	*same as above*	lady lying on bed *"Now she is resting."*	I				
23	*same as above*	*same as above*	*"That kid does not want to rest."*	I				
24	*same as above*	*same as above*	*"Make the kid jump."*	O/A				
25	*same as above*	*same as above*	*"The kid was jumping."*	I				
			Total Record the Total in the Level 1 Summary Table.					

*ER=Expected Response: I⁻ˢᵃʸ = Imitates (excluding Say); I = Imitates; P = Points; O/A = Correct action on correct object

NOTE: Remember to create Daily Real-World Exercises and use them regularly throughout the day.

	Level 8 Lesson 3 (repeat, if needed, as Lessons 6, 9, & 12)							
	Objects		Adult's Actions & Words	ER*	✔ if correct			
	Near Child	Far from Child			Lesson 3	Lesson 6	Lesson 9	Lesson 12
1	frog		*"This is a frog."*	I				
2	same as above		frog jumping *"It is jumping."*	I				
3	same as above		*"It was jumping."*	I				
4	same as above	2 trucks	trucks going *"The trucks are going."*	I				
5	same as above	same as above	*"They were going."*	I				
6	dog	2 planes	*"Dogs can run."*	I				
7	same as above	same as above	dog running *"This dog is running."*	I				
8	same as above	same as above	planes flying *"The planes are flying."*	I				
9	same as above	same as above	*"The dog was running."*	I				
10	same as above	same as above	*"The planes were flying."*	I				
11		2 boys	boys walking *"Those boys are walking."*	I				
12		same as above	boys standing *"The boys were walking."*	I				
13	man chair	2 buses	pointing to man *"A man is here."*	I/P				
14	same as above	same as above	man sitting in chair *"He is sitting."*	I				
15	same as above	same as above	man still sitting *"He is not standing."*	I				
16	same as above	same as above	pointing to buses *"Some buses are there."*	I/P				
17	same as above	same as above	*"Buses can go."*	I				
18	same as above	same as above	*"Those buses are not going."*	I				
19	kid plane		kid standing *"Kids can run."*	I				
20	same as above		*"This kid is not running."*	I				

Level 8 Lesson 3 (continued)								
	Objects		Adult's Actions & Words	ER*	✔ if correct			
	Near Child	Far from Child			Lesson 3	Lesson 6	Lesson 9	Lesson 12
21	*same as above*		*"Make the kid run."*	O/A				
22	*same as above*		*"The kid was running."*	I				
23	*same as above*		*"Planes can fly."*	I				
24	*same as above*		*"This plane is not flying."*	I				
25	*same as above*		*"Make the plane fly and then give me the plane."*	O/A				
			Record the Total in the Level 1 Summary Table.	**Total**				

*ER=Expected Response: I⁻ˢᵃʸ = Imitates (excluding Say); I = Imitates; P = Points; O/A = Correct action on correct object

NOTE: Remember to create Daily Real-World Exercises and use them regularly throughout the day.

LEVEL 9

SENTENCES IN THE FUTURE TENSE

Overview

In this level, "language beyond the present" continues to expand by introducing forms that describe future events. In daily life we refer to the future using two major forms — "going to" (as in *"We are going to the park"*) and "will" (as in *"He will be here soon"*). "Going to" tends to be used more commonly. Therefore, it is the form that is used in the exercises that follow.

Examples:

> *The dog is going to run.*
> *These kids are going to rest.*

This level introduces another dimension to the children's language. To increase the child's flexibility in dealing with language, the response to statements will be varied. Until now, the child has had to imitate each statement. Now, on some items the statement is paired with a command. For these items, the child will **NOT** imitate the statement. Instead, he or she will simply carry out the command. This is introduced for the first time in Level 9 Lesson 2 Item 10, where the item is as follows

> Adult: "A boy is there. Point to the boy."
> Child: (points to the boy without saying anything)

If the child tries to imitate the statement, stop speaking, shake your head and if it is helpful, put your finger over his or her mouth. Keep repeating this until the item is done correctly. If it takes several minutes to achieve success, stop the session for that day and then in the next session, resume where you left off.

Level 9 Summary Table
(to be filled in at the completion of each lesson)

Lesson	1	2	3	4	5	6	7	8	9	10	11	12
Date												
Total # Correct Responses												

*Criterion for Moving On: Each lesson contains 25 items. Once a child achieves 20 or more items correct on 3 out of 4 consecutive sessions, move on to the next level. (The child does not need to complete all 12 sessions in order to move on). If the child does not achieve criterion within the 12 sessions, take a break for 3-4 weeks, and then restart this level from Lesson 1.

NOTE: Continue to carry out the Daily Real-World activities. You may find it helpful to refer back to the instructions provided in Level 1 *Outside the Session.*

NOTE: Throughout the program, all figures should be in the standing position unless otherwise noted in the column labeled Adult's Actions & Words.

	Level 9 Lesson 1 (repeat, if needed, as Lessons 4, 7, & 10)							
	Objects		**Adult's Actions & Words**	**ER***	**✔ if correct**			
	Near Child	*Far from Child*			*Lesson 1*	*Lesson 4*	*Lesson 7*	*Lesson 10*
1	horse	girl bed	pointing to horse *"A horse is here."*	I/P				
2	*same as above*	*same as above*	*"The horse is going to walk."*	I				
3	*same as above*	*same as above*	horse walking *"Now the horse is walking."*	I				
4	*same as above*	*same as above*	horse standing *"The horse did walk."*	I				
5	*same as above*	*same as above*	*"But the girl did not walk."*	I				
6	*same as above*	*same as above*	*"The girl is going to rest."*	I				
7	*same as above*	*same as above*	*"Now make the girl rest."*	O/A				
8	2 dogs	man	*"These dogs are going to run."*	I				
9	*same as above*	*same as above*	dogs running *"Now they are running."*	I				
10	*same as above*	*same as above*	dogs standing *"The dogs were running."*	I				
11	*same as above*	*same as above*	*"The man was not running."*	I				
12	*same as above*	*same as above*	*"He is going to walk."*	I				
13	*same as above*	*same as above*	*"Make him walk."*	O/A				
14	*same as above*	*same as above*	*"Now give me the man and the dogs."*	O/A				
15	kid chair	2 trucks	*"This kid likes to sit."*	I				
16	*same as above*	*same as above*	*"He is going to sit."*	I				
17	*same as above*	*same as above*	kid sitting in chair *"Now he is sitting."*	I				
18	*same as above*	*same as above*	*"Make the trucks go."*	O/A				

	Objects		Adult's Actions & Words	ER*	✔ if correct			
	Near Child	**Far from Child**			Lesson 1	Lesson 4	Lesson 7	Lesson 10
19	*same as above*	*same as above*	*"The trucks were going."*	I				
20	*same as above*	*same as above*	*"Now the trucks are not going."*	I				
21	3 frogs		pointing to one frog *"This frog wants to jump."*	I/P				
22	*same as above*		*"It is not jumping."*	I				
23	*same as above*		frog jumping *"Now it is jumping."*	I				
24	*same as above*		pointing to frog that was jumping *"This one was jumping."*	I/P				
25	*same as above*		pointing to frogs that were not jumping *"Those frogs were not jumping."*	I/P				
			Total Record the Total in the Level 1 Summary Table.					

*ER=Expected Response: I^-Say^ = Imitates (excluding Say); I = Imitates; P = Points; O/A = Correct action on correct object

NOTE: Remember to create Daily Real-World Exercises and use them regularly throughout the day.

Level 9 Sample Daily Real-World Exercises

These examples show you how the new language forms taught in this level should be used in daily life. You should also continue to use the forms taught in prior levels.

Setting	Adult's Actions & Words	Expected Response
Playground	*"We are going to sit."*	I
Playground	sitting a bench *"Now we are sitting."*	I
Kitchen	pointing to an apple *"An apple is there."*	I/P
Kitchen	*"We can eat apples."*	I
Kitchen	*"Mom is going to eat this apple."*	I
Kitchen	Mom eating apple *"Now mom is doing that."*	I
Kitchen	Mom stops eating *"Mom was eating the apple."*	I
Kitchen	*"Now mom is not eating."*	I
Restaurant	*"We do not have any food yet."*	I
Restaurant	*"We are going to get some food."*	I
Restaurant	pointing to a waiter *"That man/lady is going to bring us food."*	I

	Objects		Adult's Actions & Words	ER*	✔ if correct			
	Near Child	Far from Child			Lesson 2	Lesson 5	Lesson 8	Lesson 11
Level 9 Lesson 2 (repeat, if needed, as Lessons 5, 8, & 11)								
1	bird cat horse		pointing to animals *"Some animals are here."*	I/P				
2	*same as above*		pointing to cat *"This one is a cat."*	I/P				
3	*same as above*		*"It is going to run."*	I				
4	*same as above*		cat running *"Now it is running."*	I				
5	*same as above* and 2 dogs		pointing to dogs *"Now some dogs are here."*	I/P				
6	*same as above*		pointing to one dog *"Give me this dog."*	O/A				
7	*same as above*		pointing to remaining dog *"This other dog is going to walk."*	I/P				
8	*same as above*		*"Make him walk."*	O/A				
9	*same as above*		*"Now make him rest."*	O/A				
10	*same as above*	boy 2 chairs	pointing to boy *"A boy is there. Point to the boy."*	O/A				
11	*same as above*	*same as above*	*"The boy is going to sit."*	I				
12	*same as above*	*same as above*	boy sitting in a chair *"Now the boy is sitting."*	I				
13	*same as above*	*same as above*	*"The animals are not sitting."*	I				
14	2 ladies		pointing to ladies *"Some other people are here."*	I/P				
15	*same as above*		*"They are not boys."*	I				
16	*same as above*		*"They are ladies."*	I				
17	*same as above*		*"These ladies can run."*	I				

Level 9 Lesson 2 (continued)								
	Objects		**Adult's Actions & Words**	**ER***	**✔ if correct**			
	Near Child	*Far from Child*			*Lesson 2*	*Lesson 5*	*Lesson 8*	*Lesson 11*
18	*same as above*		*"They are going to run."*	I				
19	*same as above*		*"Make them run."*	O/A				
20		2 buses	*"Those are buses."*	I				
21		*same as above*	*"They can go."*	I				
22		*same as above*	*"Make them go."*	O/A				
23		*same as above*	*"The buses were going."*	I				
24		*same as above*	*"Now they are not."*	I				
25		*same as above*	*"Give me the buses."*	O/A				
			Total Record the Total in the Level 1 Summary Table.					

*ER=Expected Response: I⁻ˢᵃʸ = Imitates (excluding Say); I = Imitates; P = Points; O/A = Correct action on correct object

NOTE: Remember to create Daily Real-World Exercises and use them regularly throughout the day.

Level 9 Lesson 3 (repeat, if needed, as Lessons 6, 9, & 12)								
	Objects		Adult's Actions & Words	ER*	✔ if correct			
	Near Child	Far from Child			Lesson 3	Lesson 6	Lesson 9	Lesson 12
1		2 frogs	pointing to frogs *"Some frogs are there."*	I/P				
2		*same as above*	*"Frogs can jump."*	I				
3		*same as above*	*"Those frogs are going to jump."*	I				
4		*same as above*	*"Make them jump."*	O/A				
5		*same as above*	*"They were jumping."*	I				
6		*same as above* and one more frog	pointing to new frog *"This is another frog."*	I/P				
7		*same as above*	*"It did not jump."*	I				
8		*same as above*	*"But it can jump."*	I				
9		*same as above*	*"Make it jump."*	O/A				
10		*same as above*	*"All these frogs did jump."*	I				
11	bird	*same as above*	pointing to bird *"A bird is here."*	I/P				
12	*same as above*	*same as above*	*"Birds can fly."*	I				
13	*same as above*	*same as above*	*"Frogs cannot fly."*	I				
14	*same as above*	*same as above*	*"This bird is going to fly.*	I				
15	*same as above*	*same as above*	bird flying *"Now the bird is flying."*	I				
16	*same as above*	*same as above*	bird not flying *"Give me the one who was flying."*	O/A				
17	*same as above*	*same as above*	pointing to two frogs *"Give me these two frogs."*	O/A				
18	*same as above*	*same as above*	*"Put this last frog over here."* pointing to a place near adult	O/A				

	Objects		Adult's Actions & Words	ER*	✔ if correct			
	Near Child	*Far from Child*			*Lesson 3*	*Lesson 6*	*Lesson 9*	*Lesson 12*
Level 9 Lesson 3 (continued)								
19			remove last frog from the table *"Now no animals are here."*	I				
20	Adult holds 3 kids in hands		giving kids to child and pointing to a spot on the table *"These are kids. Put them here."*	O/A				
21	same as above		*"All these kids can jump."*	I				
22	same as above		pointing to one kid *"Make this one jump."*	O/A				
23	same as above		*"Point to the one who was jumping."*	O/A				
24	same as above		pointing to kid who was jumping *"This kid was jumping."*	I				
25	same as above		pointing to kids who were not jumping *"These kids were not jumping."*	I				
			Total Record the Total in the Level 1 Summary Table.					

*ER=Expected Response: I^{Say} = Imitates (excluding Say); I = Imitates; P = Points; O/A = Correct action on correct object

NOTE: Remember to create Daily Real-World Exercises and use them regularly throughout the day.

LEVEL 10

SENTENCE COMBINATIONS
6 TO 8 WORDS IN LENGTH

Overview

At this level, the child learns to combine sentences that he or she has already mastered to create combinations of six to eight words in length. The combinations contain two sentences that differ by only one word.

Example: "Here is a girl. Here is a boy."

Several new verbs are introduced in this level and subsequent levels, including *has, have, do, does, & did.*

Level 10 Summary Table
(to be filled in at the completion of each lesson)

Lesson	1	2	3	4	5	6	7	8	9	10	11	12
Date												
Total # Correct Responses												

*Criterion for Moving On: Each lesson contains 25 items. Once a child achieves 20 or more items correct on 3 out of 4 consecutive sessions, move on to the next level. (The child does not need to complete all 12 sessions in order to move on). If the child does not achieve criterion within the 12 sessions, take a break for 3-4 weeks, and then restart this level from Lesson 1.

NOTE: Continue to carry out the Daily Real-World activities. You may find it helpful to refer back to the instructions provided in Level 1 *Outside the Session.*

NOTE: When saying the two sentences in sequence, do not pause between them. Both sentences are to be imitated together, not one at a time.

NOTE: Throughout the program, all figures should be in the standing position unless otherwise noted in the column labeled Adult's Actions & Words.

	Level 10 Lesson 1 (repeat, if needed, as Lessons 4, 7, & 10)						
	Objects		**Adult's Actions & Words**	**ER***	**✔ if correct**		
	Near Child	*Far from Child*			Lesson 1	Lesson 4	Lesson 7	Lesson 10
1	girl man		pointing to girl *"This is a girl."* pointing to man *"This is a man."*	I/P				
2	*same as above*		*"The girl can run. The man can run."*	I				
3	*same as above*		girl and man both running *"She is running. He is running."*	I				
4	2 planes 2 birds		pointing to birds *"These are birds."* pointing to planes *"These are planes."*	I/P				
5	*same as above*		*"Birds can fly. Planes can fly."*	I				
6	*same as above*		*"Birds have wings. Planes have wings."*	I				
7		2 cars 3 trucks	pointing to cars *"Those are cars."* pointing to trucks *"Those are trucks."*	I/P				
8		*same as above*	*"Cars can go. Trucks can go."*	I				
9		*same as above*	*"Cars have wheels. Trucks have wheels."*	I				
10		*same as above*	pointing to two trucks *"Make these trucks go."*	O/A				
11	horse		*"Some things can jump."*	I				
12	*same as above*		pointing to horse *"Here is something that can jump."*	I/P				
13	*same as above*		*"It is a horse."*	I				

	Objects		Adult's Actions & Words	ER*	✔ if correct			
	Near Child	Far from Child			Lesson 1	Lesson 4	Lesson 7	Lesson 10
14	*same as above*		*"This horse is going to jump. Make it jump."*	O/A				
15	*same as above*	2 frogs	pointing to frogs *"There are more things that can jump."*	I/P				
16	*same as above*	*same as above*	*"They are frogs."*	I				
17	*same as above*	*same as above*	*"Frogs can jump. Horses can jump."*	I				
18	*same as above*	*same as above*	*"Make the frogs jump."*	O/A				
19	*same as above*	*same as above*	*"Now give me the horse and then the frogs."*	O/A				
20	cat dog		*"These are some other animals."*	I				
21	*same as above*		*"They can run. They can walk."*	I				
22	*same as above*		*"Make them walk."*	O/A				
23	*same as above*		*"The dog was walking. The cat was walking."*	I				
24	*same as above*		*"These animals can also run."*	I				
25	*same as above*		cat and dog running *"The cat is running. The dog is running."*	I				
			Total Record the Total in the Level 1 Summary Table.					

Level 10 Lesson 1 (continued)

*ER=Expected Response: I⁻ˢᵃʸ = Imitates (excluding Say); I = Imitates; P = Points; O/A = Correct action on correct object

NOTE: Remember to create Daily Real-World Exercises and use them regularly throughout the day.

Level 10 Sample Daily Real-World Exercises

These examples show you how the new language forms taught in this level should be used in daily life. You should also continue to use the forms taught in prior levels.

Setting	Adult's Actions & Words	Expected Response
Store	pointing to apples *"Apples are there."* pointing to more apples *"More apples are over there."*	I/P
Store	*"Put an apple in the cart."*	O/A
Store	pointing to store clerk at register *"That lady is working."*	I
Restaurant	pointing to a cup *"This is a cup."* pointing to a plate *"This is a plate."*	I/P
Restaurant	pointing to a kid sitting *"That kid is sitting."* pointing to another kid sitting *"That other kid is sitting."*	I
Restaurant	pointing to a lady eating *"She is eating."* pointing to a man eating *"He is eating."*	I
Park	pointing to trees *"Some trees are here."* pointing to rocks *"Some rocks are here."*	I/P
Park	pointing to a lady with a dog *"That lady has a dog."*	I
Playground	pointing to a boy with a ball *"This boy has a ball."*	I
Playground	pointing to some kids with toys *"Those kids have toys."*	I/P

Level 10 Lesson 2 (repeat, if needed, as Lessons 5, 8, & 11)								
Objects		Adult's Actions & Words	ER*	✔ if correct				
Near Child	Far from Child			Lesson 2	Lesson 5	Lesson 8	Lesson 11	
1		kid dog	pointing to far kid *"A kid is there."* pointing to dog *"A dog is there."*	I/P				
2		*same as above*	*"Kids can jump. Dogs can jump."*	I				
3		*same as above*	*"That kid is going to jump."*	I				
4		*same as above*	far kid jumping *"Now the kid is jumping."*	I				
5	lady chair bed		*"She likes the chair. She likes the bed."*	I				
6	*same as above*		*"She wants to sit."*	I				
7	*same as above*		*"Make her sit."* (can sit on chair or bed or table)	O/A				
8	2 birds 2 planes		pointing to birds *"Some birds are here."* pointing to planes *"Some planes are here."*	I/P				
9	*same as above*		*"Birds can fly. Planes can fly."*	I				
10	*same as above*		birds flying *"The birds are flying."*	I				
11	*same as above*		birds still flying *"The planes are not flying."*	I				
12	bus car		pointing to car *"A car is here."* pointing to bus *"A bus is here."*	I/P				
13	*same as above*		*"Cars can go. Buses can go."*	I				
14	*same as above*		*"Make them go."*	O/A				
15	*same as above*		*"The car was going. The bus was going."*	I				
16	*same as above*		*"They were both going."*	I				
17	*same as above*		*"Now they are not going."*	I				
18		man dog	*"That man has a dog."*	I				

Level 10 Lesson 2 (continued)								
	Objects		Adult's Actions & Words	ER*	✔ if correct			
	Near Child	*Far from Child*			*Lesson* 2	*Lesson* 5	*Lesson* 8	*Lesson* 11
19		*same as above*	***"The man can walk. The dog can walk."***	I				
20		*same as above*	***"Make the man walk and then make the dog walk."***	O/A				
21	2 kids 2 frogs		***"These kids have frogs."***	I				
22	*same as above*		***"These kids can jump. These frogs can jump."***	I				
23	*same as above*		***"The kids are going to jump."***	I				
24	*same as above*		kids jumping ***"Now they are jumping."***	I				
25	*same as above*		kids standing ***"The kids were jumping."***	I				
Total Record the Total in the Level 1 Summary Table.								

*ER=Expected Response: I^{-Say} = Imitates (excluding Say); I = Imitates; P = Points; O/A = Correct action on correct object

NOTE: Remember to create Daily Real-World Exercises and use them regularly throughout the day.

	Objects		Adult's Actions & Words	ER*	✔ if correct			
	Near Child	Far from Child			Lesson 3	Lesson 6	Lesson 9	Lesson 12
1	2 girls 2 frogs		pointing to girls *"These are girls."* pointing to frogs *"These are frogs."*	I/P				
2	same as above		*"The frogs can jump. The girls can jump."*	I				
3	same as above		frogs jumping *"Now the frogs are jumping."*	I				
4	same as above		frogs not jumping *"The frogs did jump."*	I				
5	man car	lady car	*"He has a car. She has a car."*	I				
6	same as above	same as above	*"Cars can go."* pointing to near car *"Make this car go."*	O/A				
7	remove man same as above	remove lady same as above	pointing to near car *"This car was going."* pointing to far car *"This car was not."*	I/P				
8	girl boy 2 chairs		pointing to kids *"Some kids are here."*	I/P				
9	same as above		*"Make them sit."*	O/A				
10	same as above		kids still sitting *"He is sitting. She is sitting."*	I				
11	same as above		kids still sitting *"They are not standing."*	I				
12	same as above		kids still sitting *"Girls can run. Boys can run."*	I				
13	same as above		point to one kid *"Make this kid run."* point to other kid *"Then make that kid run."*	O/A				
14		2 birds 2 planes	*"Planes have wings. Birds have wings."*	I				
15		same as above	*"Birds can fly. Planes can fly."*	I				

Level 10 Lesson 3 (repeat, if needed, as Lessons 6, 9, & 12)

	Objects		Adult's Actions & Words	ER*	✔ if correct			
	Near Child	**Far from Child**			**Lesson 3**	**Lesson 6**	**Lesson 9**	**Lesson 12**
16		*same as above*	*"The birds are going to fly."*	I				
17		*same as above*	birds flying *"Now they are flying."*	I				
18		*same as above*	birds not flying *"The birds did fly."*	I				
19		*same as above*	*"The planes did not fly."*	I				
20	2 kids 2 ladies		pointing to kids *"Some kids are here."* pointing to ladies *"Some ladies are here."*	I/P				
21	*same as above*		pointing to kids *"They are small."* pointing to ladies *"They are big."*	I/P				
22	*same as above*		*"Make the kids walk and then give me one lady."*	O/A				
23	*same as above* & man		holding man in hand *"This is a man. Put the man near the ladies."*	O/A				
24	*same as above*		man and ladies sitting *"Now they are sitting."*	I				
25	*same as above*		kids standing *"The kids are not sitting."*	I				
			Total Record the Total in the Level 1 Summary Table.					

Level 10 Lesson 3 (continued)

*ER=Expected Response: I^Say = Imitates (excluding Say); I = Imitates; P = Points; O/A = Correct action on correct object

NOTE: Remember to create Daily Real-World Exercises and use them regularly throughout the day.

LEVEL 11

SENTENCE COMBINATIONS
UP TO 10 WORDS IN LENGTH

Overview

The sentences in this level increase in both length and complexity, with combinations up to ten words in length and sentence pairs that differ by more than one word.

Examples:

> *"Here is a girl. There is a boy."*
> *"The man is standing. The kid is sitting."*
> *"These frogs can jump. These birds can fly."*

This level also expands language by introducing *categories,* such as animals, furniture, food, fruits, clothes, and toys. This teaches the child that different objects can be categorized under a single word.

In order to expand the range of material, some items in each lesson use pictures rather than figures. The pictures are in Appendix B. Make photocopies of the pictures and keep the original as a back-up. Cut out the pictures and paste them onto cardboard to make them more durable, or you may choose to laminate them. (For an affordable, portable laminator see Purple Cows Hot and Cold Laminator available on Amazon.com (http://amzn.to/19SLqxs)). Write the picture number on the back of the picture.

Level 11 Summary Table
(to be filled in at the completion of each lesson)

Lesson	1	2	3	4	5	6	7	8	9	10	11	12
Date												
Total # Correct Responses												

*Criterion for Moving On: Each lesson contains 25 items. Once a child achieves 20 or more items correct on 3 out of 4 consecutive sessions, move on to the next level. (The child does not need to complete all 12 sessions in order to move on). If the child does not achieve criterion within the 12 sessions, take a break for 3-4 weeks, and then restart this level from Lesson 1.

NOTE: Continue to carry out the Daily Real-World activities. You may find it helpful to refer back to the instructions provided in Level 1 *Outside the Session.*

Items 18 to 25 in this lesson use pictures rather than objects. See Appendix B for the pictures.

NOTE: Throughout the program, all figures should be in the standing position unless otherwise noted in the column labeled Adult's Actions & Words.

	Level 11 Lesson 1 (repeat, if needed, as Lessons 4, 7, & 10)							
	Objects		**Adult's Actions & Words**	**ER***	**✔ if correct**			
	Near Child	*Far from Child*			*Lesson 1*	*Lesson 4*	*Lesson 7*	*Lesson 10*
1	boy	dog	pointing to boy *"This is a boy."* pointing to dog *"That is a dog."*	I/P				
2	*same as above*	*same as above*	boy and dog walking *"The boy is walking. The dog is also walking."*	I				
3	*same as above*	*same as above*	boy and dog standing *"Both of them were walking."*	I				
4	horse	frog	pointing to horse *"A horse is here."* pointing to frog *"A frog is there."*	I/P				
5	*same as above*	*same as above*	*"This horse likes to run."*	I				
6	*same as above*	*same as above*	*"It is going to run."*	I				
7	*same as above*	*same as above*	*"Make the horse run and then put him here."* pointing to a space on the table	O/A				
8	2 buses 3 planes		*"Planes can fly. Buses cannot fly."*	I				
9	*same as above*		*"Make one plane fly and then make one bus go."*	O/A				
10	*same as above*		pointing to bus that did go *"This bus did go."* pointing to bus that did not go *"This bus did not go."*	I/P				
11		kid chair cat	*"The kid has a cat. He likes his cat."*	I				
12		*same as above*	*"The kid is going to sit. Make him sit."*	O/A				
13		*same as above*	*"The cat does not want to sit. He wants to run. Make him run."*	O/A				

Level 11 Lesson 1 (continued)								
	Objects		**Adult's Actions & Words**	**ER***	**✔ if correct**			
	Near Child	*Far from Child*			*Lesson 1*	*Lesson 4*	*Lesson 7*	*Lesson 10*
14		remove items	*"The kid was sitting. The cat was running."*	I				
15	girl bird		*"The girl has a pet. It is a bird."*	I				
16	*same as above*		*"The bird is going to fly. "*	I				
17	*same as above*		bird flying *"Now the bird is flying."*	I				
18	Picture 1		*"Some kids are here."*	I				
19	*same as above*		*"They are sleeping."*	I				
20	*same as above*		*"Point to the kids."*	O/A				
21	remove picture		*"The kids were sleeping. They were not playing."*	I				
22	Picture 2		*"This is a pool."*	I				
23	*same as above*		*"Kids like to swim here."*	I				
24	*same as above*		*"A girl is swimming. A boy is swimming."*	I				
25	*same as above*		*"They are in the water."*	I				
			Total Record the Total in the Level 1 Summary Table.					

*ER=Expected Response: I-Say = Imitates (excluding Say); I = Imitates; P = Points; O/A = Correct action on correct object

NOTE: Remember to create Daily Real-World Exercises and use them regularly throughout the day.

Level 11 Sample Daily Real-World Exercises

These examples show you how the new language forms taught in this level should be used in daily life. You should also continue to use the forms taught in prior levels.

Setting	Adult's Actions & Words	Expected Response
Store	pointing to apples *"Some apples are here."* pointing to pears *"Some pears are there."*	I/P
Store	*"They are fruit."*	I
Restaurant	pointing to chairs *"These are chairs."* pointing to table *"This is a table."*	I/P
Restaurant	*"We sit on the chairs. We sit at the table."*	I
Playground	*"The lady has a baby. The baby is sleeping."*	I
Playground	*"That man has a dog."*	I
Parking Lot	pointing to a small car *"This car is little."* pointing to big car *"That car is big."* (if child has difficulty saying "little," use "small" instead)	I/P
Kitchen	*"Mom wants to eat. Dad does not want to eat."*	I
Kitchen	Mom eating *"Now Mom is eating. Dad is not eating."*	I
Playground	pointing to kids playing *"Those kids are playing.* pointing to ladies sitting *"Those ladies are sitting."*	I/P
Playground	*"The girl has a ball. The boy has a truck."*	I

267

Items 18 to 25 in this lesson use pictures rather than objects.

	Level 11 Lesson 2 (repeat, if needed, as Lessons 5, 8, & 11)							
	Objects		**Adult's Actions & Words**	**ER***	**✔ if correct**			
	Near Child	*Far from Child*			*Lesson 2*	*Lesson 5*	*Lesson 8*	*Lesson 11*
1	3 kids	3 cats	pointing to kids *"Some kids are here."* pointing to cats *"Some cats are there."*	I/P				
2	*same as above*	*same as above*	*"The kids like to jump. The cats also like to jump."*	I				
3	*same as above*	*same as above*	*"The kids are not jumping. The cats are not jumping."*	I				
4	*same as above*	*same as above*	*"Make one kid jump and then make one cat jump."*	O/A				
5	*same as above*	*same as above*	pointing to kid that was jumping *"This kid was jumping."*	I/P				
6	*same as above*	*same as above*	pointing to kids that were not jumping *"Those kids were not jumping."*	I/P				
7	1 bird	3 frogs	pointing to bird *"This is a bird."* pointing to frogs *"Those are frogs."*	I/P				
8	*same as above*	*same as above*	*"Birds move by flying."*	I				
9	*same as above*	*same as above*	*"Frogs move by hopping."*	I				
10	*same as above*	*same as above*	pointing to one frog *"This frog is going to hop. Make him hop."*	O/A				
11	2 boys 2 beds		*"These boys want to rest. They are going to rest."*	I				
12	*same as above*		*"Make them rest."*	O/A				
13	remove items		*"The boys were resting."*	I				
14	lady man		*"The man is standing. The lady is also standing."*	I				
15	*same as above*		*"They do not like to stand. They want to sit."*	I				
16	*same as above*		*"Make them sit."*	O/A				

	Objects		Adult's Actions & Words	ER*	✔ if correct			
	Near Child	Far from Child			Lesson 2	Lesson 5	Lesson 8	Lesson 11
17	same as above		lady and man sitting *"He is sitting. She is sitting."*	I				
18	Picture 3		*"Kids like to play. These kids are playing."*	I				
19	same as above		pointing to girl on swing *"This girl is on a swing. She is swinging."*	I/P				
20	same as above		pointing to girl on seesaw *"That girl is not swinging."*	I/P				
21	same as above		*"Kids like doing these things."*	I				
22	Picture 4		pointing to houses *"These are houses."*	I/P				
23	same as above		*"These are not houses for people. These are houses for dogs."*	I				
24	same as above		pointing to houses *"The dogs live here."*	I/P				
25	same as above		pointing to one house *"One dog lives here."* pointing to other house *"The other dog lives here."*	I/P				
			Total Record the Total in the Level 1 Summary Table.					

Level 11 Lesson 2 (continued)

*ER=Expected Response: I^{-Say} = Imitates (excluding Say); I = Imitates; P = Points; O/A = Correct action on correct object

NOTE: Remember to create Daily Real-World Exercises and use them regularly throughout the day.

Items 1 to 14 in this lesson use pictures rather than objects.

	Objects		Adult's Actions & Words	ER*	✔ if correct			
	Near Child	Far from Child			Lesson 3	Lesson 6	Lesson 9	Lesson 12
1	Picture 5		*"These are animals. They are bears."*	I				
2	*same as above*		pointing to big bear *"This is a big bear. She is the mother."*	I/P				
3	*same as above*		pointing to small bear *"This is a little bear. He is the baby."*	I/P				
4	Picture 6		*"All animals need water.*	I				
5	*same as above*		*"These animals need water. Point to the water."*	A				
6	Picture 7		pointing to kids *"These are kids."*	I/P				
7	*same as above*		pointing to girl *"This is a girl. She is walking."*	I/P				
8	*same as above*		*"The girl has a kite. She is happy."*	I				
9	*same as above*		pointing to boy *"This boy wants a kite."*	I/P				
10	*same as above*		*"He does not have one. He is sad."*	I				
11	Picture 8		*"Point to one baby. Then point to the other baby."*	A				
12	*same as above*		*"Babies can do some things."*	I				
13	*same as above*		*"They can sit. They can also eat."*	I				
14	*same as above*		*"The babies are sitting. They are not eating."*	I				
15	2 kids bed	2 dogs bird cat	pointing to animals *"Some animals are there."* pointing to kids *"Some kids are here."*	I/P				
16	*same as above*	*same as above*	*"Kids like to run. Kids also like to rest."*	I				

Table title: **Level 11 Lesson 3 (repeat, if needed, as Lessons 6, 9, & 12)**

	Objects		Adult's Actions & Words	ER*	✔ if correct			
	Near Child	Far from Child			Lesson 3	Lesson 6	Lesson 9	Lesson 12
17	same as above	same as above	"One kid is going to run. The other kid is going to rest."	I				
18	same as above	same as above	"Do that. Make one kid run and make the other kid rest."	O/A				
19	same as above	same as above	"Now give me the kids and the bed."	O/A				
20		same as above	"Some animals fly. Other animals do not fly."	I				
20		same as above	"Birds are animals that can fly. Make the bird fly."	O/A				
21		same as above	"Dogs do not fly. They cannot fly."	I				
22		same as above	pointing to one dog "Dogs can run. Make this dog run."	O/A				
23		same as above	"Give me the dog that was running."	O/A				
24		same as above	"Cats can also run. Make the cat run."	O/A				
25		same as above	"The cat was running."	I				
			Total Record the Total in the Level 1 Summary Table.					

*ER=Expected Response: I-Say = Imitates (excluding Say); I = Imitates; P = Points; O/A = Correct action on correct object

NOTE: Remember to create Daily Real-World Exercises and use them regularly throughout the day.

271

LEVEL 12

COMPOUND SENTENCES
UP TO 12 WORDS IN LENGTH

Overview

In this level, the child learns longer sentences that have greater variation. In addition, key words are introduced, such as "and" and "but," which play a major role in connecting ideas.

Examples:

"The girls likes to swim, and she also likes to jump."
"That boy likes to walk, but he does not like to sit."
"Cats can jump, but that cat does not want to jump."

Level 12 Summary Table
(to be filled in at the completion of each lesson)

Lesson	1	2	3	4	5	6	7	8	9	10	11	12
Date												
Total # Correct Responses												

*Criterion for Moving On: Each lesson contains 25 items. Once a child achieves 20 or more items correct on 3 out of 4 consecutive sessions, move on to the next level. (The child does not need to complete all 12 sessions in order to move on). If the child does not achieve criterion within the 12 sessions, take a break for 3-4 weeks, and then restart this level from Lesson 1.

NOTE: Continue to carry out the Daily Real-World activities. You may find it helpful to refer back to the instructions provided in Level 1 *Outside the Session.*

Items 20 to 25 in this lesson use pictures rather than objects.

NOTE: Throughout the program, all figures should be in the standing position unless otherwise noted in the column labeled Adult's Actions & Words.

	Objects		Adult's Actions & Words	ER*	✔ if correct			
	Near Child	Far from Child			Lesson 1	Lesson 4	Lesson 7	Lesson 10
1	boy	2 frogs	pointing to kid *"A kid is here,* pointing to frogs *and some frogs are there."*	I/P				
2	same as above	same as above	*"Kids can run, but this kid does not like to run."*	I				
3	same as above	same as above	*"He does like to walk. Make him walk."*	O/A				
4	same as above	same as above	*"Frogs cannot walk, but they can jump."*	I				
5	same as above	same as above	*"Make one frog jump."*	O/A				
6	girl	3 birds	pointing to girl *"This is a girl,* pointing to birds *and those are some birds."*	I/P				
7	same as above	same as above	*"The girl is not sitting, but she wants to sit."*	I				
8	same as above	same as above	*"Now make her sit."*	O/A				
9	same as above	same as above	*"Birds can fly, but those birds are not flying."*	I				
10	same as above	same as above	*"Make the birds fly."*	O/A				
11	man bed	2 buses	*"This man has a bed. He is going to rest."*	I				
12	same as above	same as above	*"Make him rest."*	O/A				
13	same as above	same as above	man lying down *"The man was standing. Now he is resting."*	I				
14	lady cat	4 kids	*"This lady has a pet. Her pet is a cat."*	I				
15	same as above	same as above	*"Cats can do many things."*	I				

Title row for the above table: **Level 12 Lesson 1 (repeat, if needed, as Lessons 4, 7, & 10)**

275

	Objects		Adult's Actions & Words	ER*	✔ if correct			
	Near Child	Far from Child			Lesson 1	Lesson 4	Lesson 7	Lesson 10
16	same as above	same as above	"They can walk. They can eat. They can jump."	I				
17	same as above	same as above	"This cat is going to walk."	I				
18	same as above	same as above	"Make this cat walk."	O/A				
19	same as above	same as above	"The cat was walking. Now he is not doing that."	I				
20	Picture 9		"This is a cat. She is sleeping on her bed."	I				
21	same as above		"Cats like to sleep. This cat likes to sleep."	I				
22	Picture 8		pointing to one baby "A baby is here, pointing to other baby and another baby is there."	I/P				
23	same as above		"Point to the baby that is holding a toy."	O/A				
24	same as above		"Babies can play, but they cannot talk."	I				
25	same as above		"These babies also cannot walk."	I				
			Total Record the Total in the Level 1 Summary Table.					

Level 12 Lesson 1 (continued)

*ER=Expected Response: I-Say = Imitates (excluding Say); I = Imitates; P = Points; O/A = Correct action on correct object

NOTE: Remember to create Daily Real-World Exercises and use them regularly throughout the day.

Setting	Adult's Actions & Words	Expected Response
Store	pointing to some socks *"Some socks are here,* pointing to a shirt *and a shirt is there."*	I/P
Store	*"They are clothes."*	I
Store	*"Put the socks in the cart."*	O/A
Restaurant	pointing to a man sitting by a window *"He is sitting near a window,* pointing to a woman sitting near a door *and she is sitting near a door."*	I/P
Restaurant	*"There are many things to eat, and there are many things to drink."*	I
Playground	*"That kid did fall, but he did not cry."*	I
Playground	*"That kid wants to swing, but the swing is broken."*	I
Kitchen	*"We are going to make some things to eat for dinner."*	I
Kitchen	pointing to apple *"This fruit is an apple,* pointing to banana *and that fruit is a banana."*	I/P
Kitchen	*"Dad is looking for a spoon, but he cannot find one."*	I
Home	*"Mom has her keys, but she cannot find her phone."*	I

Level 12 Sample Daily Real-World Exercises

These examples show you how the new language forms taught in this level should be used in daily life. You should also continue to use the forms taught in prior levels.

Level 12 Lesson 2 (repeat, if needed, as Lessons 5, 8, & 11)								
	Objects		Adult's Actions & Words	ER*	✔ if correct			
	Near Child	Far from Child			Lesson 2	Lesson 5	Lesson 8	Lesson 11
1	Picture 7		*"The girl has a kite, but the boy does not have one."*	I				
2	*same as above*		*"He wants the kite, but he cannot have it."*	I				
3	Picture 10		pointing to boy *"This boy is looking up at the sun."*	I/P				
4	*same as above*		*"He is not in the house. He is outside."*	I				
5	Picture 11		*"This cat has a ball, and he is playing with it."*	I				
6	*same as above*		pointing to food *"Some food is in the bowl, but the cat is not eating."*	I/P				
7	*same as above*		*"Cats do eat, but this cat does not want to eat."*	I				
8	Picture 8		pointing to babies *"Some babies are sitting here."*	I/P				
9	*same as above*		*"Only one baby has a toy."*	I				
10	*same as above*		*"The other baby does not have a toy."*	I				
11	2 girls	horse	pointing to girls *"Two girls are here,* pointing to horse *and a horse is there."*	I/P				
12	*same as above*	*same as above*	horse standing *"Horses can stand, and this horse is standing."*	I				
13	*same as above*	*same as above*	*"Horses can also walk."*	I				
14	*same as above*	*same as above*	*"Make that horse walk and then make it rest."*	O/A				
15	*same as above*	*same as above*	horse lying down *"That horse was walking, and now it is resting."*	I				
16	plane	man chair	*"That man has a chair, but he does not want to sit."*	I				

	Objects		Adult's Actions & Words	ER*	✔ if correct			
	Near Child	Far from Child			Lesson 2	Lesson 5	Lesson 8	Lesson 11
17	same as above	same as above	"He wants to run."	I				
18	same as above	same as above	"Make him run."	O/A				
19	same as above	same as above	"The plane can fly, and it is going to fly."	I				
20	same as above	same as above	"Make the plane fly."	O/A				
21	3 birds	2 ladies	pointing to one lady "That lady is going to sit. Make that lady sit."	O/A				
22	same as above	same as above	one lady still sitting and other lady standing "One lady is sitting, and the other lady is standing.	I				
23	same as above	same as above	pointing to birds "Some birds are here. One bird is going to fly."	I				
24	same as above	same as above	pointing to one bird "Make this bird fly."	O/A				
25	same as above	same as above	"Give me the ladies and then the birds."	O/A				

Title row: **Level 12 Lesson 2 (continued)**

Total
Record the Total in the Level 1 Summary Table.

*ER=Expected Response: I⁻ˢᵃʸ = Imitates (excluding Say); I = Imitates; P = Points; O/A = Correct action on correct object

NOTE: Remember to create Daily Real-World Exercises and use them regularly throughout the day.

Level 12 Lesson 3 (repeat, if needed, as Lessons 6, 9, & 12)								
	Objects		Adult's Actions & Words	ER*	✔ if correct			
	Near Child	Far from Child			Lesson 3	Lesson 6	Lesson 9	Lesson 12
1	3 ladies	2 cats 2 dogs	pointing to animals "Some animals are there, pointing to ladies and some ladies are here."	I/P				
2	same as above	same as above	"Animals can walk, and those cats are going to walk."	I				
3	same as above	same as above	"Make the cats walk."	O/A				
4	same as above	same as above	cats stop walking "Those cats were walking, but the dogs were not walking."	I				
5	same as above	same as above	pointing to one dog "That dog wants to run. Make him run."	O/A				
6	same as above	same as above	pointing to other dog "That dog wants to jump, and he is going to jump."	I				
7	same as above	same as above	"Make him jump."	O/A				
8	same as above	same as above	"These ladies can sit. Make the ladies sit."	O/A				
9	boy bed	girl chair	girl and boy both standing "The boy has a bed, but he does not want to rest."	I				
10	same as above	same as above	"He wants to walk. Make him walk."	O/A				
11	same as above	same as above	"That girl has a chair, and she wants to sit on it."	I				
12	same as above	same as above	"Make the girl sit on the chair."	O/A				
13	frog horse	lady kid	pointing to animals "These are animals, pointing to people and those are people."	I/P				
14	same as above	same as above	"Animals can do lots of things, but they cannot talk."	I				
15	same as above	same as above	"Some animals can fly, but these animals cannot fly."	I				
16	same as above	same as above	"They can jump. Make the animals jump."	O/A				

	Objects		Adult's Actions & Words	ER*	✔ if correct			
	Near Child	Far from Child			Lesson 3	Lesson 6	Lesson 9	Lesson 12
17	*same as above*	*same as above*	*"People can also jump, but these people are not jumping."*	I				
18	*same as above*	*same as above*	*"They are standing."*	I				
19	Picture 12		*"A door is here, and it is open. Point to the door."*	O/A				
20	*same as above*		*"This boy has a lot of toys, and he likes to play with them."*	I				
21	*same as above*		*"He also has many animals."*	I				
22	*same as above*		*"Point to an animal."*	A				
23	Picture 13		*"These are birds that do not fly."*	I				
24	*same as above*		pointing to penguin *"This bird likes to swim. It swims in the water."*	I/P				
25	*same as above*		*"The other birds do not swim, but they do walk."*	I				
			Total Record the Total in the Level 1 Summary Table.					

Table title: **Level 12 Lesson 3 (continued)**

*ER=Expected Response: I‑Say = Imitates (excluding Say); I = Imitates; P = Points; O/A = Correct action on correct object

NOTE: Remember to create Daily Real-World Exercises and use them regularly throughout the day.

LEVEL 13
STARTING QUESTIONS

Overview

At this point, we move on to the vital skill of learning how to answer questions. Even when the children can speak extensively (as they can now do at this level of the program), questions can still be extremely challenging. Often the children do not understand what the question is asking, leading them to resort to a range of ineffective strategies. One such strategy is to answer all questions with a label—that is, a word that names a person or an object. For example, when asked, "What is the boy doing?" a child may answer, "boy." Other patterns also exist. All reflect the confusion that the children experience in this domain.

A useful strategy for getting past these difficulties is to show the children in an explicit manner how questions and answers link together. This is done by having key words in the question "brought down" and incorporated in the answer. In the examples below, those carry-down words appear in bold.

Examples:
> (*Show the child a car*)
> Adult's question: "What **is this**?"
> Child's answer: "**This is** a car."
> Adult's question: "What **is that kid** doing?"
> Child's answer: "**That kid is** running."

In the first example above, the typical answer would be "a car"—with the words *This is* being understood implicitly. Similarly, for the second question, the words *That kid is* would generally be left out of the answer and only the single word "running" would be offered.

Many questions, such as those just cited, can be answered by one or two word responses. This similarity in form (one or two word responses regardless of the question form) is one source of the children's confusion. It leads them to think that all questions are alike. By making the hidden words explicit, the children are provided with clear cues that enable them to distinguish among different types of questions. They then realize that they have the ability to deal effectively with a range of questions—a realization that greatly increases their comfort with language.

Carrying down key words means that questions will always be answered with full sentences. While this is somewhat unusual, it has many benefits, including helping children improve their production of smooth and fluent language.

The questions taught at this level all involve the identification of people, animals, or objects.

> *Who is this/that?*
> *Who are they?*
> *What is this/that?*
> *What are these/those?*

"Who" is the question word used for people and domestic animals, such as pets. *"What"* is used for inanimate objects and most other animals. Simultaneous introduction of these related forms (those that involve singular, plural, animate, inanimate, etc.), helps the children see the commonality underlying them. Subsequent levels continue this pattern (i.e., clustering varying but related forms) since it facilitates the children's recognition of key patterns that underlie language.

Supporting the Transition: Key Techniques

Up until now, when the child has had to speak in a session, the language has mirrored what the adult has said. Questions represent a major change. Now the child is not going to mirror what the adult has said. Instead, the child changes the words to create a meaningful response.

To help the child master this major and complex transition, it is helpful to start by saying the question in a somewhat soft voice. Then in a louder voice, immediately provide the answer.

Example
> *Adult: (in a soft voice) "What is this?"*
> *Adult: (in a louder voice) "This is a plane."*

Then the adult once again gives the question but this time waits for the child to offer the answer. If, after five attempts, a child still does not offer the correct response, provide the answer again and then have the child repeat your model. In the initial sessions, this sequence may need to be repeated a number of times before the child recognizes what is needed. If that keeps happening (i.e., a considerable amount of time is needed to get a correct response), the session should stop once the correct response is achieved. Then in the next session, go back to where you left off and resume at that point.

A common pattern is for children to echo the question rather than provide an answer. If the child imitates part or all of the question (i.e., including saying the question and then the answer), say, "No," shake your head, and repeat the question. If the child offers anything but the answer, interrupt him or her right away by saying "no" and holding up your hand. Then repeat the above sequence.

The successful transition to questions represents a major change and its mastery may take some time. Do not be concerned if the child continues to show difficulty over the first several sessions. By the 3rd or 4th session, the difficulties generally recede, and the children begin to show clear progress. If that keeps happening (i.e., a considerable amount of time is needed to get a correct response), the session should stop once the correct response is achieved. Then in the next session, go back to where you left off and resume at that point.

Level 13 Summary Table
(to be filled in at the completion of each lesson)

Lesson	1	2	3	4	5	6	7	8	9	10	11	12
Date												
Total # Correct Responses												

*Criterion for Moving On: Each lesson contains 25 items. Once a child achieves 20 or more items correct on 3 out of 4 consecutive sessions, move on to the next level. (The child does not need to complete all 12 sessions in order to move on). If the child does not achieve criterion within the 12 sessions, take a break for 3-4 weeks, and then restart this level from Lesson 1.

NOTE: Continue to carry out the Real-World activities on a daily basis. Incorporate as much language as you can from the lessons into the outside world. The language should include material taught in previous levels as well as the new material taught in this level. Remember to use the samples provided as a guide to creating your own.

NOTE: The first several times that a new question form is used, the item is shaded in gray. For these items, you will model the correct response by asking the question and then giving the child the correct answer. You will then state the question again and wait for the child to answer. (You may choose to use this technique in unshaded items as well, if the child is having difficulty. In later lessons, once the child has learned the new form and is answering correctly, you no longer need to model the correct answer for shaded items.)

It is difficult for some children to distinguish gender; therefore, any question involving gender (e.g., Who is this?) may be answered with "This is a kid" rather than "This is a boy" or "This is a girl."

In the column ER (Expected Response), the letter P in parentheses — (P) — means that the child must point to the correct object when giving his or her response.

	Objects		Adult's Actions & Words	ER*	✔ if correct			
	Near Child	Far from Child			Lesson 1	Lesson 4	Lesson 7	Lesson 10
1		frog	*"What is that?"*	"That is a frog."				
2		3 frogs	*"What are those?"*	"Those are frogs."				
3		*same as above*	*"Give me the frogs."*	O/A				
4	girl boy		*"Who are they?"*	"They are kids."				
5	remove boy		*"Who is this?"*	"This is a kid/girl."				
6	3 birds		*"What are these?"*	"These are birds."				
7	*same as above*		*"Birds can fly, but these birds are not flying."*	I				
8	*same as above*		pointing to one bird *"Make this bird fly."*	O/A				
9	3 planes		*"These are not birds, but they can fly."*	I				
10	*same as above*		*"What are they?"*	"They are planes."				
11	*same as above*	man cat	pointing to man *"Who is that?"*	"That is a man." (P)				
12	*same as above*	*same as above*	pointing to cat *"What is that?"*	"That is a cat." (P)				

Level 13 Lesson 1 (repeat, if needed, as Lessons 4, 7, & 10)

	Objects		Adult's Actions & Words	ER*	✔ if correct			
	Near Child	Far from Child			Lesson 1	Lesson 4	Lesson 7	Lesson 10
\multicolumn{9}{c}{**Level 13 Lesson 1 (continued)**}								
13	*same as above*	*same as above*	**"Give me all the things on the table."**	O/A				
14			pointing to where man was **"A man was there,** pointing to where cat was **and a cat was there."**	I/P				
15			pointing to where planes were **"Some planes were also here."**	I/P				
16	Picture 14		pointing to bus **"What is this?"**	"This is a bus."				
17	*same as above*		pointing to kids **"Who are they?"**	"They are kids."				
18	*same as above*		**"Kids can be sad, and kids can be happy."**	I				
19	*same as above*		**"These kids are happy."**	I				
20	*same as above*		**"Point to one of the kids that is smiling."**	A				
21	Picture 15		pointing to animals **"Some animals are here."**	I/P				
22	*same as above*		pointing to dog **"What is this?"**	"This is a dog." (P)				
23	*same as above*		pointing to cat **"What are these?"**	"These are cats."				
24	*same as above*		**"Some fish are swimming."**	I				
25	*same as above*		**"Point to a fish."**	A				
				Total Record the Total in the Level 1 Summary Table.				

*ER=Expected Response: I^Say = Imitates (excluding Say); I = Imitates; P = Points; O/A = Correct action on correct object

NOTE: Remember to create Daily Real-World Exercises and use them regularly throughout the day.

Level 13 Sample Daily Real-World Exercises

These examples show you how the new language forms taught in this level should be used in daily life.
You should also continue to use the forms taught in prior levels.

Setting	Adult's Actions & Words	Expected Response
Store	pointing to some shirts *"What are these?"*	"These are shirts." (P)
Store	pointing to some coats *"What are those?"*	"Those are coats." (P)
Store	pointing to some ladies *"Who are they?"*	"They are ladies." (P)
Store	pointing to some kids *"Who are they?"*	"They are kids." (P)
Playroom	pointing to some dolls *"What are these?"*	"These are dolls." (P)
Playroom	*"Dolls have arms, and they also have legs. Point to this doll's legs."*	O/A
Playground	pointing to a kite *"This is a kite,* pointing to some balls *and those are some balls."*	I/P
Playground	*"They are toys."*	I
Home	pointing to a window *"What is that?"*	"That is a window." (P)
Home	*"This room has some windows, and it has some doors. Point to a door."*	O/A

288

Level 13 Lesson 2 (repeat, if needed, as Lessons 5, 8, & 11)							
	Objects		Adult's Actions & Words	ER*	✔ if correct		
	Near Child	Far from Child			Lesson 2	Lesson 5	Lesson 8	Lesson 11
1	3 cars bus	2 trucks plane	pointing to bus "What is this?"	"This is a bus." (P)				
2	same as above	same as above	pointing to plane "What is that?"	"That is a plane." (P)				
3	same as above	same as above	pointing to a location next to the bus "Put the plane here."	O/A				
4	same as above	same as above	pointing to cars "What are these?"	"These are cars." (P)				
5	same as above	same as above	pointing to trucks "What are those?"	"Those are trucks." (P)				
6		man	"Who is that?"	"That is a man."				
7		same as above	"The man likes cars, but he does not have one."	I				
8	2 ladies 2 chairs		pointing to ladies "Who are they?"	"They are ladies." (P)				
9	same as above		"Some ladies are here, and some chairs are also here."	I				
10	same as above		"Ladies can stand, and they can sit."	I				
11	same as above		"These ladies are standing, but they are going to sit. Make them sit in the chairs."	O/A				
12	2 birds		"What are these?"	"These are birds."				
13	same as above		"Make them fly."	O/A				
14	same as above		"The birds were flying, but now they are resting."	I				

	Objects		Adult's Actions & Words	ER*	✔ if correct			
	Near Child	*Far from Child*			Lesson 2	Lesson 5	Lesson 8	Lesson 11
	Level 13 Lesson 2 (continued)							
15		2 frogs	*"What are those?"*	"Those are frogs."				
16		*same as above*	*"Frogs can jump, but those frogs are not jumping."*	I				
17		*same as above*	*"Make both frogs jump."*	O/A				
18		*same as above*	pointing to one frog *"Now make that frog jump again."*	O/A				
19	Picture 3		pointing to kids *"Who are they?"*	"They are kids." (P)				
20	*same as above*		*"Kids can do many things in this place."*	I				
21	*same as above*		*"They can swing, and they can slide."*	I				
22	*same as above*		*"Point to the kid that is swinging."*	A				
23	Picture 16		pointing to cats *"What are these?"*	"These are cats." (P)				
24	*same as above*		*"These cats are playing with a ball."*	I				
25	*same as above*		*"Point to the ball."*	A				
				Total Record the Total in the Level 1 Summary Table.				

*ER=Expected Response: I-Say = Imitates (excluding Say); I = Imitates; P = Points; O/A = Correct action on correct object

NOTE: Remember to create Daily Real-World Exercises and use them regularly throughout the day.

	Objects		Adult's Actions & Words	ER*	✔ if correct			
	Near Child	Far from Child			Lesson 3	Lesson 6	Lesson 9	Lesson 12
1	Picture 17		pointing to ducks *"What are these?"*	"These are ducks." (P)				
2	*same as above*		*"Ducks can fly, and they can also swim."*	I				
3	*same as above*		*"Point to the duck that is swimming."*	A				
4	*same as above*		*"Now point to the duck that is flying."*	A				
5	Picture 18		pointing to kids *"Who are they?"*	"They are kids." (P)				
6	*same as above*		*"These kids have some food, and they are all eating."*	I				
7	*same as above*		*"They want to drink, but they do not have anything to drink."*	I				
8	*same as above*		pointing to middle kid *"This kid is getting some food from a bag."*	I/P				
9	Picture 16		pointing to ball *"What is this?"*	"This is a ball." (P)				
10	*same as above*		*"The cats have a ball, and they like to play with it."*	I				
11	bed 2 frogs	lady chair 2 horses	pointing to bed *"What is this?"*	"This is a bed." (P)				
12	*same as above* & kid	*same as above*	giving the child a kid *"Put this kid on the bed."*	O/A				
13	*same as above*	*same as above*	*"Now the kid is resting."*	I				
14	*same as above*	*same as above*	*"Kids can rest, but they can also walk. Make the kid walk."*	O/A				

Level 13 Lesson 3 (repeat, if needed, as Lessons 6, 9, & 12)

	Objects		Adult's Actions & Words	ER*	✔ if correct			
	Near Child	Far from Child			Lesson 3	Lesson 6	Lesson 9	Lesson 12
15	*same as above*	*same as above*	*"Now give me the kid and the bed."*	O/A				
16	*same as above*	*same as above*	pointing to the lady *"Who is that?"*	"That is a lady." (P)				
17	*same as above*	*same as above*	*"Ladies can do many things."*	I				
18	*same as above*	*same as above*	*"They can sit, but that lady is not sitting."*	I				
19	*same as above*	*same as above*	*"Make that lady sit in the chair."*	O/A				
20	*same as above*	*same as above*	pointing to horses *"What are those?"*	"Those are horses." (P)				
21	*same as above*	*same as above*	pointing to frogs *"What are these?"*	"These are frogs." (P)				
22	*same as above*	*same as above*	*"Frogs are animals, and horses are also animals."*	I				
23	*same as above*	*same as above*	*"Many animals can jump."*	I				
24	*same as above*	*same as above*	*"Make both horses jump, and then* pointing to one frog *make this frog jump."*	O/A				
25	*same as above*	*same as above*	*"Now give me all of the animals."*	O/A				
				Total Record the Total in the Level 1 Summary Table.				

Level 13 Lesson 3 (continued)

*ER=Expected Response: I^Say = Imitates (excluding Say); I = Imitates; P = Points; O/A = Correct action on correct object

NOTE: Remember to create Daily Real-World Exercises and use them regularly throughout the day.

LEVEL 14
QUESTIONS ABOUT ACTION

Overview

At this level, the lessons expand to include questions about actions (e.g., "What is the boy doing?"). The answers to these sorts of questions require the use of verbs (e.g., "The boy is walking.").

The question forms taught here are

> *What is (this/that) _____ doing?*
> *What are (these/those) _____ doing?*

Examples:
> *Adult: (dog walking) "What is the dog doing?"*
> *Child: "The dog is walking."*
> *Adult: (kids running) "What are they doing?"*
> *Child: "They are running."*

The "actors" may be named directly, as in, *"the kid," "the frog,"* etc., or they may be referred to by pronouns (*he, she, it,* and *they*).

As in the previous level, the first several times that the new question form is introduced, you will model the correct answer for the child. These items are shaded in gray.

This level also introduces the child to a new format, where a statement is immediately followed by a question. As you may recall, in earlier lessons, some items involved a statement followed by a command. In those items the child did not imitate the statement. He or she simply followed the command. Analogously, at this level for items where a statement is immediately followed by a question, the child should not imitate the statement but only answer the question. (For an example, see Lesson 1 Item 10).

It may take some time for the child to make the adjustment. To help in the transition, you can modify the timing and tone of voice in which the material is presented. For example, for items where the child should not repeat the statement, do not pause after the statement. Instead, immediately proceed with the question. It may also help to say the statement in a softer voice, and then say the question in a louder voice.

Level 14 Summary Table
(to be filled in at the completion of each lesson)

Lesson	1	2	3	4	5	6	7	8	9	10	11	12
Date												
Total # Correct Responses												

*Criterion for Moving On: Each lesson contains 25 items. Once a child achieves 20 or more items correct on 3 out of 4 consecutive sessions, move on to the next level. (The child does not need to complete all 12 sessions in order to move on). If the child does not achieve criterion within the 12 sessions, take a break for 3-4 weeks, and then restart this level from Lesson 1.

NOTE: Continue to carry out the Real-World activities on a daily basis. Incorporate as much language as you can from the lessons into the outside world. The language should include material taught in previous levels as well as the new material taught in this level. Remember to use the samples provided as a guide to creating your own.

NOTE: Throughout the program, whenever the question asks about what a vehicle is doing, the answer can either include the action word "going" or "moving." Both are acceptable.

	Level 14 Lesson 1 (repeat, if needed, as Lessons 4, 7, & 10)							
	Objects		**Adult's Actions & Words**	**ER***	**✔ if correct**			
	Near Child	*Far from Child*			*Lesson 1*	*Lesson 4*	*Lesson 7*	*Lesson 10*
1	cat 2 dogs	lady 2 kids	pointing to cat *"What is this?"*	"This is a cat." (P)				
2	*same as above*	*same as above*	cat walking *"What is the cat doing?"*	"The cat is walking."				
3	*same as above*	*same as above*	pointing to lady *"Who is that?"*	"That is a lady." (P)				
4	*same as above*	*same as above*	lady sitting *"What is the lady doing?"*	"The lady is sitting."				
5	*same as above*	*same as above*	dogs standing *"What are these dogs doing?"*	"These dogs are standing."				
6	*same as above*	*same as above*	kids jumping *"What are those kids doing?"*	"Those kids are jumping."				
7	truck		*"What is this?"*	"This is a truck."				
8	*same as above*		truck going *"What is it doing?"*	"It is going."				
9	*same as above*		truck not going *"The truck was going, but now it is not going."*	I				
10		man chair bed	pointing to far objects *"Some things are there."* pointing to chair *"What is that one?"*	"That one is a chair." (P)				
11		*same as above*	man sitting in chair *"What is the man doing?"*	"The man is sitting."				
12		*same as above*	*"He is sitting, but he is going to stand."*	I				
13		*same as above*	*"Now make him stand."*	O/A				
14		*same as above*	man lying on bed *"The man was standing. Now he is resting."*	I				

Level 14 Lesson 1 (continued)								
	Objects		**Adult's Actions & Words**	**ER***	**✔ if correct**			
	Near Child	*Far from Child*			*Lesson 1*	*Lesson 4*	*Lesson 7*	*Lesson 10*
15	girl boy		*"Who are they?"*	"They are kids."				
16	*same as above*		kids jumping *"What are they doing?"*	"They are jumping."				
17	*same as above*		kids standing *"These kids did jump, but they did not run. Make them run."*	O/A				
18	Picture 16		*"What are these?"*	"These are cats."				
19	*same as above*		*"Cats can play, and cats can sleep."*	I				
20	*same as above*		*"What are these cats doing?"*	"These cats are playing."				
21	Picture 19		*"Who are they?"*	"They are kids."				
22	*same as above*		*"Some of the kids are swimming. Point to the kids who are swimming."*	A				
23	*same as above*		*"Kids like to swim, and they also like to run."*	I				
24	*same as above*		point to kids running *"What are these kids doing?"*	"These kids are running." (P)				
25	*same as above*		*"They are not swimming, they are running."*	I				
			Total Record the Total in the Level 1 Summary Table.					

*ER=Expected Response: I-Say = Imitates (excluding Say); I = Imitates; P = Points; O/A = Correct action on correct object

NOTE: Remember to create Daily Real-World Exercises and use them regularly throughout the day.

Setting	Adult's Actions & Words	Expected Response
Restaurant	pointing to a kid eating *"Who is that?"*	"That is a kid."
Restaurant	pointing to a kid eating *"What is that kid doing?"*	"That kid is eating."
Restaurant	pointing to a lady standing *"Who is that?"*	"That is a lady."
Restaurant	pointing to a lady standing *"What is the lady doing?"*	"The lady is standing."
Home	Dad talking on the phone *"What is Dad doing?"*	"Dad is talking."
Home	Dad stops talking on the phone and lays down *"Dad was talking, but now he is resting."*	I
Outdoors	pointing to a dog walking *"What is this?"*	"This is a dog."
Outdoors	pointing to a dog walking *"What is the dog doing?"*	"The dog is walking."
Playground	pointing to some kids playing *"Who are they?*	"They are kids."
Playground	pointing to some kids playing *"What are they doing?"*	"They are playing."

Level 14 Sample Daily Real-World Exercises
These examples show you how the new language forms taught in this level should be used in daily life.
You should also continue to use the forms taught in prior levels.

Level 14 Lesson 2 (repeat, if needed, as Lessons 5, 8, & 11)								
	Objects		Adult's Actions & Words	ER*	✔ if correct			
	Near Child	Far from Child			Lesson 2	Lesson 5	Lesson 8	Lesson 11
1	Picture 9		*"What is this?"*	"This is a cat."				
2	*same as above*		*"Cats are animals, and all animals sleep."*	I				
3	*same as above*		*"What is this cat doing?"*	"This cat is sleeping."				
4	Picture 20		*"These are babies."*	I				
5	*same as above*		*"They have some cookies."*	I				
6	*same as above*		*"What are these babies doing?"*	"These babies are eating."				
7	Picture 21		*"What are these?"*	"These are ducks."				
8	*same as above*		*"What are the ducks doing?"*	"The ducks are swimming."				
9	*same as above*		*"The ducks are swimming. They can also fly."*	I				
10	*same as above*		*"These ducks are not flying now."*	I				
11		frog	*"What is that?"*	"That is a frog."				
12		*same as above*	frog jumping *"What is the frog doing?"*	"The frog is jumping."				
13		*same as above*	*"The frog was jumping. Now it is not doing that."*	I				
14	2 cars	plane	pointing to cars *"What are these?"*	"These are cars." (P)				
15	*same as above*	*same as above*	cars going *"What are the cars doing?"*	"The cars are going."				
16	*same as above*	*same as above*	pointing to plane *"What is that?"*	"That is a plane." (P)				

	Objects		Adult's Actions & Words	ER*	✔ if correct			
	Near Child	Far from Child			Lesson 2	Lesson 5	Lesson 8	Lesson 11
				Level 14 Lesson 2 (continued)				
17	*same as above*	*same as above*	plane flying **"What is the plane doing?"**	"The plane is flying."				
18	2 ladies 2 beds	2 cats 3 dogs	pointing to ladies lying on beds **"Who are they?"**	"They are ladies." (P)				
19	*same as above*	*same as above*	**"What are they doing?"**	"They are resting."				
20	*same as above*	*same as above*	ladies walking **"The ladies are not resting now. They are walking."**	I				
21	*same as above*	*same as above*	pointing to cats **"What are those?"**	"Those are cats." (P)				
22	*same as above*	*same as above*	cats jumping **"What are the cats doing?"**	"The cats are jumping."				
23	*same as above*	*same as above*	cats standing **"Cats can jump, and these cats were doing that."**	I				
24	*same as above*	*same as above*	**"The dogs did not jump."** pointing to one dog **"Make that dog jump."**	O/A				
25	*same as above*	*same as above*	pointing to dogs that did not jump **"Those dogs did not jump. Give me those dogs."**	O/A				
				Total				
			Record the Total in the Level 1 Summary Table.					

*ER=Expected Response: I^Say = Imitates (excluding Say); I = Imitates; P = Points; O/A = Correct action on correct object

NOTE: Remember to create Daily Real-World Exercises and use them regularly throughout the day.

299

NOTE: If the child has mastered the new language form, do not model the items shaded in gray.

Level 14 Lesson 3 (repeat, if needed, as Lessons 6, 9, & 12)							
Objects		Adult's Actions & Words	ER*	✔ if correct			
Near Child	Far from Child			Lesson 3	Lesson 6	Lesson 9	Lesson 12
1 Picture 22		pointing to boy *"Who is this?"*	"This is a boy." (P)				
2 *same as above*		*"What is he doing?"*	"He is sitting."				
3 *same as above*		*"He has many animals. All the animals are pets."*	I				
4 *same as above*		*"Point to the pets."*	A				
5 Picture 18		*"Who are they?"*	"They are kids."				
6 *same as above*		*"What are the kids doing?"*	"The kids are eating."				
7 Picture 17		*"These birds are doing different things."*	I				
8 *same as above*		pointing to the bird swimming *"What is this bird doing?"*	"This bird is swimming." (P)				
9 *same as above*		pointing to the bird flying *"What is that bird doing?"*	"That bird is flying." (P)				
10 girl boy chair	3 ladies	pointing to the chair *"This is something people sit on. What is it?"*	"It is a chair."				
11 *same as above*	*same as above*	pointing to the kids *"Who are they?"*	"They are kids."				
12 *same as above*	*same as above*	pointing to boy *"This kid is going to sit in the chair."*	I/P				
13 *same as above*	*same as above*	*"Do that. Make him sit in the chair."*	O/A				
14 *same as above*	*same as above*	*"One kid is sitting, but the other kid is not sitting."*	I				

Level 14 Lesson 3 (continued)							
Objects		**Adult's Actions & Words**	**ER***	**✔ if correct**			
Near Child	**Far from Child**			**Lesson 3**	**Lesson 6**	**Lesson 9**	**Lesson 12**
15	*same as above*	*same as above*	*"Ladies can also sit, but those ladies are not doing that."*	I				
16	*same as above*	*same as above*	ladies walking *"What are the ladies doing?"*	"The ladies are walking."				
17	car 2 trucks	bird 3 planes	pointing to trucks *"What are these?"*	"These are trucks." (P)				
18	*same as above*	*same as above*	*"Trucks can go, and cars can also go."*	I				
19	*same as above*	*same as above*	*"Make the car go, and then give me one truck."*	O/A				
20	*same as above*	*same as above*	*"Cars do not fly, and trucks do not fly."*	I				
21	*same as above*	*same as above*	*"But planes can fly. Make one plane fly."*	O/A				
22	*same as above*	*same as above*	*"Birds have wings, and they can fly."*	I				
23	*same as above*	*same as above*	*"Make the bird fly."*	O/A				
24		2 horses 3 frogs	pointing to animals *"Some animals are there."*	I/P				
25		*same as above*	*"They can all jump, but they are not jumping."*	I				
			Total Record the Total in the Level 1 Summary Table.					

*ER=Expected Response: I^Say = Imitates (excluding Say); I = Imitates; P = Points; O/A = Correct action on correct object

NOTE: Remember to create Daily Real-World Exercises and use them regularly throughout the day.

LEVEL 15

QUESTIONS ABOUT LOCATION

Overview

In this level the language expands to include questions about location.

> *Where is _____? Where are _____?*

Questions about location can often be answered with prepositional phrases (e.g., "Where is the box?" "On the floor.") Responses like these involve spatial relations that can be difficult for children on the spectrum (e.g., *in, on, under, etc.*) At this stage, these difficulties are avoided by structuring the situation so that the questions can be answered with the words "here" and "there."

Examples:
> *Adult: (places bird on table close to the child) "Where is the bird?"*
> *Child: (points to the bird) "The bird is here."*
> *Adult: (places some kids on the table far from the child) "Where are the kids?"*
> *Child: (points to the kids) "The kids are there."*

As you will see, when a question asks the child about the location of a particular figure, other figures are also present since this makes the question more meaningful (e.g., if the question is "where is the car?" the car will be shown with other objects. If the car was by itself, there would be little need for the question). In addition, in answering the question, the child points to the figure at the same time that he or she gives the correct verbal response.

Terms like "here" and "there" in everyday language reflect distance from the observer. If a glass is near you, you would say, "A glass is here." If a glass is far from you, you would say, "A glass is there." We try to teach this by using *"here"* for figures that are close to the child, and *"there"* for figures far from the child. Despite this aid, the distinction may prove elusive for some children. **If after Lesson 6 in this level, the child continues to show difficulty differentiating *"here"* from *"there,"* allow the child to use the forms interchangeably for all questions about location.**

Level 15 Summary Table
(to be filled in at the completion of each lesson)

Lesson	1	2	3	4	5	6	7	8	9	10	11	12
Date												
Total # Correct Responses												

*Criterion for Moving On: Once a child achieves 20 or more items correct on 3 out of 4 consecutive sessions, move on to the next level. If the child does not achieve criterion within the 12 sessions, take a break for 3-4 weeks, and then restart this level from Lesson 1.

NOTE: Continue to carry out the Real-World activities on a daily basis. Incorporate as much language as you can from the lessons into the outside world. The language should include material taught in previous levels as well as the new material taught in this level. Remember to use the samples provided as a guide to creating your own.

NOTE: It is important that the child carry down as many words as possible from the question into the answer. Therefore, the child's response to questions should match what is shown in the column labeled ER* (Expected Response).

Level 15 Lesson 1 (repeat, if needed, as Lessons 4, 7, & 10)								
Objects		**Adult's Actions & Words**	**ER***	**✔ if correct**				
Near Child	**Far from Child**			**Lesson 1**	**Lesson 4**	**Lesson 7**	**Lesson 10**	
1	dog	2 ladies	*"Where is the dog?"*	"The dog is here." (P)				
2	*same as above*	*same as above*	dog walking *"What is it doing?"*	"It is walking."				
3	*same as above*	*same as above*	dog lying down *"The dog was walking, but now it is resting."*	I				
4	*same as above*	*same as above*	*"Where are the ladies?"*	"The ladies are there." (P)				
5	*same as above*	*same as above*	ladies sitting *"What are they doing?"*	"They are sitting."				
6	*same as above*	*same as above*	*"The ladies want to run, and they are going to run. Make them run."*	O/A				
7	*same as above*	*same as above*	ladies standing *"What were the ladies doing?"*	"The ladies were running."				
8	3 kids 2 cars	2 trucks	*"Where are the kids?"*	"The kids are here." (P)				
9	*same as above*	*same as above*	one kid jumping *"What is this kid doing?"*	"This kid is jumping."				
10	*same as above*	*same as above*	all kids standing *"Give me the kids that were not jumping."*	O/A				
11	*same as above*	*same as above*	*"Where are the trucks?"*	"The trucks are there." (P)				
12	*same as above*	*same as above*	trucks going *"What are the trucks doing?"*	"The trucks are going."				
13	2 planes	bus bird	*"Where are the planes?"*	"The planes are here." (P)				
14	*same as above*	*same as above*	planes flying *"What are they doing?"*	"They are flying."				

	Objects		Adult's Actions & Words	ER*	✔ if correct			
	Near Child	Far from Child			Lesson 1	Lesson 4	Lesson 7	Lesson 10
15	*same as above*	*same as above*	*"Birds can also fly, but that bird did not fly."*	I				
16	*same as above*	*same as above*	*"Make that bird fly and then make the bus go."*	O/A				
17	Picture 15	Picture 24	pointing to animals *"Some animals are here."* pointing to the snake *"This one is a snake."*	I/P				
18	*same as above*	*same as above*	pointing to bugs *"What are these?"*	"These are bugs." (P)				
19	*same as above*	*same as above*	pointing to lady bug *"This bug has wings, but* pointing to other bugs *those bugs do not have wings."*	I/P				
20	*same as above*	*same as above*	*"Some bugs have wings, and they can fly."*	I				
21	Picture 12		*"The boy has some pets, and he likes to play with them."*	I				
22	*same as above*		*"Some of his pets are sitting, but one pet is standing. Point to the one that is standing."*	A				
23	*same as above*		*"He also has some toys."*	I				
24	*same as above*		pointing to plane *"Here is one toy, and* pointing to robot *here is another toy."*	I/P				
25	*same as above*		*"Point to the one that can fly."*	A				
			Total Record the Total in the Level 1 Summary Table.					

Level 15 Lesson 1 (continued)

*ER=Expected Response: I⁻ˢᵃʸ = Imitates (excluding Say); I = Imitates; P = Points; O/A = Correct action on correct object

NOTE: Remember to create Daily Real-World Exercises and use them regularly throughout the day.

Level 15 Sample Daily Real-World Exercises

These examples show you how the new language forms taught in this level should be used in daily life.
You should also continue to use the forms taught in prior levels.

Setting	Adult's Actions & Words	Expected Response
Home	*"Where is the bathroom?"*	"The bathroom is here/there." (P)
Home	*"Walk to the bathroom and then wash your hands."*	O/A
Restaurant	*"Where is the bread?"*	"The bread is here/there." (P)
Restaurant	*"Where is the water?"*	"The water is here/there." (P)
Restaurant	Mom drinking *"What is Mom doing?"*	"Mom is drinking."
Pool	*"Where is the lady?"*	"The lady is here/there." (P)
Pool	*"What is she doing?"*	"She is swimming."
Toy Store	pointing to a toy bear *"What is this?"*	"This is a bear." (P)
Toy Store	*"Where are the dolls?"*	"The dolls are here/there." (P)
Home	several items on a shelf including a book *"Where is the book?"*	"The book is here/there." (P)

	Objects		Adult's Actions & Words	ER*	✔ if correct			
	Near Child	Far from Child			Lesson 2	Lesson 5	Lesson 8	Lesson 11
1	2 cars	man 2 frogs	*"Where is the man?"*	"The man is there." (P)				
2	*same as above*	*same as above*	*"The man has some frogs, and the frogs can jump."*	I				
3	*same as above*	*same as above*	*"Make them jump."*	O/A				
4	*same as above*	*same as above*	frogs not jumping *"The frogs were jumping, but now they are resting."*	I				
5	*same as above*	*same as above*	*"Where are the cars?"*	"The cars are here." (P)				
6	*same as above*	*same as above*	cars going *"What are the cars doing?"*	"The cars are going."				
7	lady bed		*"Where is the lady?"*	"The lady is here." (P)				
8	*same as above*		lady standing *"What is she doing?"*	"She is standing."				
9	*same as above*		*"The lady is tired, and she wants to rest. Make the lady rest."*	O/A				
10	*same as above*		lady lying on bed *"The lady was standing, but now she is resting."*	I				
11	2 cats	2 dogs	*"Where are the dogs?"*	"The dogs are there." (P)				
12	*same as above*	*same as above*	dogs running *"What are the dogs doing?"*	"The dogs are running."				
13	*same as above*	*same as above*	*"Where are the cats?"*	"The cats are here." (P)				
14	*same as above*	*same as above*	cats walking *"What are they doing?"*	"They are walking."				
15	*same as above*	*same as above*	cats and dogs all standing *"The dogs did run, and the cats did walk."*	I				

Level 15 Lesson 2 (repeat, if needed, as Lessons 5, 8, & 11)

	Objects		Adult's Actions & Words	ER*	✔ if correct			
	Near Child	*Far from Child*			*Lesson 2*	*Lesson 5*	*Lesson 8*	*Lesson 11*
				Level 15 Lesson 2 (continued)				
16	Picture 10		*"Where is the man?"*	"The man is here." (P)				
17	*same as above*		*"What is he doing?"*	"He is resting."				
18	*same as above*		*"Where is the sun?"*	"The sun is here." (P)				
19	*same as above*		*"Where is the house?"*	"The house is here." (P)				
20	Picture 25		*"This boy has some food, and he wants to eat it."*	I				
21	*same as above*		*"Where is the food?"*	"The food is here." (P)				
22	Picture 7		*"Where is the kite?"*	"The kite is here." (P)				
23	*same as above*		*"The girl has a kite, and she is happy."*	I				
24	*same as above*		*"The boy wants the kite, but he cannot have it."*	I				
25	*same as above*		*"He is sad."*	I				
				Total Record the Total in the Level 1 Summary Table.				

*ER=Expected Response: I^{Say} = Imitates (excluding Say); I = Imitates; P = Points; O/A = Correct action on correct object

NOTE: Remember to create Daily Real-World Exercises and use them regularly throughout the day.

NOTE: If the child has mastered the new language form, do not model the items shaded in gray for Lessons 3 to 12.

	Objects		Adult's Actions & Words	ER*	✔ if correct			
	Near Child	Far from Child			Lesson 3	Lesson 6	Lesson 9	Lesson 12
1	Picture 5		*"Where are the bears?"*	"The bears are here." (P)				
2	same as above		*"Bears are animals, and animals need water to drink."*	I				
3	same as above		*"These bears are looking for water."*	I				
4	Picture 6		*"Now they are drinking."*	I				
5	Picture 16		pointing to cats *"What are these?"*	"These are cats." (P)				
6	same as above		*"The cats have a ball, and they are playing with it."*	I				
7	same as above		*"Point to the ball."*	A				
8	Picture 26		*"Many toys are here."*	I				
9	same as above		*"Where is the doll?"*	"The doll is here." (P)				
10	same as above		*"Where is the plane?"*	"The plane is here." (P)				
11	boy plane		*"Where is the kid?"*	"The kid is here." (P)				
12	same as above		*"This kid has a plane, and the plane can fly."*	I				
13	same as above		plane flying *"What is the plane doing?"*	"The plane is flying."				
14	same as above		*"Planes can fly, but kids cannot fly."*	I				
15	2 horses	2 cats	*"These are animals. Where are the cats?"*	"The cats are there." (P)				

(table title: Level 15 Lesson 3 (repeat, if needed, as Lessons 6, 9, & 12))

	Objects		Adult's Actions & Words	ER*	✔ if correct			
	Near Child	*Far from Child*			*Lesson 3*	*Lesson 6*	*Lesson 9*	*Lesson 12*
16	*same as above*	*same as above*	"Cats can walk, and they can also jump."	I				
17	*same as above*	*same as above*	"Make one cat walk and then make the other cat jump."	O/A				
18	*same as above*	*same as above*	cats standing "Give me the one that was jumping."	O/A				
19	*same as above*	*same as above*	"Horses can also jump, but these horses did not jump."	I				
20	*same as above*	*same as above*	"They are going to run."	I				
21	*same as above*	*same as above*	horses running "Now they are running."	I				
22	2 dogs	lady chair	"Where is the lady?"	"The lady is there." (P)				
23	*same as above*	*same as above*	"She has a chair, and she wants to sit. Make her sit."	O/A				
24	*same as above*	*same as above*	"Where are the dogs?"	"The dogs are here." (P)				
25	*same as above*	*same as above*	dogs jumping "What are the dogs doing?"	"The dogs are jumping."				
				Total Record the Total in the Level 1 Summary Table.				

*ER=Expected Response: I^{Say} = Imitates (excluding Say); I = Imitates; P = Points; O/A = Correct action on correct object

NOTE: If after Lesson 6, the child continues to show difficulty differentiating "here" from "there," allow the child to use the terms interchangeably.

NOTE: Remember to create Daily Real-World Exercises and use them regularly throughout the day.

LEVEL 16

QUESTIONS THAT USE "WHICH ONE" FOR IDENTIFICATION

Overview

The question word *"which"* is added at this level and it is used to ask the child to identify people, animals, and objects based on name, properties, or actions. The following question forms are taught:

Which one is a ____? Which ones are ____?
Which one is ____ing? Which ones are ____ing?
Which one has ____? Which ones have ____?

Examples:

(On the table are a bird, car, a lady sitting, and a lady standing)
Adult: "Which one is a bird?"
Child: (points to the bird) "This one is a bird."
Adult: "Which lady is sitting?"
Child: (points to lady sitting) "This lady is sitting."
Adult: "Which one is standing?"
Child: (points to lady standing) "This one is standing."
Adult: "Which one has wheels?"
Child: (points to car) "This one has wheels."

Some of the responses are slightly unusual. For example, for the question *"Which ones are frogs?"* the response is, *"These ones are frogs."* This is necessary to maintain the pattern of carrying down all possible key words from the question to the answer; thereby showing the child how the same strategy applies to a range of questions.

Understandably, the child may try to offer other types of answers. For example, when looking at two figures (a lady standing and a kid sitting) and asked, *"Which one is sitting?"* the child might answer, *"the kid"* or *"The kid is sitting."* Technically, these answers are correct. However, they do not fit the pattern of carrying down all possible key words from the question to the answer. Therefore, allowing such answers takes away from the child a key tool for understanding the range of questions that he or she may encounter. This ultimately interferes with their progress. Hence, to the question *"Which <u>one is sitting</u>?"* the correct answer would be, *"This <u>one is sitting</u>,"* along with the child pointing to the correct object.

As in previous levels, when the new question form is introduced, be prepared to offer a number of trials of repetition until the child answers the question correctly.

Level 16 Summary Table
(to be filled in at the completion of each lesson)

Lesson	1	2	3	4	5	6	7	8	9	10	11	12
Date												
Total # Correct Responses												

*Criterion for Moving On: Once a child achieves 20 or more items correct on 3 out of 4 consecutive sessions, move on to the next level. If the child does not achieve criterion within the 12 sessions, take a break for 3-4 weeks, and then restart this level from Lesson 1.

NOTE: Continue to carry out the Real-World activities on a daily basis. Incorporate as much language as you can from the lessons into the outside world. The language should include material taught in previous levels as well as the new material taught in this level. Remember to use the samples provided as a guide to creating your own.

	Objects		Adult's Actions & Words	ER*	✔ if correct			
	Near Child	Far from Child			Lesson 1	Lesson 4	Lesson 7	Lesson 10
1	boy girl frog	car	*"Which one is a frog?"*	"This one is a frog." (P)				
2	*same as above*	*same as above*	frog jumping *"What is the frog doing?"*	"The frog is jumping."				
3	*same as above*	*same as above*	*"Which one is a car?"*	"That one is a car." (P)				
4	*same as above*	*same as above*	car going *"What is the car doing?"*	"The car is going."				
5	*same as above*	*same as above*	*"Which ones are kids?"*	"These ones are kids." (P)				
6	*same as above*	*same as above*	*"Kids can run, but they are not going to do that."*	I				
7	*same as above*	*same as above*	*"They are going to sit. Do that. Make them sit."*	O/A				
8	2 ladies	dog cat	ladies sitting *"Which ones are sitting?"*	"These ones are sitting." (P)				
9	*same as above*	*same as above*	ladies walking *"The ladies were sitting, but now they are walking."*	I				
10	*same as above*	*same as above*	*"Where are the animals?"*	"The animals are there." (P)				
11	*same as above*	*same as above*	*"Animals can walk, but these animals are not doing that."*	I				
12	2 trucks bus	man	*"Which one has arms?"*	"That one has arms." (P)				
13	*same as above*	*same as above*	*"Which ones have wheels?"*	"These ones have wheels." (P)				

Level 16 Lesson 1 (repeat, if needed, as Lessons 4, 7, & 10)

315

	Objects		Adult's Actions & Words	ER*	✔ if correct			
	Near Child	*Far from Child*			Lesson 1	Lesson 4	Lesson 7	Lesson 10
14	*same as above*	*same as above*	*"Trucks can go. Buses can also go."*	I				
15	*same as above*	*same as above*	*"Make one truck go."*	O/A				
16	*same as above*	*same as above*	point to truck that did not go *"This truck did not go. Give me this truck and then give me the bus."*	O/A				
17	Picture 12		point to boy *"Who is this?"*	"This is a boy/kid."				
18	*same as above*		*"He has some animals. Point to an animal."*	A				
19	*same as above*		*"He also has some toys."*	I				
20	*same as above*		*"Which one is a plane?"*	"This one is a plane." (P)				
21	Picture 17		*"What are these?"*	"These are birds/ ducks." (P)				
22	*same as above*		*"Ducks have wings. They can fly."*	I				
23	*same as above*		*"Ducks can also swim."*	I				
24	*same as above*		*"Point to the duck that is flying."*	A				
25	*same as above*		*"Which one is swimming?"*	"This one is swimming." (P)				
				Total Record the Total in the Level 1 Summary Table.				

*ER=Expected Response: I⁻ˢᵃʸ = Imitates (excluding Say); I = Imitates; P = Points; O/A = Correct action on correct object

NOTE: Remember to create Daily Real-World Exercises and use them regularly throughout the day.

Level 16 Sample Daily Real-World Exercises

These examples show you how the new language forms taught in this level should be used in daily life.
You should also continue to use the forms taught in prior levels.

Setting	Adult's Actions & Words	Expected Response
Home	looking at many objects on a table *"Which one is a pen?"*	"This/That one is a pen." (P)
Home	looking at many objects on a shelf *"Which ones are books?"*	"These/Those ones are books." (P)
Home	standing near a box with many toys, including some cars *"Which ones are balls?"*	"These ones are balls." (P)
Home	places a phone, keys, and wallet in front of the child *"Which one is a phone?"*	"This one is a phone." (P)
Restaurant	looking at many objects on a table *"Which one is a bowl?"*	"This/That one is a bowl." (P)
Restaurant	looking at many objects on a table *"Which ones are spoons?"*	"These/Those ones are spoons." (P)
Playground	near several dogs standing, sitting, or walking *"Which one is sitting?"*	"This/That one is sitting." (P)
Playground	near several kids on swings and slides *"Some kids are here. Which ones are swinging?"*	"These/Those ones are swinging." (P)
Playground	near a kid playing with a ball and some kids playing with other toys *"Some kids are here. Which one has a ball?"*	"This/That one has a ball." (P)
Playroom	place 2 dolls, a ball, and crayons near the child *"Which ones have eyes?"*	"These ones have eyes." (P)

317

Level 16 Lesson 2 (repeat, if needed, as Lessons 5, 8, & 11)								
	Objects		Adult's Actions & Words	ER*	✔ if correct			
	Near Child	Far from Child			Lesson 2	Lesson 5	Lesson 8	Lesson 11
1	man bird	2 cars	*"Which one is a bird?"*	"This one is a bird." (P)				
2	*same as above*	*same as above*	*"Birds can fly. Make this one fly."*	O/A				
3	*same as above*	*same as above*	*"Which ones are cars?"*	"Those ones are cars." (P)				
4	*same as above*	*same as above*	*"Cars have wheels. Make those cars go."*	O/A				
5	*same as above*	*same as above*	*"The cars did go, and the bird did fly."*	I				
6	3 kids	plane truck	plane flying *"Which one is flying?"*	"That one is flying." (P)				
7	*same as above*	*same as above*	plane not flying *"That plane was flying. Now it is not."*	I				
8	*same as above*	*same as above*	*"Which ones have legs?"*	"These ones have legs." (P)				
9	*same as above*	*same as above*	*"Kids use legs to walk."*	I				
10	*same as above*	*same as above*	*"Make two kids walk."*	O/A				
11	2 cats 2 dogs	truck	*"Where are the cats?"*	"The cats are here." (P)				
12	*same as above*	*same as above*	*"The cats are going to run, but the dogs are not going to do that. Make the cats run."*	O/A				
13	*same as above*	*same as above*	*"Now turn over the dogs."*	O/A				
14	*same as above*	*same as above*	*"Which one is a truck?"*	"That one is a truck." (P)				
15	*same as above*	*same as above*	*"Give me the truck and then give me one animal."*	O/A				
16	Picture 15		pointing to animals *"Some more animals are here."*	I/P				

	Objects		Adult's Actions & Words	ER*	✔ if correct			
	Near Child	Far from Child			Lesson 2	Lesson 5	Lesson 8	Lesson 11
			**Level 16 Lesson 2 (continued)**					
17	*same as above*		*"Which one is a snake?"*	"This one is a snake." (P)				
18	*same as above*		*"Which one is sleeping?"*	"This one is sleeping." (P)				
19	Picture 18		*"Who are they?"*	"They are kids."				
20	*same as above*		*"What are the kids doing?"*	"The kids are eating."				
21	*same as above*		*"These kids have food to eat, but they do not have any drinks."*	I				
22	Picture 2		*"Some more kids are here."*	I				
23	*same as above*		*"Kids like to do many things."*	I				
24	*same as above*		*"These kids like to swim, and they also like to run."*	I				
25	*same as above*		*"What are these kids doing?"*	"These kids are swimming."				
			Total Record the Total in the Level 1 Summary Table.					

*ER=Expected Response: I⁻ˢᵃʸ = Imitates (excluding Say); I = Imitates; P = Points; O/A = Correct action on correct object

NOTE: Remember to create Daily Real-World Exercises and use them regularly throughout the day.

NOTE: If the child has mastered the new language form, do not model the items shaded in gray for Lessons 3 to 12.

	Level 16 Lesson 3 (repeat, if needed, as Lessons 6, 9, & 12)							
	Objects		**Adult's Actions & Words**	**ER***	**✔ if correct**			
	Near Child	*Far from Child*			*Lesson 3*	*Lesson 6*	*Lesson 9*	*Lesson 12*
1	Picture 29		pointing to dogs *"Two dogs are running. One dog is sitting."*	I/P				
2	*same as above*		*"Which one is sitting?"*	"This one is sitting." (P)				
3	*same as above*		*"Which ones are running?"*	"These ones are running." (P)				
4	Picture 1		pointing to one boy *"This is not a man. Who is this?"*	"This is a kid/boy." (P)				
5	*same as above*		*"He likes to rest, and he is doing that now."*	I				
6	Picture 27		pointing to bears *"Some bears are here."*	I/P				
7	*same as above*		*"They are hungry. They have some food."*	I				
8	*same as above*		*"They are going to eat."*	I				
9	Picture 28		pointing to plants *"These are not kids, and these are not animals. What are they?"*	"They are plants."				
10	*same as above*		*"Some of the plants are trees. Which ones are trees?"*	"These ones are trees." (P)				
11	bird cat	2 ladies	pointing to the animals *"Some animals are here."*	I/P				
12	*same as above*	*same as above*	*"Which one is a cat?"*	"This one is a cat." (P)				
13	*same as above*	*same as above*	*"Where are the ladies?"*	"The ladies are there." (P)				

	Level 16 Lesson 3 (continued)							
	Objects		**Adult's Actions & Words**	**ER***	**✔ if correct**			
	Near Child	*Far from Child*			*Lesson 3*	*Lesson 6*	*Lesson 9*	*Lesson 12*
14	*same as above*	*same as above*	one lady sitting *"Which one is sitting?"*	"That one is sitting." (P)				
15	*same as above*	*same as above*	*"These ladies are going to walk."*	I				
16	*same as above*	*same as above*	ladies walking *"Now they are walking."*	I				
17	girl car	2 birds	*"Which one has arms?"*	"This one has arms." (P)				
18	*same as above*	*same as above*	*"Girls have arms, but they do not have wings."*	I				
19	*same as above*	*same as above*	*"Which ones have wings?"*	"Those ones have wings." (P)				
20	*same as above*	*same as above*	*"Those birds can fly, but they are not flying."*	I				
21	*same as above*	*same as above*	*"Now give me the birds."*	O/A				
22	man plane	dog	man sitting, dog standing *"Which one is standing?"*	"That one is standing." (P)				
23	*same as above*	*same as above*	*"Dogs can do many things. Right now, he is only standing."*	I				
24	*same as above*	*same as above*	*"Where is the man?"*	"The man is here." (P)				
25	*same as above*	*same as above*	*"What is he doing?"*	"He is sitting."				
				Total Record the Total in the Level 1 Summary Table.				

*ER=Expected Response: I^{Say} = Imitates (excluding Say); I = Imitates; P = Points; O/A = Correct action on correct object

NOTE: Remember to create Daily Real-World Exercises and use them regularly throughout the day.

LEVEL 17
QUESTIONS ABOUT DESIRE AND ABILITY

Overview

Until now, although the child has been imitating sentences involving items not in view, no questions of that sort have appeared. All questions have been limited to information that is in view. This holds for the questions about identity *(what are these?)*, location *(where is that?)*, action *(what are they doing?)*, and possession *(which one has arms?)*. Now we make the important move of raising questions about what is not in view. This is an early step in enabling the child to access the phenomenal potential of language to discuss anything and everything—without the need for there to be any material in view. Examples include discussions about a family trip, a planned birthday party, events that took place in school, and so on.

As always, we start at a simple level with questions about abilities (as reflected in words such as *can*) and desires (as reflected in words such as *likes*). The following question forms are introduced:

> *Which one can ____? Which ones can ____?*
> *Which one likes to ____? Which ones like to ____?*

Examples:
> *"Which one can fly?"*
> *"Which ones can talk?"*
> *"Which one likes to jump?"*
> *"Which ones like to run?"*

In the child's response to each question, he or she must point at the correct object.

Level 17 Summary Table
(to be filled in at the completion of each lesson)

Lesson	1	2	3	4	5	6	7	8	9	10	11	12
Date												
Total # Correct Responses												

*Criterion for Moving On: Once a child achieves 20 or more items correct on 3 out of 4 consecutive sessions, move on to the next level. If the child does not achieve criterion within the 12 sessions, take a break for 3-4 weeks, and then restart this level from Lesson 1.

NOTE: Continue to carry out the Real-World activities on a daily basis. Incorporate as much language as you can from the lessons into the outside world. The language should include material taught in previous levels as well as the new material taught in this level. Remember to use the samples provided as a guide to creating your own.

	Objects		Adult's Actions & Words	ER*	✔ if correct			
	Near Child	Far from Child			Lesson 1	Lesson 4	Lesson 7	Lesson 10
1	boy	car	pointing to boy *"A boy is here,* pointing to car *and a car is there."*	I/P				
2	same as above	same as above	*"Which one can walk?"*	"This one can walk." (P)				
3	same as above	same as above	*"Make the boy walk, and then make the car go."*	O/A				
4	plane bird truck		*"Some of these can fly. Which ones can fly?"*	"These ones can fly." (P)				
5	same as above		pointing to truck *"What is this?"*	"This is a truck." (P)				
6	same as above		*"Trucks cannot fly, but they can go. Make the truck go."*	O/A				
7		2 birds 3 frogs	*"Some of those animals like to jump. Which ones like to jump?"*	"Those ones like to jump." (P)				
8		same as above	*"Frogs like to jump, but those frogs are not doing that."*	I				
9	truck 2 cars	2 ladies	*"Which one is a truck?"*	"This one is a truck." (P)				
10	same as above	same as above	*"Make the truck go."*	O/A				
11	same as above	same as above	*"The truck was going. Now make the cars go."*	O/A				
12	same as above	same as above	*"Which ones can walk?"*	"Those ones can walk." (P)				
13	same as above	same as above	*"Ladies can run. They can also walk."*	I				
14	same as above	same as above	*"Now they are going to walk. Make them do that."*	O/A				
15	same as above	same as above	*"The cars were going, and the ladies were walking."*	I				

Level 17 Lesson 1 (repeat, if needed, as Lessons 4, 7, & 10)

325

Level 17 Lesson 1 (continued)							
Objects		Adult's Actions & Words	ER*	✔ if correct			
Near Child	Far from Child			Lesson 1	Lesson 4	Lesson 7	Lesson 10
16	Picture 30		pointing to tree *"A tree is here,* pointing to dog *and a dog is here."*	I/P				
17	*same as above*		*"Which one can run?"*	"This one can run." (P)				
18	*same as above*		*"Dogs can run. Trees cannot do that."*	I				
19	Picture 31		*"This girl is happy. She likes dogs."*	I				
20	*same as above*		*"The dog can jump, but it is not doing that. It is sitting."*	I				
21	Picture 22		*"This boy has some animals."*	I				
22	*same as above*		*"Which ones are swimming?"*	"These ones are swimming." (P)				
23	Picture 13		*"Some birds are here. Point to one."*	A				
24	*same as above*		*"Many birds can fly, but these birds cannot do that."*	I				
25	*same as above*		*"They do not fly. They move by walking."*	I				
Total Record the Total in the Level 1 Summary Table.								

*ER=Expected Response: I-Say = Imitates (excluding Say); I = Imitates; P = Points; O/A = Correct action on correct object

NOTE: Remember to create Daily Real-World Exercises and use them regularly throughout the day.

Level 17 Sample Daily Real-World Exercises

These examples show you how the new language forms taught in this level should be used in daily life.
You should also continue to use the forms taught in prior levels.

Setting	Adult's Actions & Words	Expected Response
Playground	pointing to a baby nearby *"A baby is here,* pointing to some kids at a distance *and some kids are there.* *Which ones can walk?"*	"Those ones can walk." (P)
Outdoors	pointing to a bird at a distance *"A bird is there,* pointing to a dog nearby *and a dog is here.* *Which one likes to fly?"*	"That one likes to fly." (P)
Playground	pointing to some trees nearby *"Some trees are here,* pointing to some kids at a distance *and some kids are there.* *Which ones can run?"*	"Those ones can run." (P)
Playroom	pointing to some planes and some cars *"Which ones can fly?"*	"These ones can fly." (P)

	Objects		Adult's Actions & Words	ER*	✔ if correct			
	Near Child	Far from Child			Lesson 2	Lesson 5	Lesson 8	Lesson 11
1	3 cars	2 boys	pointing to boys *"Who are they?"*	"They are boys." (P)				
2	*same as above*	*same as above*	pointing to cars *"What are these?"*	"These are cars." (P)				
3	*same as above*	*same as above*	*"Which ones can sit?"*	"Those ones can sit." (P)				
4	*same as above*	*same as above*	*"Make them sit."*	O/A				
5	*same as above*	*same as above*	two cars going *"Which ones are going?"*	"These ones are going." (P)				
6		plane truck	pointing to plane *"A plane is there* pointing to truck *and a truck is there."*	I/P				
7		*same as above*	*"Which one can fly?"*	"That one can fly." (P)				
8		*same as above*	*"That plane is not flying, but it is going to fly."*	I				
9		*same as above*	plane flying *"Now it is flying."*	I				
10	2 trucks	3 frogs	pointing to frogs *"Some frogs are there,* pointing to trucks *and some trucks are here."*	I/P				
11	*same as above*	*same as above*	*"Which ones like to jump?"*	"Those ones like to jump." (P)				
12	*same as above*	*same as above*	*"Make one frog jump."*	O/A				
13	*same as above*	*same as above*	*"Give me the frogs that were not jumping."*	O/A				
14	Picture 15		pointing to picture *"Some animals are here."*	I/P				
15	*same as above*		*"Which ones are swimming?"*	"These ones are swimming." (P)				

Level 17 Lesson 2 (repeat, if needed, as Lessons 5, 8, & 11)

	Objects		Adult's Actions & Words	ER*	✔ if correct			
	Near Child	Far from Child			Lesson 2	Lesson 5	Lesson 8	Lesson 11
16	same as above		*"Fish can swim, but they cannot run."*	I				
17	same as above		*"Point to an animal that can run."*	A				
18	Picture 24		pointing to bugs *"Some bugs are here* pointing to kids *and some kids are here."*	I/P				
19	same as above		*"Which ones can talk?"*	"These ones can talk." (P)				
20	same as above		*"Bugs cannot talk, but they can do other things."*	I				
21	same as above		*"Some bugs fly, and some bugs walk."*	I				
22	Picture 12		pointing to boy *"Who is this?"*	"This is a boy/kid."				
23	same as above		*"He has some animals. Point to an animal."*	A				
24	same as above		*"He also has some toys."*	I				
25	same as above		*"Which one can fly?"*	"This one can fly." (P)				
				Total Record the Total in the Level 1 Summary Table.				

*ER=Expected Response: I^{-Say} = Imitates (excluding Say); I = Imitates; P = Points; O/A = Correct action on correct object

NOTE: Remember to create Daily Real-World Exercises and use them regularly throughout the day.

NOTE: If the child has mastered the new language form, do not model the items shaded in gray for Lessons 3 to 12.

Level 17 Lesson 3 (repeat, if needed, as Lessons 6, 9, & 12)								
	Objects		Adult's Actions & Words	ER*	✔ if correct			
	Near Child	Far from Child			Lesson 3	Lesson 6	Lesson 9	Lesson 12
1	Picture 5		pointing to bears *"Some animals are here,* pointing to trees *and some plants are here."*	I/P				
2	*same as above*		*"Which ones like to eat?"*	"These ones like to eat." (P)				
3	Picture 16		*"Some cats are here. Point to the cats."*	A				
4	*same as above*		*"They are playing with a ball."*	I				
5	*same as above*		*"Where is the ball?"*	"The ball is here." (P)				
6	lady	2 birds 3 cats	pointing to animals *"Some animals are there."*	I/P				
7	*same as above*	*same as above*	*"Which ones like to fly?"*	"Those ones like to fly." (P)				
8	*same as above*	*same as above*	*"Birds fly. Cats cannot fly, but they can walk."*	I				
9	*same as above*	*same as above*	*"Make one cat walk."*	O/A				
10	2 boys girl		girl lying down *"Some kids are here. Which one is resting?"*	"This one is resting." (P)				
11	*same as above*		girls jumping *"The girl was resting. Now what is she doing?"*	"Now she is jumping." OR "She is jumping now."				
12	*same as above*		all kids standing *"Give me the other kids—the kids that were not jumping."*	O/A				
13	3 frogs	2 planes bus	*"Where are the planes?"*	"The planes are there." (P)				

	Objects		Adult's Actions & Words	ER*	✔ if correct			
	Near Child	Far from Child			Lesson 3	Lesson 6	Lesson 9	Lesson 12
			Level 17 Lesson 3 (continued)					
14	same as above	same as above	"Planes can fly. Make those planes fly."	O/A				
15	same as above	same as above	"Which ones can jump?"	"These ones can jump." (P)				
16	same as above	same as above	pointing to two frogs "Make these frogs jump."	O/A				
17	same as above	same as above	"Some frogs were jumping, but one was not jumping."	I				
18	same as above	same as above	"Give me the one that was not jumping."	O/A				
19	3 cars	2 kids	"Which ones have wheels?"	"These ones have wheels." (P)				
20	same as above	same as above	"Cars have wheels, and they can go."	I				
21	same as above	same as above	"These cars are not going."	I				
22	same as above	same as above	one car going "Now one car is going."	I				
23	same as above	same as above	"Which ones can walk?"	"Those ones can walk." (P)				
24	same as above	same as above	"Kids have legs, and they can walk."	I				
25	same as above	same as above	"Kids can also jump. Make one kid walk and then make one kid jump."	O/A				
			Total Record the Total in the Level 1 Summary Table.					

*ER=Expected Response: I-Say = Imitates (excluding Say); I = Imitates; P = Points; O/A = Correct action on correct object

NOTE: Remember to create Daily Real-World Exercises and use them regularly throughout the day.

LEVEL 18
QUESTIONS USING "NOT"

Overview

The activities in this level continue to expand the child's mastery of language by raising questions that involve the word "not." The question forms are the ones that the child has already learned in previous levels, but they are now modified to include *"not."*

> *Which one is not a ____? Which ones are not ____?*
> *Which one is not ____ing? Which ones are not ____ing?*
> *Which one cannot ____? Which ones cannot____?*
> *Which one does not ____? Which ones do not ____?*
> *Which one does not have ____? Which ones do not have ____?*

Examples:

> *Adult: (places bird, plane, and 3 dogs near child) "Which one is not a dog?"*
> *Child: (points to bird) "This one is not a dog."*
> *Adult: "Which ones cannot fly?"*
> *Child: (points to dogs) "These ones cannot fly."*
> *Adult: "Which one does not have legs?"*
> *Child: (points to plane) "This one does not have legs."*

Techniques for handling errors

Because many children have had extensive experience labeling objects that they see, they may initially have difficulty adjusting to questions of this type. For example, when shown three cars and a dog and asked the question, *"Which one is not a car,"* a common initial response is to use what they have learned to date, so they pick up a car and say, *"This one is not a car."*

If this happens, pick up the correct object (in this case, the dog), model the correct response, and then repeat the item from the beginning. Rather than moving on to the next exercise in Lesson 1, go to the table at the end of Lesson 1 which provides several trials of this sort, each time with a new set of objects. These should be repeated until the child learns the concept of *"not."* In each trial, the objects include three or four items that are the same and one that is different (e.g., 3 girls and a cat; 3 dogs and a bird; 4 kids and a plane; etc.)

After a few trials, the children realize that selecting the object that was named in the question is not the way to go. They are then left with only one alternative: to choose the object that is NOT named in the question. By carefully controlling the materials and presenting a clear two-choice situation, (i.e., selecting the object named versus selecting the object not named), the child is given the tools to master questions that deal with a complex, abstract concept such as *"not."* Once the concept of *"not"* is mastered, the child can proceed with the remainder of Lesson 1.

Level 18 Summary Table
(to be filled in at the completion of each lesson)

Lesson	1	2	3	4	5	6	7	8	9	10	11	12
Date												
Total # Correct Responses												

*Criterion for Moving On: Once a child achieves 20 or more items correct on 3 out of 4 consecutive sessions, move on to the next level. If the child does not achieve criterion within the 12 sessions, take a break for 3-4 weeks, and then restart this level from Lesson 1.

NOTE: Continue to carry out the Real-World activities on a daily basis. Incorporate as much language as you can from the lessons into the outside world. The language should include material taught in previous levels as well as the new material taught in this level. Remember to use the samples provided as a guide to creating your own.

NOTE: If the child has difficulty with items 1 and 3 in Lesson 1, go to the table that follows Lesson 1 called "Trials to teach the concept of not." Repeat these trials until the child has learned the concept. Then return to Lesson 1.

NOTE: Throughout the program, all figures should be in the standing position unless otherwise noted.

Level 18 Lesson 1 (repeat, if needed, as Lessons 4, 7, & 10)								
Objects		Adult's Actions & Words	ER*	✔ if correct				
Near Child	Far from Child			Lesson 1	Lesson 4	Lesson 7	Lesson 10	
1	3 horses cat		*"Some animals are here. Which one is not a horse?"*	"This one is not a horse." (P)				
2	*same as above*		*"What is it?"*	"It is a cat."				
3	plane 3 cars		*"Which one is not a car?"*	"This one is not a car." (P)				
4	*same as above*		*"What is it?"*	"It is a plane."				
5	*same as above*		*"Planes can fly. Make the plane fly."*	O/A				
6	2 ladies	3 kids	all figures standing pointing to kids *"Some kids are there. What are they doing?"*	"They are standing."				
7	*same as above*	*same as above*	two kids sitting *"Now some of them are sitting. Which one is not sitting?"*	"That one is not sitting." (P)				
8	*same as above*	*same as above*	pointing to ladies *"They are not kids. Who are they?"*	"They are ladies." (P)				
9	*same as above*	*same as above*	pointing to one lady lying down *"What is she doing?"*	"She is resting." (P)				
10	*same as above*	*same as above*	*"One lady is resting and one is not. Point to the one that is standing."*	A				
11	3 birds		*"These are some birds. They can fly."*	I				
12	*same as above*		two birds flying *"Which one is not flying?"*	"This one is not flying." (P)				
13	*same as above*	3 dogs horse	*"Those are some more animals. Which one is not a dog?"*	"That one is not a dog." (P)				
14	*same as above*	*same as above*	pointing to horse *"What is that?"*	"That is a horse." (P)				

	Objects		Adult's Actions & Words	ER*	✔ if correct			
	Near Child	*Far from Child*			Lesson 1	Lesson 4	Lesson 7	Lesson 10
15	*same as above*	*same as above*	*"Horses can do many things. They can run and they can jump."*	I				
16	*same as above*	*same as above*	*"Make that horse jump."*	O/A				
17	Picture 31		pointing to trees *"Some trees are here* pointing to dog *and a dog is here."*	I/P				
18	*same as above*		*"Which one can run?"*	"This one can run." (P)				
19	*same as above*		*"Dogs can run, but this dog is not doing that."*	I				
20	*same as above*		*"This dog is sitting."*	I				
21	Picture 17		*"Some ducks are here. Which one is not swimming?"*	"This one is not swimming." (P)				
22	*same as above*		*"What is it doing?"*	"It is flying."				
23	*same as above*		*"One duck is flying, and another one is swimming."*	I				
24	Picture 13		*"These are some more birds."*	I				
25	*same as above*		*"These birds can do many things, but they cannot fly."*	I				
				Total Record the Total in the Level 1 Summary Table.				

*ER=Expected Response: I-Say = Imitates (excluding Say); I = Imitates; P = Points; O/A = Correct action on correct object

NOTE: Remember to create Daily Real-World Exercises and use them regularly throughout the day.

	Trials to Teach the Concept of "Not"				
	Objects		**Adult's** Actions & Words	**ER***	**✔ if correct**
	Near Child	*Far from Child*			
1	3 buses cat		*"Which one is not a bus?"*	"This one is not a bus." (P)	
2	plane 3 cars		*"Which one is not a car?"*	"This one is not a car." (P)	
3	4 kids horse		*"Which one is not a kid?"*	"This one is not a kid." (P)	
4	3 trucks lady		*"Which one is not a truck?"*	"This one is not a truck." (P)	
5	bed 3 birds		*"Which one is not a bird?"*	"This one is not a bird." (P)	
6	3 frogs plane		*"Which one is not a frog?"*	"This one is not a frog." (P)	
7	4 kids chair		*"Which one is not a kid?"*	"This one is not a kid." (P)	
8	3 dogs man		*"Which one is not a dog?"*	"This one is not a dog." (P)	
9	boy 3 cats		*"Which one is not a cat?"*	"This one is not a cat." (P)	
10	4 kids horse		*"Which one is not a kid?"*	"This one is not a kid." (P)	

Level 18 Sample Daily Real-World Exercises

These examples show you how the new language forms taught in this level should be used in daily life.
You should also continue to use the forms taught in prior levels.

Setting	Adult's Actions & Words	Expected Response
Playground	pointing to some kids playing *"Which ones do not have a ball?"*	"These ones do not have a ball." (P)
Playground	pointing to baby *"A baby is here,* pointing to lady *and a lady is here."*	I/P
Playground	*"Which one does not walk?"*	"This one does not walk." (P)
Outdoors	pointing to bird *"A bird is here,* pointing to dog *and a dog is here."*	I/P
Outdoors	*"Which one does not fly?"*	"This one does not fly." (P)
Store	apples, pears, oranges, and bread in a cart *"Which one is not a fruit?"*	"This one is not a fruit." (P)
Store	*"What is it?"*	"It is bread."
Playroom	two dolls standing and two dolls lying down *"Some dolls are here. Which ones are not sitting?"*	"These ones are not eating." (P)
Playroom	*"What are they doing?"*	"They are standing."

	Objects		Adult's Actions & Words	ER*	✔ if correct			
	Near Child	**Far from Child**			**Lesson 2**	**Lesson 5**	**Lesson 8**	**Lesson 11**

Level 18 Lesson 2 (repeat, if needed, as Lessons 5, 8, & 11)

	Objects Near Child	Objects Far from Child	Adult's Actions & Words	ER*	Lesson 2	Lesson 5	Lesson 8	Lesson 11
1	3 ladies		*"Who are they?"*	"They are ladies."				
2	*same as above*		two ladies sitting and one lady standing *"Which one is not sitting?"*	"This one is not sitting." (P)				
3	*same as above*	3 boys	two boys jumping *"Some boys are jumping. Which one is not jumping?"*	"That one is not jumping." (P)				
4	3 planes	truck	pointing to planes *"Some planes are here,* pointing to trucks *and a truck is there."*	I/P				
5	*same as above*	*same as above*	*"Which one does not fly?"*	"That one does not fly." (P)				
6	*same as above*	*same as above*	*"These planes are not flying, but they are going to fly."*	I				
7	*same as above*	*same as above*	*"Make the planes fly, and then make the truck go."*	O/A				
8		3 frogs 2 birds	pointing to animals *"Some animals are there. Which ones are not frogs?"*	"Those ones are not frogs." (P)				
9		*same as above*	pointing to birds *"What are they?"*	"They are birds." (P)				
10		*same as above*	*"Birds have wings, but frogs do not have wings."*	I				
11	2 birds horse	*same as above*	pointing to near animals *"Some more animals are here. Which one does not have wings?"*	"This one does not have wings." (P)				
12	boy 2 girls	bed 2 chairs	pointing to furniture *"Some furniture is there. Which one is not a chair?"*	"That one is not a chair." (P)				
13	*same as above*	*same as above*	*"What is it?*	"It is a bed."				
14	*same as above*	*same as above*	pointing to boy *"This kid wants to rest. Make him rest on the bed."*	O/A				

Level 18 Lesson 2 (continued)							
	Objects		**Adult's Actions & Words**	**ER***	**✔ if correct**		
	Near Child	*Far from Child*			Lesson 2	Lesson 5	Lesson 8	Lesson 11
15	*same as above*	*same as above*	pointing to two girls *"These kids like to sit. Make them sit in the chairs."*	O/A				
16	Picture 15		pointing to picture *"Some animals are here. Which ones do not have legs?"''*	"These ones do not have legs." (P)				
17	*same as above*		*"Fish do not have legs, but other animals do."*	I				
18	*same as above*		*"Dogs have legs. Point to the legs on the dog."*	A				
19	*same as above*		*"Snakes do not have arms or legs."*	I				
20	*same as above*		*"Point to the snake."*	A				
21	Picture 24		pointing to ladybug *"This is a bug,* pointing to boy *and this is a boy."*	I/P				
22	*same as above*		*"Which one can fly?"*	"This one can fly." (P)				
23	*same as above*		*"And which one cannot fly?"*	"This one cannot fly." (P)				
24	*same as above*		*"The boy does not have wings. He cannot fly."*	I				
25	*same as above*		*"He has legs, and he can walk."*	I				
				Total Record the Total in the Level 1 Summary Table.				

*ER=Expected Response: I^{-Say} = Imitates (excluding Say); I = Imitates; P = Points; O/A = Correct action on correct object

NOTE: Remember to create Daily Real-World Exercises and use them regularly throughout the day.

Level 18 Lesson 3 (repeat, if needed, as Lessons 6, 9, & 12)								
	Objects		Adult's Actions & Words	ER*	✔ if correct			
	Near Child	Far from Child			Lesson 3	Lesson 6	Lesson 9	Lesson 12
1	boy	car	pointing to boy *"A boy is here,* pointing to car *and a car is there."*	I/P				
2	*same as above*	*same as above*	*"Which one cannot walk?"*	"That one cannot walk." (P)				
3	*same as above*	*same as above*	*"Make the boy walk, and then make the car go."*	O/A				
4	plane bird bus		*"Some of these can fly, but some cannot. Which one cannot fly?"*	"This one cannot fly." (P)				
5	*same as above*		pointing to bus *"What is this?"*	"This is a bus." (P)				
6	*same as above*		*"Buses cannot fly, but they can go. Make the bus go."*	O/A				
7		2 birds frog horse	*"Some of those animals are birds. Which ones are not birds?"*	"Those ones are not birds." (P)				
8		*same as above*	*"Give me the birds and then make the frog jump."*	O/A				
9	truck 2 cars	2 ladies	*"Where are the ladies?"*	"The ladies are there." (P)				
10	*same as above*	*same as above*	*"Ladies can walk. Make those ladies walk."*	O/A				
11	*same as above*	*same as above*	*"Which ones cannot walk?"*	"These ones cannot walk." (P)				
12	boy girl	2 dogs	girl lying down pointing to kids *"Some kids are here. Which one is resting?"*	"This one is resting." (P)				
13	*same as above*	*same as above*	girls jumping *"The girl was resting. Now what is she doing?"*	"Now she is jumping." OR "She is jumping now."				

341

	Objects		Adult's Actions & Words	ER*	✔ if correct			
	Near Child	Far from Child			Lesson 3	Lesson 6	Lesson 9	Lesson 12
	Level 18 Lesson 3 (continued)							
14	*same as above*	*same as above*	*"Which ones are not kids?"*	"Those ones are not kids." (P)				
15	*same as above*	*same as above*	*"Those are dogs. They like to run. Make them run."*	O/A				
16	Picture 18		*"Who are they?"*	"They are kids."				
17	*same as above*		*"What are they doing?"*	"They are eating."				
18	*same as above*		*"The kids have food to eat, but they do not have any drinks."*	I				
19	Picture 19		*"Some more kids are here."*	I				
20	*same as above*		*"Kids like to do many things."*	I				
21	*same as above*		*"They like to swim. They also like to run."*	I				
22	*same as above*		*"Which ones are swimming?"*	"These ones are swimming." (P)				
23	*same as above*		*"Which ones are not swimming?"*	"These ones are not swimming." (P)				
24	Picture 29		*"Some dogs are here. Which one is not running?"*	"This one is not running." (P)				
25	*same as above*		*"What is he doing?"*	"He is sitting."				
				Total Record the Total in the Level 1 Summary Table.				

*ER=Expected Response: I-Say = Imitates (excluding Say); I = Imitates; P = Points; O/A = Correct action on correct object

NOTE: Remember to create Daily Real-World Exercises and use them regularly throughout the day.

LEVEL 19

QUESTIONS THAT REFER
TO PAST ACTIONS

Overview

This level continues the development of higher level communication by teaching the child to handle questions about past actions.

What was ____ doing? What were ____ doing?

The items are presented in two different formats described below.

Format #1

The figure performs an action and the child is asked to name the action. The action then stops, and the child is asked to name the past action.

Examples:

Adult: (bird flying) "What is the bird doing?"
Child: "The bird is flying."
Adult: (flying stops and bird is removed from view) "What was the bird doing?"
Child: "The bird was flying."
Adult: (2 dogs running) "What are the dogs doing?"
Child: "The dogs are running."
Adult: (running stops and dogs are removed from view) "What were the dogs doing?"
Child: "The dogs were running."

Format #2

Once the child has mastered the format above, he or she moves on to a more difficult format. The figure once again performs an action and the child identifies it, but then the figure moves on to a different action and the child has to name the previous action. The child is, therefore, describing the past action while viewing a new action taking place. This demand is more difficult and its mastery represents a critical achievement. The child is now able to recognize that, despite what is going on, he or she can use memory to recall the action that was performed.

Examples:

> *Adult: (kid walking) "What is the kid doing?"*
> *Child: "The kid is walking."*
> *Adult: (kid jumping) "What was the kid doing?"*
> *Child: "The kid was walking."*
>
> *Adult: (2 ladies sitting) "What are the ladies doing?"*
> *Child: "The ladies are sitting."*
> *Adult: (ladies walking) "What were the ladies doing?"*
> *Child: "The ladies were sitting."*

Level 19 Summary Table

(to be filled in at the completion of each lesson)

Lesson	1	2	3	4	5	6	7	8	9	10	11	12
Date												
Total # Correct Responses												

*Criterion for Moving On: Once a child achieves 20 or more items correct on 3 out of 4 consecutive sessions, move on to the next level. If the child does not achieve criterion within the 12 sessions, take a break for 3-4 weeks, and then restart this level from Lesson 1.

NOTE: Continue to carry out the Real-World activities on a daily basis. Incorporate as much language as you can from the lessons into the outside world. The language should include material taught in previous levels as well as the new material taught in this level. Remember to use the samples provided as a guide to creating your own.

	Objects		Adult's Actions & Words	ER*	✔ if correct			
	Near Child	Far from Child			Lesson 1	Lesson 4	Lesson 7	Lesson 10
1	car		car going "What is the car doing?"	"The car is going."				
2	remove car		"What was the car doing?"	"The car was going."				
3		2 girls	girls walking "What are the girls doing?"	"The girls are walking."				
4		remove girls	"What were the girls doing?"	"The girls were walking."				
5			"Girls can run, but those girls were walking."	I				
6	3 buses plane		"Which one is not a bus?"	"This one is not a bus." (P)				
7	same as above		"What is it?"	"It is a plane."				
8	same as above		"Planes can fly. Make the plane fly."	O/A				
9	remove plane		"What was the plane doing?"	"The plane was flying."				
10	same as above		buses going "What are these buses doing?"	"These buses are going." (P)				
11	remove buses		"What were the buses doing?"	"The buses were going." (P)				
12			"The buses were going, and the plane was flying."	I				
13	2 planes	2 dogs	"Which ones cannot fly?"	"Those ones cannot fly." (P)				
14	same as above	same as above	pointing to dogs "What are those?"	"Those are dogs."				
15	same as above	same as above	dogs walking "What are those dogs doing?"	"Those dogs are walking."				

Level 19 Lesson 1 (repeat, if needed, as Lessons 4, 7, & 10)

345

	Objects		Adult's Actions & Words	ER*	✔ if correct			
	Near Child	Far from Child			Lesson 1	Lesson 4	Lesson 7	Lesson 10

	Near Child	Far from Child	Adult's Actions & Words	ER*	Lesson 1	Lesson 4	Lesson 7	Lesson 10
16	*same as above*	remove dogs	*"What were the dogs doing?"*	"The dogs were walking."				
17	*same as above*		*"Dogs can also run, but those dogs were not running."*	I				
18	*same as above*		*"They were walking."*	I				
19	Picture 3		*"Who are they?"*	"They are kids."				
20	*same as above*		*"Kids like to do many things. Some kids like to swing."*	I				
21	*same as above*		*"Point to the ones that are not swinging."*	A				
22	Picture 28		pointing to plants *"These are not kids, and these are not animals. What are they?"*	"They are plants."				
23	*same as above*		*"Some of the plants are trees. Which ones are trees?"*	"These ones are trees." (P)				
24	Picture 29		*"Two dogs are running. One dog is sitting."*	I				
25	*same as above*		*"Which one is sitting?"*	"This one is sitting." (P)				
			Total Record the Total in the Level 1 Summary Table.					

The table title spans: **Level 19 Lesson 1 (continued)**

*ER=Expected Response: I^{-Say} = Imitates (excluding Say); I = Imitates; P = Points; O/A = Correct action on correct object

NOTE: Remember to create Daily Real-World Exercises and use them regularly throughout the day.

346

Level 19 Sample Daily Real-World Exercises		
These examples show you how the new language forms taught in this level should be used in daily life. You should also continue to use the forms taught in prior levels.		
Setting	**Adult's Actions & Words**	**Expected Response**
Kitchen	Dad eating *"What is dad doing?"*	"Dad is eating."
Kitchen	Dad stops eating *"What was Dad doing?"*	"Dad was eating."
Home	Mom lying down *"What is Mom doing?"*	"Mom is resting."
Home	Mom walking *"What was Mom doing?"*	"Mom was resting."
Playground	pointing to a kid running *"What is that kid doing?"*	"That kid is running."
Playground	kid stops running *"What was that kid doing?"*	"That kid was running."
Playground	pointing to a lady sitting *"What is the lady doing?"*	"The lady is sitting."
Playground	lady stands up *"What was the lady doing?"*	"The lady was sitting."

Level 19 Lesson 2 (repeat, if needed, as Lessons 5, 8, & 11)								
Objects		Adult's Actions & Words	ER*	✔ if correct				
Near Child	Far from Child			Lesson 2	Lesson 5	Lesson 8	Lesson 11	
1		boy	*"Who is that?"*	"That is a boy."				
2		*same as above*	boy jumping *"What is he doing?"*	"He is jumping."				
3		remove boy	*"What was the boy doing?"*	"The boy was jumping."				
4	2 ladies	truck	*"Where are the ladies?"*	"The ladies are here." (P)				
5	*same as above*	*same as above*	ladies walking *"What are they doing?"*	"They are walking."				
6	*same as above*	*same as above*	ladies standing *"What were they doing?"*	"They were walking."				
7	3 planes	*same as above*	pointing to planes *"What are these?"*	"These are planes." (P)				
8	*same as above*	*same as above*	*"These planes are not flying now, but they are going to do that."*	I				
9	*same as above*	*same as above*	planes flying *"What are the planes doing?"*	"The planes are flying."				
10	*same as above*	*same as above*	planes not flying *"What were the planes doing?"*	"The planes were flying."				
11	*same as above*	*same as above*	pointing to truck *"What is that?"*	"That is a truck."				
12	*same as above*	*same as above*	truck going *"What is the truck doing?"*	"The truck is going."				
13	*same as above*	*same as above*	truck not going *"What was the truck doing?"*	"The truck was going."				
14	3 birds	cat	*"Which one does not fly?"*	"That one does not fly." (P)				
15	*same as above*	*same as above*	*"Cats do not fly, but they can walk. Make the cat walk."*	O/A				

Level 19 Lesson 2 (continued)								
	Objects		**Adult's Actions & Words**	**ER***	**✔ if correct**			
	Near Child	*Far from Child*			*Lesson 2*	*Lesson 5*	*Lesson 8*	*Lesson 11*
16	*same as above*	*same as above*	cat standing *"What was the cat doing?"*	"The cat was walking."				
17	Picture 15		pointing to picture *"Some animals are here."*	I/P				
17	*same as above*		*"Which ones are swimming?"*	"These ones are swimming." (P)				
18	*same as above*		*"Fish can swim, but they cannot run."*	I				
19	*same as above*		*"Point to an animal that can run."*	A				
20	Picture 12		point to boy *"Who is this?"*	"This is a boy/kid." (P)				
21	*same as above*		*"He has some animals. Point to an animal."*	A				
22	*same as above*		*"He also has some toys."*	I				
23	*same as above*		*"One of his toys is a plane. Where is the plane?"*	"The plane is here." (P)				
24	Picture 31		*"This girl is happy. She likes dogs."*	I				
25	*same as above*		*"What is the dog doing?"*	"The dog is sitting."				
			Total Record the Total in the Level 1 Summary Table.					

*ER=Expected Response: I^(-Say) = Imitates (excluding Say); I = Imitates; P = Points; O/A = Correct action on correct object

NOTE: Remember to create Daily Real-World Exercises and use them regularly throughout the day.

NOTE: If the child has mastered the new language form, do not model the items shaded in gray for Lessons 3 to 12.

Level 19 Lesson 3 (repeat, if needed, as Lessons 6, 9, & 12)								
Objects		**Adult's Actions & Words**	**ER***	**✔ if correct**				
Near Child	*Far from Child*			*Lesson 3*	*Lesson 6*	*Lesson 9*	*Lesson 12*	
1	truck 2 horses		*"Which ones are animals?"*	"These ones are animals." (P)				
2	*same as above*		*"Horses are animals. Trucks are not animals."*	I				
3	*same as above*		horses walking *"What are the horses doing?"*	"The horses are walking."				
4	*same as above*		horses jumping *"What were the horses doing?"*	"The horses were walking."				
5	*same as above*	2 girls	*"Where are the girls?"*	"The girls are there." (P)				
6	*same as above*	*same as above*	girls lying down *"What are the girls doing?"*	"The girls are resting."				
7	*same as above*	*same as above*	girls walking *"What were the girls doing?"*	"The girls were resting."				
8	*same as above*	*same as above*	girls still walking *"The girls were resting, but now they are walking."*	I				
9		man chair	pointing to man standing *"Who is that?"*	"That is a man." (P)				
10		*same as above*	*"What is he doing?"*	"He is standing."				
11		*same as above*	man sitting in chair *"What was he doing?"*	"He was standing."				
12		*same as above*	*"He was standing, but now he is sitting in a chair."*	I				
13		*same as above*	*"Make the man walk and then give me the man and the chair."*	O/A				
14	girl dog		*"A girl is here. She has a dog."*	I				

Level 19 Lesson 3 (continued)								
	Objects		**Adult's Actions & Words**	**ER***	**✔ if correct**			
	Near Child	*Far from Child*			Lesson 3	Lesson 6	Lesson 9	Lesson 12
15	*same as above*		*"Dogs can run. This dog is going to run."*	I				
16	*same as above*		dog running *"Now he is running."*	I				
17	*same as above*		dog standing *"What was he doing?"*	"He was running."				
18	Picture 10		*"Where is the house?"*	"The house is here." (P)				
19	*same as above*		*"Where is the sun?"*	"The sun is here." (P)				
20	*same as above*		*"Some kids like to rest under the sun. Point to the kid who is doing that."*	A				
21	Picture 28		pointing to plants *"These are not kids, and these are not animals. What are they?"*	"They are plants."				
22	*same as above*		*"Some of the plants are trees. Which ones are trees?"*	"These ones are trees." (P)				
23	Picture 29		pointing to dogs *"Two dogs are running. One dog is sitting."*	I				
24	*same as above*		*"Which one is sitting?"*	"This one is sitting." (P)				
25	*same as above*		*"Which ones are not sitting?"*	"These ones are not sitting." (P)				
				Total Record the Total in the Level 1 Summary Table.				

*ER=Expected Response: I^Say = Imitates (excluding Say); I = Imitates; P = Points; O/A = Correct action on correct object

NOTE: Remember to create Daily Real-World Exercises and use them regularly throughout the day.

LEVEL 20

QUESTIONS THAT REFER TO FUTURE ACTIONS

Overview

Continuing the expansion of language, the activities in this level enable the child to understand and respond to questions about future actions:

> *What is _____ going to do?*
> *What are _____ going to do?*

In contrast to the past, questions about the future are open-ended. Many actions could reasonably occur in the future. To help the child make the transition to this new form, the first few trials are set up so that you tell the child what future action will occur. This provides the child with a model for how to answer this question form

Example from the first few trials:
> *(Place a bird on the table in front of the child)*
> *Adult (in soft tone of voice): "What is the bird going to do?"*
> *Adult (in louder tone of voice): "The bird is going to fly."*
> *Adult (in soft tone of voice): "What is the bird going to do?"*
> *(Waits for the child to respond)*
> *Child: "The bird is going to fly."*
> *(This is always followed by the action taking place, either by having the adult or the child carry out the action).*
> *Adult: "Make the bird fly."*
> *(Child makes bird fly)*

The first few items may need to be repeated several times until the child learns this new form. You can help with the transition by using the techniques described above. (See Level 13 "Techniques to support the child's transition to questions" for more detail). In brief, this involves saying the question in a soft tone of voice, then immediately providing the answer in a louder voice. Then once again ask the question, but this time wait for the child to offer the answer.

Once the child has learned the new form, you no longer provide the correct answer. Instead, the child should come up with an appropriate answer. For example, if asked, *"What is the girl going to do?"* the child may say, *"The girl is going to run"* or *"The girl Is going to jump"* or *"The girl is going to walk,"* etc. Any reasonable response is fine. However, a response such as, *"The girl is going to fly"* would not be acceptable.

Example from later trial:
> *(Place a horse on the table in front of the child)*
> Adult: *"What is the horse going to do?"*
> Child: *"The horse is going to run."*
> Adult: *"Make the horse run."*
> *(Child makes horse run)*

Level 20 Summary Table
(to be filled in at the completion of each lesson)

Lesson	1	2	3	4	5	6	7	8	9	10	11	12
Date												
Total # Correct Responses												

*Criterion for Moving On: Once a child achieves 20 or more items correct on 3 out of 4 consecutive sessions, move on to the next level. If the child does not achieve criterion within the 12 sessions, take a break for 3-4 weeks, and then restart this level from Lesson 1.

NOTE: Continue to carry out the Real-World activities on a daily basis. Incorporate as much language as you can from the lessons into the outside world. The language should include material taught in previous levels as well as the new material taught in this level. Remember to use the samples provided as a guide to creating your own.

Level 20 Lesson 1 (repeat, if needed, as Lessons 4, 7, & 10)							
Objects		Adult's Actions & Words	ER*	✔ if correct			
Near Child	Far from Child			Lesson 1	Lesson 4	Lesson 7	Lesson 10
1	man		man standing soft *"What is the man going to do?"* loud *"The man is going to sit."* pause soft *"What is the man going to do?"*	"The man is going to sit."				
2	*same as above*		*"Make the man sit."*	O/A				
3	*same as above*		man sitting *"Now the man is sitting."*	I				
4	2 girls		girls sitting soft *"What are these girls going to do?"* loud *"These girls are going to walk."* pause soft *"What are these girls going to do?"*	"These girls are going to walk."				
5	*same as above*		*"Do that. Make the girls walk."*	O/A				
6	*same as above*		girls standing *"These girls were walking, but now they are not walking."*	I				
7	*same as above*		*"They are standing."*	I				
8	2 buses	cat	cat standing soft *"What is that cat going to do?"* loud *"That cat is going to run."* pause soft *"What is that cat going to do?"*	"That cat is going to run."				
9	*same as above*	*same as above*	*"Make the cat run, and then make the buses go."*	O/A				
10	*same as above*	*same as above*	*"What were the buses doing?"*	"The buses were going."				

Level 20 Lesson 1 (continued)								
	Objects		**Adult's Actions & Words**	**ER***	**✔ if correct**			
	Near Child	*Far from Child*			*Lesson 1*	*Lesson 4*	*Lesson 7*	*Lesson 10*
11	2 planes	2 dogs	*"Which ones are not dogs?"*	"These ones are not dogs." (P)				
12	*same as above*	*same as above*	pointing to planes *"What are these?"*	"These are planes." (P)				
13	*same as above*	*same as above*	planes at rest soft *"What are the planes going to do?"* loud *"The planes are going to fly."* pause soft *"What are the planes going to do?"*	"The planes are going to fly."				
14	*same as above*	*same as above*	planes flying *"Now the planes are flying."*	I				
15	*same as above*	*same as above*	planes not flying *"These planes did fly, but now they are not flying."*	I				
16	*same as above*	*same as above*	dogs jumping *"What are those dogs doing?"*	"Those dogs are jumping."				
17	*same as above*	*same as above*	dogs walking *"What were those dogs doing?"*	"Those dogs were jumping."				
18	Picture 32		pointing to kids *"Some kids are here."*	I/P				
19	*same as above*		soft *"What are these kids going to do?"* loud *"These kids are going to swim."* pause soft *"What are these kids going to do?"*	"These kids are going to swim."				
20	Picture 2		*"Now the kids are swimming."*	I				
21	*same as above*		*"They are happy. They like to swim."*	I				

Level 20 Lesson 1 (continued)								
	Objects		Adult's Actions & Words	ER*	✔ if correct			
	Near Child	*Far from Child*			*Lesson 1*	*Lesson 4*	*Lesson 7*	*Lesson 10*
22	Picture 4		***"These are some dogs. They have houses."***	I				
23	*same as above*		***"The dogs are sitting in the houses."***	I				
24	*same as above*		***"The dogs can run, but they are not running now."***	I				
25	Picture 33		***"Now these dogs are running."***	I				
Total Record the Total in the Level 1 Summary Table.								

*ER=Expected Response: I^{-Say} = Imitates (excluding Say); I = Imitates; P = Points; O/A = Correct action on correct object

NOTE: Remember to create Daily Real-World Exercises and use them regularly throughout the day.

Setting	Adult's Actions & Words	Expected Response
Home	Dad standing near a chair soft *"What is Dad going to do?"* loud *"Dad is going to sit."* pause soft *"What is Dad going to do?"*	"Dad is going to sit."
Home	Dad sitting *"Now Dad is sitting."*	I
Restaurant	pointing to a table nearby where a waiter has brought food but a child has not yet started eating it soft *"What is that kid going to do?"* loud *"That kid is going to eat."* pause soft *"What is that kid going to do?"*	"That kid is going to eat."
Restaurant	after boy starts eating *"Now he is eating."*	I
Playground	Mom standing soft *"What is Mom going to do?"* loud *"Mom is going to swing."* pause soft *"What is Mom going to do?"*	"Mom is going to swing."
Playground	Mom swinging *"Now Mom is swinging."*	I
Playroom	pointing to a toy doll *"What is that doll going to do?"*	"That doll is going to ____." *(accept any reasonable response)*
Playroom	*"Do that. Make the doll ____."* *(use child's response from previous item)*	O/A

Level 20 Sample Daily Real-World Exercises

These examples show you how the new language forms taught in this level should be used in daily life. You should also continue to use the forms taught in prior levels.

Level 20 Lesson 2 (repeat, if needed, as Lessons 5, 8, & 11)							
Objects		Adult's Actions & Words	ER*	✔ if correct			
Near Child	Far from Child			Lesson 2	Lesson 5	Lesson 8	Lesson 11
1	lady		lady sitting "What is the lady going to do?"	"The lady is going to ____." (accept any reasonable response)				
2	same as above		"Do that. Make the lady____." (use child's response from previous item)	O/A				
3		2 boys	boys standing "What are the boys going to do?"	"The boys are going to ____." (accept any reasonable response)				
4		same as above	"Do that. Make the boys ____." (use child's response from previous item)	O/A				
5	2 cars		"What are these?"	"These are cars."				
6	same as above		cars going "What are the cars doing?"	"The cars are going."				
7	same as above		cars not going "What were the cars doing?"	"The cars were going."				
8	same as above	2 horses	"Where are the horses?"	"The horses are there." (P)				
9	same as above	same as above	"Horses are animals. Animals eat and drink."	I				
10	same as above	same as above	"Cars are not animals. They do not eat and drink."	I				
11	bird 3 frogs		"Which one is not a frog?"	"This one is not a frog." (P)				
12	same as above		"What is it?"	"It is a bird."				
13	same as above		"Birds can fly. Make this bird fly."	O/A				
14	same as above		bird not flying "The bird did fly, but now it is resting."	I				

	Objects		Adult's Actions & Words	ER*	✔ if correct			
	Near Child	Far from Child			Lesson 2	Lesson 5	Lesson 8	Lesson 11
			Level 20 Lesson 2 (continued)					
15	*same as above*		*"Which ones do not fly?"*	"These ones do not fly." (P)				
16	*same as above*		*"Frogs do not fly, but they can jump. Make them jump."*	O/A				
17	Picture 8		*"Some babies are here. They are sitting"*	I				
18	*same as above*		*"These babies are not eating, but they are going to eat."*	I				
19	*same as above*		*"What are the babies going to do?"*	"The babies are going to eat."				
20	Picture 20		*"Now they are eating."*	I				
21	Picture 11		pointing to cat *"A cat is here. Cats can play and cats can sleep."*	I/P				
22	*same as above*		*"This cat is playing, but it is going to stop."*	I				
23	turn picture over so cat is not in view		pointing to the picture that has been turned over *"What was this cat doing?"*	"This cat was playing."				
24	Picture 9		*"This cat is sleeping."*	I				
25	*same as above*		*"Like other cats, this cat likes to sleep."*	I				
			Total Record the Total in the Level 1 Summary Table.					

*ER=Expected Response: I[-Say] = Imitates (excluding Say); I = Imitates; P = Points; O/A = Correct action on correct object

NOTE: Remember to create Daily Real-World Exercises and use them regularly throughout the day.

Level 20 Lesson 3 (repeat, if needed, as Lessons 6, 9, & 12)							
	Objects		**Adult's Actions & Words**	**ER***	**✔ if correct**		
	Near Child	*Far from Child*			*Lesson 3*	*Lesson 6*	*Lesson 9*	*Lesson 12*
1	frog		*"What is this frog going to do?"*	"This frog is going to ____." *(accept any reasonable response)*				
2	*same as above*		*"Do that. Make the frog____."* *(use child's response from previous item)*	O/A				
3	2 kids		kids standing *"What are these kids going to do?"*	"These kids are going to ____." *(accept any reasonable response)*				
4	*same as above*		*"Do that. Make these kids ____."* *(use child's response from previous item)*	O/A				
5	2 cats	plane	*"Where is the plane?"*	"The plane is there." (P)				
6	*same as above*	*same as above*	*"Many planes fly, but this plane is not flying."*	I				
7	*same as above*	*same as above*	*"Which ones have legs?"*	"These ones have legs." (P)				
8	*same as above*	*same as above*	*"Cats have legs, and they can run."*	I				
9	*same as above*	*same as above*	*"What are these cats going to do?"*	"These cats are going to ____." *(accept any reasonable response)*				
10	*same as above*	*same as above*	*"Do that. Make the cats____."* *(use child's response from previous item)*	O/A				
11	2 buses	2 dogs horse	*"Which ones are not animals?"*	"These ones are not animals." (P)				
12	*same as above*	*same as above*	*"Where are the animals?"*	"The animals are there." (P)				
13	*same as above*	*same as above*	*"Dogs are animals, and horses are animals."*	I				

361

Level 20 Lesson 3 (continued)							
Objects		**Adult's Actions & Words**	**ER***	**✔ if correct**			
Near Child	*Far from Child*			*Lesson 3*	*Lesson 6*	*Lesson 9*	*Lesson 12*
14	*same as above*	*same as above*	horse running *"What is the horse doing?"*	"The horse is running."				
15	*same as above*	*same as above*	horse standing *"What was the horse doing?"*	"The horse was running."				
16	Picture 5		pointing to bears *"Some bears are here."*	I/P				
17	*same as above*		*"These bears want to drink, and they are going to drink."*	I				
18	*same as above*		*"What are these bears going to do?"*	"These bears are going to drink."				
19	Picture 6		*"Now they are drinking."*	I				
20	Picture 29		pointing to dogs *"What are these?"*	"These are dogs." (P)				
21	*same as above*		pointing to running dogs *"These dogs are running. Soon they are going to rest."*	I				
22	Picture 4		*"Now they are resting."*	I				
23	Picture 15		*"Some animals are here. One of them can fly. Which one can fly?"*	"This one can fly." (P)				
24	*same as above*		*"This bird can fly, but it cannot swim."*	I				
25	*same as above*		*"Point to an animal that can swim."*	A				
			Total Record the Total in the Level 1 Summary Table.					

*ER=Expected Response: I-Say = Imitates (excluding Say); I = Imitates; P = Points; O/A = Correct action on correct object

NOTE: Remember to create Daily Real-World Exercises and use them regularly throughout the day.

LEVEL 21
YES/NO QUESTIONS

Overview

In this level the child learns to respond to Yes/No questions. These questions cover a wide range of language groupings including the following:

- *Objects or Persons:* *"Is this a cat?" "Are these kids?"*
- *Actions:* *"Is the boy running?" "Were the ladies sitting?"*
- *Abilities:* *"Can birds fly?" "Do frogs jump?"*
- *Possession:* *"Does the man have a dog?" "Do cars have wheels?"*

Though *yes/no* questions appear simple, they are, in fact, more complex than the questions taught up to this point. With all previous questions, the answer was a single form that mirrored the question. *Yes/no* is the first form where this is not the case. The answer to the question is open to two possibilities:

- *Yes* – where the answer does mirror the question (e.g., pointing to a cat and asking, "Is this a cat?" The appropriate answer is, "Yes, this is a cat.")
- *No* – where the answer does not simply mirror the question but rather contains the word "not" (e.g., pointing to a cat and asking, "Is this a dog?" The appropriate answer is, "No, this is not a dog.")

This step up in complexity may lead to some difficulty for the child. For any difficulties that arise, say the question in a soft voice; then immediately provide the answer in a louder voice (so that you are modeling the full sequence). Then ask the question, but this time wait for the child to answer. Refer back to the techniques described in Level 13 for additional guidance.

If the child says *"yes"* and does not complete the sentence, then model the full response for the child (emphasizing the words that the child did not say) and then repeat the item from the beginning.

Example:
> *Adult: (pointing to a plane) "Is this a plane?"*
> *Child: "Yes."*

*Adult: (pointing to a plane) "Is this a plane? Yes, **this is a plane**."*
Adult: Is this a plane?
Child: "Yes, this is a plane."

Some of the responses may seem unusual since they differ from typical conversation. For example, in everyday talk, a question like "Do kids eat?" can be answered in a variety of ways (e.g., "Yes," or "Yes, they do" or "Yes, kids eat.") In this program, there is a single response. It is "Yes, kids do eat."

The variability of natural language can be overwhelming for the children. By keeping the pattern consistent, the child has a clear, reliable tool that empowers them. It sends the message that they can crack the code of language.

Level 21 Summary Table

(to be filled in at the completion of each lesson)

Lesson	1	2	3	4	5	6	7	8	9	10	11	12
Date												
Total # Correct Responses												

*Criterion for Moving On: Once a child achieves 20 or more items correct on 3 out of 4 consecutive sessions, move on to the next level. If the child does not achieve criterion within the 12 sessions, take a break for 3-4 weeks, and then restart this level from Lesson 1.

NOTE: Continue to carry out the Real-World activities on a daily basis. Incorporate as much language as you can from the lessons into the outside world. The language should include material taught in previous levels as well as the new material taught in this level. Remember to use the samples provided as a guide to creating your own.

Level 21 Lesson 1 (repeat, if needed, as Lessons 4, 7, & 10)							
Objects		**Adult's Actions & Words**	**ER***	**✔ if correct**			
Near Child	*Far from Child*			*Lesson 1*	*Lesson 4*	*Lesson 7*	*Lesson 10*
1 man		*"Is this a man?"*	"Yes, this is a man."				
2 *same as above*		man standing *"What is he doing?"*	"He is standing."				
3 dog		*"Is this a dog?"*	"Yes, this is a dog."				
4 *same as above*		*"Dogs can walk. Make this dog walk."*	O/A				
5	bird	*"Is that a bird?"*	"Yes, that is a bird."				
6	*same as above*	bird flying *"Is the bird flying?"*	"Yes, the bird is flying."				
7	*same as above*	bird not flying *"What was the bird doing?"*	"The bird was flying."				
8	car	*"Is that a plane?"*	"No, that is not a plane."				
9	*same as above*	*"What is it?"*	"It is a car."				
10	*same as above*	car going *"What is the car doing?"*	"The car is going."				
11 3 planes	horse	*"Which one cannot fly?"*	"That one cannot fly." (P)				
12 *same as above*	*same as above*	*"What is that?"*	"That is a horse."				
13 *same as above*	*same as above*	horse walking *"Is the horse jumping?"*	"No, the horse is not jumping."				
14 *same as above*	*same as above*	horse still walking *"What is it doing?"*	"It is walking."				
15 *same as above*	*same as above*	horse not walking *"The horse was walking. Now it is going to jump."*	I				

Level 21 Lesson 1 (continued)								
	Objects		**Adult's Actions & Words**	**ER***	**✔ if correct**			
	Near Child	*Far from Child*			*Lesson 1*	*Lesson 4*	*Lesson 7*	*Lesson 10*
16	*same as above*	*same as above*	*"What is the horse going to do?"*	"The horse is going to jump."				
17	*same as above*	*same as above*	*"Do that. Make the horse jump."*	O/A				
18	3 frogs	boy dog	*"Where are the frogs?"*	"The frogs are here." (P)				
19	*same as above*	*same as above*	*"What are the frogs going to do?"*	"The frogs are going to _____." *(accept any reasonable response)*				
20	*same as above*	*same as above*	*"Do that. Make the frogs _____." (use child's response from previous item)*	O/A				
21	Picture 12		pointing to boy *"Is this a boy?"*	"Yes, this is a boy." (P)				
22	*same as above*		*"This boy has many animals, but he does not have a snake."*	I				
23	Picture 11		pointing to cat *"Is this a dog?"*	"No, this is not a dog." (P)				
24	*same as above*		*"What is it?"*	"It is a cat."				
25	*same as above*		*"The cat has some food, but it is not eating."*	I				
				Total Record the Total in the Level 1 Summary Table.				

*ER=Expected Response: I^{-Say} = Imitates (excluding Say); I = Imitates; P = Points; O/A = Correct action on correct object

NOTE: Remember to create Daily Real-World Exercises and use them regularly throughout the day.

Level 21 Sample Daily Real-World Exercises

These examples show you how the new language forms taught in this level should be used in daily life.
You should also continue to use the forms taught in prior levels.

Setting	Adult's Actions & Words	Expected Response
Home	Dad not reading *"Is Dad reading?"*	"No, Dad is not reading."
Restaurant	pointing to waitress *"Is this lady eating?"*	"No, this lady is not eating."
Restaurant	pointing to waitress *"Is she standing?"*	"Yes, she is standing."
Restaurant	pointing to a man eating *"Does that man have food?"*	"Yes, that man has food."
Outdoors	pointing to some ants *"Are these bugs?"*	"Yes, these are bugs."
Outdoors	*"Do these bugs crawl?"*	"Yes, these bugs do crawl."
Playroom	Mom drawing a picture *"Is Mom drawing?"*	"Yes, Mom is drawing."
Playroom	*"Can kids draw?"*	"Yes, kids can draw."
Kitchen	pointing to some forks *"Are these spoons?"*	"No, these are not spoons."

Level 21 Lesson 2 (repeat, if needed, as Lessons 5, 8, & 11)								
	Objects		Adult's Actions & Words	ER*	✔ if correct			
	Near Child	*Far from Child*			Lesson 2	Lesson 5	Lesson 8	Lesson 11
1	2 birds	horse	pointing to horse *"Is that a horse?"*	"Yes, that is a horse." (P)				
2	*same as above*	*same as above*	*"Can that horse fly?"*	"No, that horse cannot fly."				
3	*same as above*	*same as above*	soft *"What can the horse do?"* loud *"The horse can walk."* pause soft *"What can the horse do?"*	"The horse can walk."				
4	*same as above*	*same as above*	*"Make the horse walk."*	O/A				
5	*same as above*	*same as above*	pointing to birds *"What are these?"*	"These are birds." (P)				
6	*same as above*	*same as above*	*"Can they fly?"*	"Yes, they can fly."				
7	*same as above*	*same as above*	*"Do that. Make them fly."*	O/A				
8	*same as above*	*same as above*	*"What were the birds doing?"*	"The birds were flying."				
9	chair table	dog 2 cats frog	pointing to furniture *"Are these animals?"*	"No, these are not animals." (P)				
10	*same as above*	*same as above*	*"Where are the animals?"*	"The animals are there." (P)				
11	*same as above*	*same as above*	*"Which ones are cats?"*	"Those one are cats." (P)				
12	*same as above*	*same as above*	cats lying down *"Are the cats running?"*	"No, the cats are not running."				
13	*same as above*	*same as above*	cats lying down *"What are they doing?"*	"They are resting."				
14	2 girls		girls jumping *"Are these girls resting?"*	"No, these girls are not resting."				
15	*same as above*		girls still jumping *"What are they doing?"*	"They are jumping."				

Level 21 Lesson 2 (continued)								
	Objects		**Adult's Actions & Words**	**ER***	**✔ if correct**			
	Near Child	*Far from Child*			*Lesson 2*	*Lesson 5*	*Lesson 8*	*Lesson 11*
16	*same as above*		girls sitting *"What were they doing?"*	"They were jumping."				
17	*same as above*		*"Now what are they going to do?"*	"They are going to ____." *(accept any reasonable response)*				
18	*same as above*	*same as above*	*"Do that. Make these girls ____."* *(use child's response from previous item)*	O/A				
19	Picture 16		pointing to cats *"Are these turtles?"*	"No, these are not turtles."				
20	*same as above*		*"What are they?"*	"They are cats."				
21	*same as above*		*"Do the cats have a ball?"*	"Yes, the cats do have a ball."				
22	*same as above*		*"The cats have a ball, and they are playing with it."*	I				
23	Picture 19		*"Some of these kids are swimming. Which ones are swimming?"*	"These ones are swimming." (P)				
24	*same as above*		*"Which ones are not swimming?"*	"These ones are not swimming." (P)				
25	*same as above*		*"What are they doing?"*	"They are running."				
				Total Record the Total in the Level 1 Summary Table.				

*ER=Expected Response: I^{Say} = Imitates (excluding Say); I = Imitates; P = Points; O/A = Correct action on correct object

NOTE: Remember to create Daily Real-World Exercises and use them regularly throughout the day.

NOTE: If the child has mastered the new language form, do not model the items shaded in gray for Lessons 3 to 12.

	Objects		Adult's Actions & Words	ER*	✔ if correct			
	Near Child	*Far from Child*			*Lesson 3*	*Lesson 6*	*Lesson 9*	*Lesson 12*
			Level 21 Lesson 3 (repeat, if needed, as Lessons 6, 9, & 12)					
1	Picture 7		*"Does the girl have a kite?"*	"Yes, the girl has a kite."				
2	*same as above*		*"Does the boy have a kite?"*	"No, the boy does not have a kite."				
3	*same as above*		*"The boy wants a kite, but he does not have one."*	I				
4	Picture 10		pointing to house *"Is this a house?"*	"Yes, this is a house." (P)				
5	*same as above*		pointing to the boy *"A boy is here. What is he doing?"*	"He is resting."				
6	Picture 28		pointing to trees *"Are those animals?"*	"No, those are not animals." (P)				
7	*same as above*		*"What are those?"*	"Those are trees."				
8	*same as above*		*"Can trees walk?"*	"No, trees cannot walk."				
9	*same as above*		*"Many animals can walk, but trees cannot do that."*	I				
10	Picture 31		*"This dog is sitting, but he wants to play with the girl."*	I				
11	*same as above*		*"Can girls play?"*	"Yes, girls can play."				
12	2 frogs 3 cats	2 kids	pointing to kids *"Are they animals?"*	"No, they are not animals." (P)				
13	*same as above*	*same as above*	*"What are they?"*	"They are kids."				
14	*same as above*	*same as above*	*"Can kids play?"*	"Yes, kids can play.				

Level 21 Lesson 3 (continued)								
	Objects		Adult's Actions & Words	ER*	✔ if correct			
	Near Child	Far from Child			Lesson 3	Lesson 6	Lesson 9	Lesson 12
15	*same as above*	*same as above*	kids lying down *"Are those kids playing?*	"No, those kids are not playing."				
16	*same as above*	*same as above*	kids still lying down *"What are they doing?"*	"They are resting."				
17	*same as above*	*same as above*	frogs jumping *"Frogs can rest, but these frogs are not doing that."*	I				
18	*same as above*	*same as above*	jumping stops *"What were these frogs doing?"*	"These frogs were jumping."				
19	3 buses		*"What are these?"*	"These are buses."				
20	*same as above*		*"Do buses have wheels?"*	"Yes, buses have wheels."				
21	*same as above*		*"Buses can go to many places."*	I				
22	*same as above*		pointing to one bus *"Make this bus go."*	O/A				
23	2 planes	3 birds	*"Do planes have wings?"*	"Yes, planes do have wings."				
24	*same as above*	*same as above*	*"Planes have wings, and birds also have them."*	I				
25	*same as above*	*same as above*	*"Make one plane fly, and then make one bird fly."*	O/A				
				Total Record the Total in the Level 1 Summary Table.				

*ER=Expected Response: I^Say = Imitates (excluding Say); I = Imitates; P = Points; O/A = Correct action on correct object

NOTE: Remember to create Daily Real-World Exercises and use them regularly throughout the day.

LEVEL 22

INTRODUCING "YOU" AND "I"

Overview

It is well known that the pronouns "*I*" (first person) and "*you*" (second person) pose particular difficulties for children on the spectrum. These seemingly simple words are far from simple. In contrast to names such as "*mommy*" and "*daddy*" that stay consistent, "*you*" and "*I*" steadily change. When you are speaking to someone, you call that someone "*you*," but then when that person responds, he (she) refers to himself (herself) as "*I*."

Discussions involving third person pronouns (*he, she, it, they*) do not present these difficulties. If you pose a question about a third person (e.g., "What is he doing?) the person you are speaking to can use that same pronoun in offering a response (e.g., "He is sitting"). The greater simplicity of third person pronouns is a major factor in our having used them as the basis for the tasks in all the levels until now.

The ability to use first and second person pronouns effectively rests with an understanding of what is called "role relationships" — that is, understanding the role you have relative to another person. For example, even though you refer to yourself as "*I*," you know that you are the same person that others refer to as "*you*." This is an area of subtle social understanding, and problems in this realm are central to ASD. That is why it poses such difficulty for the children.

In this level, the teaching will convey some selected aspects of using first and second person pronouns. The most common demands that children face with these forms involve "*you*" questions that require "*I*" responses (e.g., "What are you going to do?" "I am going to play."). It is less common and also less important for them to face "*I*" questions that demand "*you*" responses (e.g., "What am I doing?" "You are eating.") Accordingly, this level will focus on teaching the child to use "*I*" in response to questions containing "*you*." This eases the complexity that the children confront and thereby gives them a smoother entry into this important realm of exchange.

The following question forms are taught in this level:

- Identifying an Action: *What are you doing? Are you _____ing? What were you doing? Were you _____ing? What did you do? Did you _____?*

- ◻ <u>Identifying Possession:</u> *What do you have? Do you have ____? What did you have? Did you have ____? What are you holding? Are you holding ____?*
- ◻ <u>Identifying Ability:</u> *Can you ____?*

As with the Yes/No question that imposed greater variability than the other question forms, the child may show some difficulty at first with the "you − I" questions. If this happens, say the question in a soft voice; then immediately provide the answer in a louder voice (so that you are modeling the full sequence). Then ask the question, but this time wait for the child to answer. Refer back to the techniques described in Level 13 for additional guidance.

Level 22 Summary Table
(to be filled in at the completion of each lesson)

Lesson	1	2	3	4	5	6	7	8	9	10	11	12
Date												
Total # Correct Responses												

*Criterion for Moving On: Once a child achieves 20 or more items correct on 3 out of 4 consecutive sessions, move on to the next level. If the child does not achieve criterion within the 12 sessions, take a break for 3-4 weeks, and then restart this level from Lesson 1.

NOTE: Continue to carry out the Real-World activities on a daily basis. Incorporate as much language as you can from the lessons into the outside world. The language should include material taught in previous levels as well as the new material taught in this level. Remember to use the samples provided as a guide to creating your own.

Level 22 Lesson 1 (repeat, if needed, as Lessons 4, 7, & 10)								
Objects		Adult's Actions & Words	ER*	✔ if correct				
Near Child	Far from Child			Lesson 1	Lesson 4	Lesson 7	Lesson 10	
1			*"Stand up."*	A				
2			*"What are you doing?"*	"I am standing."				
3			*"Now sit down."*	A				
4			*"Now what are you doing?"*	"Now I am sitting." OR "I am sitting now."				
5	dog		*"Pick up the dog and hold it in your hand."*	O/A				
6	same as above (child holding dog in hand)		*"What are you holding?"*	"I am holding a/the dog."				
7	same as above		*"Is the dog walking?"*	"No, the dog is not walking."				
8	same as above		*"Make the dog walk."*	O/A				
9	same as above		*"What was the dog doing?"*	"The dog was walking."				
10	3 kids	2 cats horse bird	*"Where are the animals?"*	"The animals are there."(P)				
11	same as above	same as above	*"Many animals are there. One of them can fly."*	I				
12	same as above	same as above	*"Which one can fly?"*	"That one can fly." (P)				
13	same as above	same as above	pointing to kids *"Some kids are here. Can they fly?"*	"No, they cannot fly."				
14	same as above	same as above	*"Kids cannot fly, but they can do many other things."*	I				
15	same as above	same as above	pointing to one kid sitting *"What is this kid doing?"*	"This kid is sitting." (P)				

375

	Objects		Adult's Actions & Words	ER*	✔ if correct			
	Near Child	**Far from Child**			**Lesson 1**	**Lesson 4**	**Lesson 7**	**Lesson 10**
16	*same as above*	*same as above*	pointing to two kids standing **"What are these kids doing?"**	"These kids are standing." (P)				
17	*same as above*	*same as above*	pointing to two kids standing **"What are these kids going to do?"**	"These kids are going to ____." *accept any reasonable response*				
18	*same as above*	*same as above*	**"Do that. Make the kids ____."** *use response from previous item*	O/A				
19	Picture 24		pointing to ladybug **"This is a ladybug,** pointing to boy **and this is a boy."**	I/P				
20	*same as above*		**"Which one can fly?"**	"This one can fly." (P)				
21	*same as above*		**"Which one cannot fly?"**	"This one cannot fly." (P)				
22	*same as above*		**"The boy does not have wings. He cannot fly."**	I				
23	*same as above*		**"He has legs, and he can walk."**	I				
24	Picture 29		**"Some dogs are here. Which one is not running?"**	"This one is not running." (P)				
25	*same as above*		**"What is he doing?"**	"He is sitting."				
				Total Record the Total in the Level 1 Summary Table.				

Level 22 Lesson 1 (continued)

*ER=Expected Response: I-Say = Imitates (excluding Say); I = Imitates; P = Points; O/A = Correct action on correct object

NOTE: Remember to create Daily Real-World Exercises and use them regularly throughout the day.

Level 22 Sample Daily Real-World Exercises

These examples show you how the new language forms taught in this level should be used in daily life. You should also continue to use the forms taught in prior levels.

Setting	Adult's Actions & Words	Expected Response
Kitchen	child sitting at the table eating *"What are you doing?"*	"I am eating."
Kitchen	*"Are you also sitting?"*	"Yes, I am also sitting."
Outdoors	child walking *"What are you doing?"*	"I am walking."
Playground	child holding ball *"Do you have a ball?"*	"Yes, I do have a ball."
Restaurant	*"Do you want to eat?"*	"Yes, I do want to eat."
Outdoors	Offering child a ball *"Can you throw the ball?"*	"Yes, I can throw the ball." OR "No, I cannot throw the ball."

Level 22 Lesson 2 (repeat, if needed, as Lessons 5, 8, & 11)								
	Objects		Adult's Actions & Words	ER*	✔ if correct			
	Near Child	Far from Child			Lesson 2	Lesson 5	Lesson 8	Lesson 11
1		2 frogs 2 cats	*"Can you point?"*	"Yes, I can point."				
2		*same as above*	*"Point to the frogs."*	A				
3		*same as above*	*"Frogs do not walk. They jump. Make them jump."*	O/A				
4			*"Can you stand?"*	"Yes, I can stand."				
5			*"Do that. Stand up."*	A				
6			*"Are you sitting now?"*	"No, I am not sitting now." OR "No, now I am not sitting."				
7			*"What are you doing now?"*	"Now I am standing." OR "I am standing now."				
8			*"Now sit down again."*	A				
9			*"What were you doing?"*	"I was standing."				
10	2 dogs bird		pointing to animals *"Pick up these animals and keep them in your hands."*	O/A				
11	*same as above (child holding animals)*		*"Are you holding some animals?"*	"Yes, I am holding some animals."				
12	*same as above*		*"Give me the dogs and then make the bird fly."*	O/A				
13			*"Did you have some dogs?"*	"Yes, I did have some dogs."				
14	3 kids		*"Kids can do many things. Some kids can swim. Can you swim?"*	"Yes, I can swim." OR "No, I cannot swim."				
15	*same as above*		*"Some kids like to run. Are these kids running?"*	"No, these kids are not running."				

Level 22 Lesson 2 (continued)								
	Objects		**Adult's Actions & Words**	**ER***	**✔ if correct**			
	Near Child	*Far from Child*			Lesson 2	Lesson 5	Lesson 8	Lesson 11
16	*same as above*		kids lying down *"What are they doing?"*	"They are resting."				
17	*same as above*		kids standing *"What were they doing?"*	"They were resting."				
18	2 cars 3 planes		pointing to cars *"Some cars are here, and* pointing to planes *some planes are here."*	I/P				
19	*same as above*		*"Pick up a plane and hold it in your hand."*	A				
20	*same as above*		*"What do you have?"*	"I have a plane."				
21	*same as above*		*"Do you have a bus?"*	"No, I do not have a bus."				
22	chair boy		pointing to chair *"A chair is here, but the boy is not sitting on it."*	I/P				
23	(remove chair & boy)		pointing to the place the chair was *"A chair was here. Was the boy sitting on it?"*	"No, the boy was not sitting on it."				
24			*"Are you sitting?"*	"Yes, I am sitting."				
25			*"What are you sitting on?"*	"I am sitting on a chair."				
			Total Record the Total in the Level 1 Summary Table.					

*ER=Expected Response: I⁻ˢᵃʸ = Imitates (excluding Say); I = Imitates; P = Points; O/A = Correct action on correct object

NOTE: Remember to create Daily Real-World Exercises and use them regularly throughout the day.

Level 22 Lesson 3 (repeat, if needed, as Lessons 6, 9, & 12)								
	Objects		Adult's Actions & Words	ER*	✔ if correct			
	Near Child	Far from Child			Lesson 3	Lesson 6	Lesson 9	Lesson 12
1		bird 2 cars kid	*"Pick up the bird and hold it in your hand."*	A				
2		*same as above* (child holding bird)	*"What are you holding?"*	"I am holding a/the bird."				
3		*same as above*	*"Give me the bird and then pick up a car."*	O/A				
4		*same as above* (child holding a car)	*"What are you holding now?"*	"Now I am holding a/the car." OR "I am holding a/the car now."				
5	plane		*"What is this?"*	"This is a plane."				
6	*same as above*		*"What is the plane going to do?"*	"The plane is going to ___." *(accept any reasonable response)*				
7	*same as above*		*"Do that. Make the plane ___."* (use child's response from previous item)	O/A				
8	frog		frog jumping *"What is this frog doing?"*	"This frog is jumping."				
9	(remove frog)		pointing to place the frog was *"A frog was here. What was it doing?"*	"It was jumping."				
10	*same as above*		*"Frogs can jump. Kids can also jump. Can you jump?"*	"Yes, I can jump."				
11	*same as above*		*"Do that. Stand up and jump."*	A				
12	*same as above*		*"Now sit back down."*	A				
13	*same as above*		*"Did you jump?"*	"Yes, I did jump."				
14	man truck		*"This man likes trucks."*	I				

	Objects		Adult's Actions & Words	ER*	✔ if correct			
	Near Child	**Far from Child**			**Lesson 3**	**Lesson 6**	**Lesson 9**	**Lesson 12**

Level 22 Lesson 3 (continued)

#	Near Child	Far from Child	Adult's Actions & Words	ER*	Lesson 3	Lesson 6	Lesson 9	Lesson 12
15	*same as above*		*"What does this man like?"*	"This man likes trucks."				
16	Picture 15		*"Some animals are here. One of them can fly. Which one can fly?"*	"This one can fly." (P)				
17	*same as above*		*"This bird can fly, but it cannot swim."*	I				
18	*same as above*		*"Point to an animal that can swim."*	A				
19	Picture 28		pointing to plants *"These are not kids, and these are not animals. What are they?"*	"They are plants."				
20	*same as above*		*"Some of the plants are trees. Which ones are trees?"*	"These ones are trees." (P)				
21	Picture 19		*"Some of these kids are swimming. Which ones are swimming?"*	"These ones are swimming." (P)				
22	*same as above*		*"Which ones are not swimming?"*	"These ones are not swimming." (P)				
23	*same as above*		*"What are they doing?"*	"They are running."				
24	2 dogs	horse	*"Where are the dogs?"*	"The dogs are here." (P)				
25	*same as above*	*same as above*	dogs jumping *"What are the dogs doing?"*	"The dogs are jumping."				
			Total Record the Total in the Level 1 Summary Table.					

*ER=Expected Response: I^{-Say} = Imitates (excluding Say); I = Imitates; P = Points; O/A = Correct action on correct object

NOTE: Remember to create Daily Real-World Exercises and use them regularly throughout the day.

LEVEL 23

QUESTIONS ABOUT "WHAT HAS BEEN SAID"

Overview

At this point, the program makes another important advance. So far, all of the comments and questions have dealt with objects and experiences in the world that the child observed. This is reflected in exchanges where the child sees a car moving and is asked, *"What is the car doing?"* We refer to this type of language as *Language About Perception* (LAP).

Many comments and questions in everyday life fall into a different category. They concern information that has been put forth in language alone, such as saying to a child *"We are going to the store,"* and then asking, *"Where are we going?"* We refer to this type of language as *Language about Language* (LAL).

LAL is vital to effective language use. For example, it is the foundation of stories—where the information comes via sentences steadily building one upon the other. It is also essential to understanding conversations where, as with stories, information is provided verbally and not through direct experience. The ability to understand stories and conversations is vital for expanding a child's communication skills, but these are only accessible to the child who has a foundation in LAL.

This level introduces questions involving LAL. Objects and pictures are still used, but they do not represent the full set of information that a child needs for a correct response. Instead, some of the information is provided through language that the child must then use to formulate an effective response.

Examples:
> *(Two frogs are in view)*
> *Adult: (pointing) "This frog can jump, but that one cannot jump. Which one can jump?"*
> *Child: (pointing) "This one can jump."*

(Two ladies and two kids are in view)
Adult: "These ladies like sitting, but these kids do not like sitting. Do these kids like sitting?"
Child: "No, these kids do not like sitting."

Level 23 Summary Table

(to be filled in at the completion of each lesson)

Lesson	1	2	3	4	5	6	7	8	9	10	11	12
Date												
Total # Correct Responses												

*Criterion for Moving On: Once a child achieves 20 or more items correct on 3 out of 4 consecutive sessions, move on to the next level. If the child does not achieve criterion within the 12 sessions, take a break for 3-4 weeks, and then restart this level from Lesson 1.

NOTE: Continue to carry out the Real-World activities on a daily basis. Incorporate as much language as you can from the lessons into the outside world. The language should include material taught in previous levels as well as the new material taught in this level. Remember to use the samples provided as a guide to creating your own.

Level 23 Lesson 1 (repeat, if needed, as Lessons 4, 7, & 10)								
	Objects		Adult's Actions & Words	ER*	✔ if correct			
	Near Child	Far from Child			Lesson 1	Lesson 4	Lesson 7	Lesson 10
1	boy	boy	pointing to near kid *"This kid likes to walk,* pointing to far kid *but that kid likes to run. Who likes to walk?"*	"This kid likes to walk." (P)				
2	same as above	same as above	pointing to near kid *"Make him walk."*	O/A				
3	frog horse		*"The frog wants to jump, but the horse does not want to jump. Which one does not want to jump?"*	"The horse does not want to jump."				
4	same as above		*"Make the frog jump."*	O/A				
5	same as above		*"The frog was jumping. The horse was not jumping."*	I				
6	cat	cat	pointing to near cat *"This cat is going to walk,* pointing to far cat *but that cat is not going to walk. Which one is going to walk?"*	"This one is going to walk." (P)				
7	same as above	same as above	near cat walking *"Now it is walking."*	I				
8	same as above	same as above	pointing to far cat *"Did that cat walk?"*	"No, that cat did not walk." (P)				
9	same as above	same as above	pointing to near cat *"Did this cat walk?"*	"Yes, this cat did walk." (P)				
10	girl		*"Some kids can swim, but some kids cannot do that."*	I				
11	same as above		*"This kid cannot swim. Can she swim?"*	"No, she cannot swim."				
12	same as above		*"She cannot swim, but she can do other things."*	I				
13	same as above		girl walking *"What is she doing?"*	"She is walking."				
14	2 buses		*"Pick up these buses and hold them in your hands."*	O/A				

Level 23 Lesson 1 (continued)								
	Objects		**Adult's Actions & Words**	**ER***	**✔ if correct**			
	Near Child	*Far from Child*			*Lesson 1*	*Lesson 4*	*Lesson 7*	*Lesson 10*
15	*same as above* (child holding buses)		*"What are you holding?"*	"I am holding (some) buses."				
16	*same as above*		*"Give me the buses. What were you holding?"*	"I was holding (some) buses."				
17	Picture 14		*"Some kids are here. They are standing."*	I				
18	*same as above*		*"These kids like to run, but they are not running. Do these kids like to run?"*	"Yes, these kids like to run."				
19	Picture 7		pointing to girl *"This girl is happy. She has a kite."*	I/P				
20	*same as above*		pointing to boy *"This boy is not happy."*	I/P				
21	*same as above*		*"He wants a kite, but he does not have a kite. What does this boy want?"*	"This boy does want a kite."				
22	Picture 8		*"These babies can sit, but they cannot walk. Can these babies walk?"*	"No, these babies cannot walk."				
23	*same as above*		*"Which one has a toy?"*	"This one has a toy." (P)				
24	*same as above*		*"Are these babies eating?"*	"No, these babies are not eating."				
25	*same as above*		*"Are you eating?"*	"No, I am not eating."				
				Total Record the Total in the Level 1 Summary Table.				

*ER=Expected Response: I-Say = Imitates (excluding Say); I = Imitates; P = Points; O/A = Correct action on correct object

NOTE: Remember to create Daily Real-World Exercises and use them regularly throughout the day.

Level 23 Sample Daily Real-World Exercises

These examples show you how the new language forms taught in this level should be used in daily life.
You should also continue to use the forms taught in prior levels.

Setting	Adult's Actions & Words	Expected Response
Kitchen	"Mom likes to cook, and Dad likes to eat. Who likes to eat?"	"Dad likes to eat."
Kitchen	"Mom does not want to eat, but Dad does want to eat. Who does not want to eat?"	"Mom does not want to eat."
Playground	pointing to a boy running "That boy likes running, point to a lady sitting and this lady likes sitting. Who likes running?"	"That boy likes running." (P)
Playground	pointing to a baby "That baby cannot walk, pointing to a toddler walking nearby but this baby can walk. Which one can walk?"	"This one can walk." (P)
Store	"We are going to shop. What are we going to do?"	"We are going to shop."
Store	"We did all the shopping. We are going to leave now. What are we going to do?"	"Now we are going to leave." OR "We are going to leave now."
Outdoors	pointing to a ball "We are going to play with this ball. What are we going to do?"	"We are going to play with this ball."

Level 23 Lesson 2 (repeat, if needed, as Lessons 5, 8, & 11)								
	Objects		Adult's Actions & Words	ER*	✔ if correct			
	Near Child	*Far from Child*			*Lesson 2*	*Lesson 5*	*Lesson 8*	*Lesson 11*
1	horse	horse	pointing to near horse **"This horse can jump,** pointing to far horse **but that horse cannot jump. Which one can jump?"**	"This one can jump." (P)				
2	*same as above*	*same as above*	near horse jumping **"This horse is jumping, but it wants to rest. Does this horse want to rest?"**	"Yes, this horse does want to rest."				
3	*same as above*	*same as above*	near horse lying down pointing to near horse **"This horse was jumping, but now it is resting."**	I/P				
4	2 girls	dog	pointing to one girl **"This girl likes to talk,** pointing to other girl **but this girl does not like to talk. Which one likes to talk?"**	"This one likes to talk." (P)				
5	*same as above*	*same as above*	**"Dogs cannot talk, but they can do many other things. Can dogs run?"**	"Yes, dogs can run."				
6	*same as above*	*same as above*	dog running **"What is the dog doing?"**	"The dog is running."				
7	*same as above*	*same as above*	dog stops running **"Was the dog swimming?"**	"No, the dog was not swimming."				
8	*same as above*	*same as above*	**"What was he doing?"**	"He was running."				
9		2 ladies	**"Are those ladies?"**	"Yes, those are ladies."				
10		*same as above*	**"Ladies can walk, but those ladies are not going to do that."**	I				
11		*same as above*	**"They are going to sit. What are the ladies going to do?"**	"The ladies are going to sit."				

	Objects		Adult's Actions & Words	ER*	✔ if correct			
	Near Child	Far from Child			Lesson 2	Lesson 5	Lesson 8	Lesson 11
			Level 23 Lesson 2 (continued)					
12		*same as above*	ladies sitting **"What are they doing?"**	"They are sitting."				
13		*same as above*	ladies standing **"What were they doing?"**	"They were sitting."				
14		*same as above*	ladies lying down **"What are they doing now?"**	"Now they are resting." OR "They are resting now."				
15	3 boys		pointing to one boy **"What is this boy going to do?"**	"This boy is going to ____." *(accept any reasonable response)*				
16	*same as above*		pointing to one boy **"Make this boy ____."** *(use child's response from previous item)*	O/A				
17	Picture 22		**"This boy likes animals, and he also likes toys. Does this boy like toys?"**	"Yes, this boy does like toys."				
18	*same as above*		**"He likes toys, but he does not have any. Does he have toys?"**	"No, he does not have toys."				
19	Picture 9		**"Is the cat walking?"**	"No, the cat is not walking."				
20	*same as above*		**"What is the cat doing?"**	"The cat is sleeping."				
21	Picture 13		**"Most birds can fly.** pointing to penguin **"This is a bird that cannot fly."**	I/P				
22	*same as above*		pointing to penguin **"This bird cannot fly, but it can swim. Can this bird swim?"**	"Yes, this bird can swim." (P)				

389

Level 23 Lesson 2 (continued)								
	Objects		**Adult's Actions & Words**	**ER***	**✔ if correct**			
	Near Child	*Far from Child*			*Lesson 2*	*Lesson 5*	*Lesson 8*	*Lesson 11*
23	Picture 30		*"This dog was running, but now it is sitting. What was the dog doing?"*	"The dog was running."				
24	*same as above*		*"Now what is the dog doing?"*	"Now the dog is sitting." OR "The dog is sitting now."				
25	*same as above*		*"Are you sitting?"*	"Yes, I am sitting."				
				Total Record the Total in the Level 1 Summary Table.				

*ER=Expected Response: I^Say = Imitates (excluding Say); I = Imitates; P = Points; O/A = Correct action on correct object

NOTE: Remember to create Daily Real-World Exercises and use them regularly throughout the day.

Level 23 Lesson 3 (repeat, if needed, as Lessons 6, 9, & 12)								
	Objects		Adult's Actions & Words	ER*	✔ if correct			
	Near Child	Far from Child			Lesson 3	Lesson 6	Lesson 9	Lesson 12
1	3 kids	2 planes	pointing to kids *"Some kids are here, and* pointing to planes *some planes are there."*	I/P				
2	*same as above*	*same as above*	*"Some kids like cars, but these kids like planes. What do these kids like?"*	"These kids like planes."				
3	*same as above*	*same as above*	*"Planes can fly, but they do not fly all the time."*	I				
4	*same as above*	*same as above*	*"Are those planes flying now?"*	"No, those planes are not flying now." OR "No, now those planes are not flying."				
5	*same as above*	*same as above*	*"Those planes were not flying, but they are going to fly. What are those planes going to do?"*	"Those planes are going to fly."				
6	*same as above*	*same as above*	*"Do that. Make the planes fly."*	O/A				
7	boy bed	boy	pointing to near boy *"This boy likes to rest,* pointing to far boy *but that boy does not like to rest. Which one likes to rest?"*	"This one likes to rest." (P)				
8	*same as above*	remove boy	pointing to bed *"A bed is here. This boy is going to rest. What is he going to do?"*	"He is going to rest."				
9	*same as above*		*"Do that. Make this boy rest."*	O/A				
10		cat horse dog	*"Are those cars?"*	"No, those are not cars."				

391

Level 23 Lesson 3 (continued)							
Objects		**Adult's Actions & Words**	**ER***	**✔ if correct**			
Near Child	*Far from Child*			Lesson 3	Lesson 6	Lesson 9	Lesson 12
11	*same as above*	*"What are those?"*	"Those are animals."				
12	*same as above*	*"Animals can eat. Are those animals eating?"*	"No, those animals are not eating."				
13	*same as above*	*"What are they doing?"*	"They are standing."				
14	*same as above*	cat walking *"What is the cat doing?"*	"The cat is walking."				
15	*same as above*	cat lying down *"What was the cat doing?"*	"The cat was walking."				
16	*same as above*	*"Now what is the cat going to do?"*	"Now the cat is going to ___." OR "The cat is going to ___ now." *(accept any reasonable response)*				
17	*same as above*	*"Do that. Make the cat ___."* *(use child's response from previous item)*	O/A				
18	Picture 16		*"Some cats are here. They are playing with a ball."*	I				
19	*same as above*		*"Point to the ball."*	A				
20	*same as above*		*"These cats like to play. They do not like to rest."*	I				
21	*same as above*		*"What do these cats like to do?"*	"These cats do like to play."				
22	*same as above*		*"Do they like to rest?"*	"No, they do not like to rest."				

	Objects		Adult's Actions & Words	ER*	✔ if correct			
	Near Child	Far from Child			Lesson 3	Lesson 6	Lesson 9	Lesson 12
				Level 23 Lesson 3 (continued)				
23	Picture 17		pointing to swimming duck **"What is this duck doing?"**	"This duck is swimming."				
24	*same as above*		pointing to flying duck **"What is that duck doing?"**	"That duck is flying."				
25	*same as above*		**"Ducks can swim. They can also fly."**	I				
				Total Record the Total in the Level 1 Summary Table.				

*ER=Expected Response: I-Say = Imitates (excluding Say); I = Imitates; P = Points; O/A = Correct action on correct object

NOTE: Remember to create Daily Real-World Exercises and use them regularly throughout the day.

LEVEL 24
SUMMARIZING EVENTS

Overview

By this point, the child has mastered a wide range of questions. This has been achieved by teaching each question form separately and intensively. As you have seen, in any session, the new form appears repeatedly — with slight variations from item to item (e.g., in teaching the past tense, one item may be "What was the girl doing?" while the next item might be "What were the dogs doing?") While this eases the learning for the child, it does not lend itself to showing how a "topic" or "theme" (e.g., a discussion about a trip to the zoo) is maintained over a set of exchanges which can vary greatly from one sentence to the next.

If a child is to become adept at verbal communication, topic maintenance is a key skill. It is also central to reading comprehension since books maintain an idea over sets of pages.

This current level begins to address this aspect of language. It is aimed at introducing the child to topic maintenance. Each session uses the language forms that the child has already mastered to craft a sustained exchange on a particular topic. The exchange then ends with the child producing a short summary of the key points.

A key support offered to the child in this work is sentence completion. In this technique, you provide a near-complete sentence that the child has to complete. He or she then has to produce the complete sentence independently.

Example of a Guided Summary (following a discussion about an animal who was hungry):
> *Adult: This animal (pointing to a picture) wanted some* _____.
> *Child: food*
> *Adult: Good, now say that again.*
> *Child: This animal wanted some food.*
> *Adult: He found some* _____.
> *Child: food*
> *Adult: Good, now say that again.*
> *Child: He found some food.*

Adult: Now tell me the whole thing
Child: The animal wanted food. He found some food.

In these activities, the techniques from earlier levels still apply. For example, If the child provides an incorrect response or no response, give the child the answer, and then repeat the item from the beginning.

Level 24 Summary Table
(to be filled in at the completion of each lesson)

Lesson	1	2	3	4	5	6	7	8	9	10	11	12
Date												
Total # Correct Responses												

*Criterion for Moving On: Once a child achieves 20 or more items correct on 3 out of 4 consecutive sessions, move on to the next level. If the child does not achieve criterion within the 12 sessions, take a break for 3-4 weeks, and then restart this level from Lesson 1.

NOTE: Continue to carry out the Real-World activities on a daily basis. Incorporate as much language as you can from the lessons into the outside world. The language should include material taught in previous levels as well as the new material taught in this level. Remember to use the samples provided as a guide to creating your own.

NOTE: In the items where the child is asked to summarize the events previously discussed, you first show the child the picture and the turn it over. The summary of events is then stated in the past tense without the picture in view.

	Objects		Adult's Actions & Words	ER*	✔ if correct
	Near Child	**Far from Child**			
1	Picture 27		pointing to bears "Some bears are here."	I/P	
2	*same as above*		pointing to small bear "This bear is small. It is a baby."	I/P	
3	*same as above*		pointing to big bear "This bear is big. It is the mother."	I/P	
4	*same as above*		pointing to the jar "The bears have some food. Point to the food."	A	
5	*same as above*		"The bears do not have water, but they want some water."	I	
6	*same as above*		"They are going to get water."	I	
7	*same as above*		"What are the bears going to get?"	"They are going to get water."	
8	Picture 5		"Now the bears are walking. They are looking for water."	I	
9	*same as above*		"Are the bears walking?"	"Yes, the bears are walking."	
10	*same as above*		"Are they looking for food?"	"No, they are not looking for food."	
11	*same as above*		"What are they looking for?"	"They are looking for water."	
12	Picture 6		"The bears found some water, and now they are drinking."	I	
13	*same as above*		"Are the bears eating?"	"No, the bears are not eating."	
14	*same as above*		"What are they doing?"	"They are drinking."	
15	Show Picture 27 then turn it over		pointing to back of Picture 27 "These animals wanted____."	"water"	

Level 24 Lesson 1

Level 24 Lesson 1 (continued)				
Objects		Adult's Actions & Words	ER*	✔ if correct
Near Child	Far from Child			
16	*same as above*		*"Good, now say that again."*	"These animals wanted water."	
17	Show Picture 6 then turn it over		pointing to back of Picture 6 *"These bears were looking for water. They found some ____."*	"water"	
18	*same as above*		*"Good, now say that again."*	"They found some water."	
17	*same as above*		*"Good, now tell me the whole thing."*	"These animals wanted water. They found some water."	
18	none		*"Animals drink water. People also drink water."*	I	
19	none		*"Do you drink water?"*	"Yes, I do drink water."	
20	Picture 19		pointing to water in the pool *"Some water is here, but it is not water to drink."*	I/P	
21	*same as above*		pointing to swimming pool *"This water is in a pool, and these kids are swimming. What are these kids doing?"*	"These kids are swimming."	
22	*same as above*		pointing to kids running *"Are those kids swimming?"*	"No, those kids are not swimming."	
23	*same as above*		*"What are those kids doing?"*	"Those kids are running."	
24	Remove picture		*"Were some kids swimming?"*	"Yes, some kids were swimming."	
25	*same as above*		*"Were some kids also running?"*	"Yes, some kids were also running."	
				Total Record the Total in the Level 1 Summary Table.	

*ER=Expected Response: I^{Say} = Imitates (excluding Say); I = Imitates; P = Points; O/A = Correct action on correct object

NOTE: Remember to create Daily Real-World Exercises and use them regularly throughout the day.

Level 24 Sample Daily Real-World Exercises

NOTE: These activities require that you take photographs to use during the exchange with the child (in the same way that pictures are used in the lessons). These exercises take place with the child seated at a table viewing photos of real-world activities. The activities are not taking place during the exchange. In the summary items, you first show the child the picture and the turn it over. The summary of events is then stated in the past tense without the picture in view.

Setting	Adult's Actions & Words	Expected Response
Kitchen	Show child a photo of dad sitting at kitchen table *"Dad wants to eat some eggs."*	I
Kitchen	*"He is going to cook some eggs."*	I
Kitchen	Show child a photo of dad cooking eggs *"What is Dad doing?"*	"Dad is cooking (some eggs)."
Kitchen	Show child a photo of dad eating *"Now what is Dad doing?"*	"Now Dad is eating." OR "Dad is eating now."
Kitchen	Show child photo of dad sitting at kitchen table and then turn it over *"Dad wanted to eat some ____."*	"eggs"
Kitchen	*"Good, now say that again."*	"Dad wanted to eat some eggs."
Kitchen	Show child photo of dad cooking eggs and then turn it over *"So he cooked some ____."*	"eggs"
Kitchen	*"Good, now say that again."*	"So he cooked some eggs."
Kitchen	*"Good, now tell me the whole thing."*	"Dad wanted to eat some eggs, so he cooked some eggs."

NOTE: In the items where the child is asked to summarize the events previously discussed, you first show the child the picture and the turn it over. The summary of events is then stated in the past tense without the picture in view.

	Level 24 Lesson 2				
	Objects		**Adult's Actions & Words**	**ER***	**✔ if correct**
	Near Child	*Far from Child*			
1	Picture 35		pointing to man *"A man is here."*	I/P	
2	*same as above*		*"He likes to fix toys."*	I	
3	*same as above*		*"What does he like to do?"*	"He likes to fix toys."	
4	*same as above*		*"This man has a truck. The truck is broken."*	I	
5	*same as above*		*"Where is the truck?"*	"The truck is here." (P)	
6	*same as above*		*"He has a robot, and the robot is also broken."*	I	
7	*same as above*		*"Point to the robot."*	A	
8	*same as above*		*"The man is going to fix the robot."*	I	
9	*same as above*		*"The robot has its legs, but it does not have its arms."*	I	
10	*same as above*		*"Does the robot have its arms?"*	"No, the robot does not have its arms."	
11	Picture 36		*"Now the man is fixing the robot."*	I	
12	Picture 37		*"The man did fix the robot. Now the robot is better."*	I	
15	Show Picture 35 then turn it over		pointing to the back of Picture 35 *"The robot was ____."*	"broken"	
16	*same as above*		*"Good, now say that again."*	"The robot was broken."	
17	Show picture 37 then turn it over		pointing to the back of Picture 37 *"The man fixed the robot. Now it is ____."*	"better"	

400

	Objects		Adult's Actions & Words	ER*	✔ if correct
	Near Child	Far from Child			
18	*same as above*		*"Good, now say that again."*	"Now it is better."	
19	*same as above*		*"Good, now tell me the whole thing."*	"The robot was broken, and now it is better."	
20			*"I would like you to stand up."*	A	
21			*"What are you doing?"*	"I am standing."	
22			*"Now I would like you to sit down again."*	A	
23			*"Now what are you doing?"*	"Now I am sitting." OR "I am sitting now."	
24			*"Were you running?"*	"No, I was not running."	
25			*"Were you standing?"*	"Yes, I was standing."	
				Total Record the Total in the Level 1 Summary Table.	

Level 24 Lesson 2 (continued)

*ER=Expected Response: I-Say = Imitates (excluding Say); I = Imitates; P = Points; O/A = Correct action on correct object

NOTE: Remember to create Daily Real-World Exercises and use them regularly throughout the day.

NOTE: In the items where the child is asked to summarize the events previously discussed, you first show the child the picture and the turn it over. The summary of events is then stated in the past tense without the picture in view.

	Objects		Adult's Actions & Words	ER*	✔ if correct
	Near Child	**Far from Child**			
Level 24 Lesson 3					
1	Picture 32		pointing to kids *"Some kids are here."*	I/P	
2	*same as above*		*"They are sitting near a pool."*	I	
3	*same as above*		*"Are the kids swimming?"*	"No, the kids are not swimming."	
4	*same as above*		*"What are they doing?"*	"They are sitting (near a pool)."	
5	*same as above*		*"Kids can do many things. These kids are sitting, but they can also swim. Can these kids swim?"*	"Yes, these kids can swim."	
6	*same as above*		*"The kids want to swim. They are going to jump into the pool."*	I	
7	*same as above*		*"What are the kids going to do?"*	"The kids are going to jump into the pool."	
8	Picture 34		*"Now the kids are jumping into the pool."*	I	
9	Picture 2		*"The kids did jump, and now they are swimming."*	I	
10	Show Picture 32 then turn it over		pointing to the back of Picture 32 *"Some kids were sitting by a ____."*	"pool"	
11	*same as above*		*"Good, now say that again."*	"Some kids were sitting by a pool."	
12	Show Picture 34 then turn it over		pointing to the back of Picture 34 *"They wanted to swim, so they jumped in the ____."*	"pool"	
15	*same as above*		*"Good, now say that again."*	"They jumped in the pool."	

	Objects		Adult's Actions & Words	ER*	✔ if correct
	Near Child	Far from Child			
16	*same as above*		*"Good, now tell me the whole thing."*	"Some kids wanted to swim, so they jumped in the pool."	
17	Picture 21		*"Many animals can also swim."*	I	
18	*same as above*		*"What are these?"*	"These are ducks/ birds."	
19	*same as above*		*"What are they doing?"*	"They are swimming."	
20	*same as above*		*"Can these birds also fly?"*	"Yes, these birds can also fly."	
21	Picture 17		*"Now one bird is swimming, and the other bird is flying."*	I	
22	*same as above*		*"Which one is not flying?"*	"This one is not flying." (P)	
23	boy bed		pointing to boy *"A boy is here. He is tired, and he wants to rest."*	I/P	
24	*same as above*		*"Make the boy rest on the bed."*	O/A	
25	*same as above*		boy standing *"Did the boy rest?"*	"Yes, the boy did rest."	
24	*same as above*		*"Is he resting now?"*	"No, he is not resting now." OR "No, now he is not resting."	
25	*same as above*		*"What is he doing?"*	"He is standing."	
				Total Record the Total in the Level 1 Summary Table.	

*ER=Expected Response: I^{-Say} = Imitates (excluding Say); I = Imitates; P = Points; O/A = Correct action on correct object

NOTE: Remember to create Daily Real-World Exercises and use them regularly throughout the day.

When the child has successfully completed Level 24, he or she is ready to move on to the program called *Steps to Stories*. For more information, go to www.ASDreading.com.

APPENDIX
B

PICTURES
FOR LANGUAGE
ACTIVITIES

Picture 1 (top) & Picture 2 (bottom)

Picture 3 (top) & Picture 4 (bottom)

Picture 5 (top) & Picture 6 (bottom)

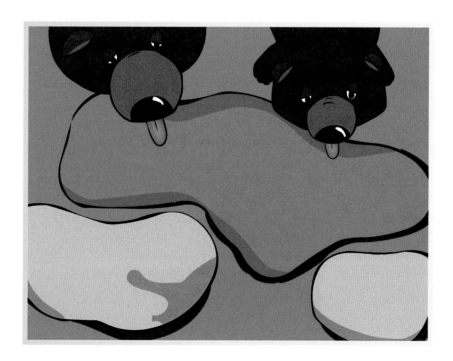

Picture 7 (top) & Picture 8 (bottom)

Picture 9 (top) & Picture 10 (bottom)

Picture 11 (top) & Picture 12 (bottom)

Picture 13 (top) & Picture 14 (bottom)

Picture 15 (top) & Picture 16 (bottom)

Picture 17 (top) & Picture 18 (bottom)

Picture 19 (top) & Picture 20 (bottom)

Picture 21 (top) & Picture 22 (bottom)

Picture 23 (top) & Picture 24 (bottom)

Picture 25 (top) & Picture 26 (bottom)

Picture 27 (top) & Picture 28 (bottom)

Picture 29 (top) & Picture 30 (bottom)

Picture 31 (top) & Picture 32 (bottom)

Picture 33 (top) & Picture 34 (bottom)

Picture 35 (top) & Picture 36 (bottom)

Picture 37